Europe and its Shadows

Coloniality after Empire

Hamid Dabashi

First published 2019 by Pluto Press
345 Archway Road, London N6 5AA

www.plutobooks.com

Copyright © Hamid Dabashi 2019

The right of Hamid Dabashi to be identified as the author of this work has been asserted
by him in accordance with the Copyright, Designs and Patents Act 1988.

British Library Cataloguing in Publication Data
A catalogue record for this book is available from the British Library

ISBN 978 0 7453 3841 5 Hardback
ISBN 978 0 7453 3840 8 Paperback
ISBN 978 1 7868 0398 6 PDF eBook
ISBN 978 1 7868 0400 6 Kindle eBook
ISBN 978 1 7868 0399 3 EPUB eBook

Typeset by Westchester Publishing Services

Simultaneously printed in the United Kingdom and United States of America

Europe and its Shadows

For
Ismael Nashef and Ayman El Desouky
From the River to the Sea

Contents

Acknowledgments

This book has been brewing in me for quite some time, and David Shulman, my editor at Pluto, has been the main engine behind my writing it. I am grateful to him for seeing this book through the labyrinth of my commitment to write it and his determination to publish it.

Three anonymous reviewers (I do not know who they are) read my proposal of this book and wrote detailed, at times deeply insightful, critical comments. Their collective wisdom vastly improved what you are about to read. I am grateful to them. Their critical thoughts helped me shape the trajectory of this book.

I wrote much of this book while vacationing with my children in Ocho Rios in Jamaica. Sitting at a beach where my children swam with dark-skinned children like them and their parents against the beautiful blue of the Caribbean Sea was the apt environment for the history that informs this book. As I wrote this book, I could see, in my mind's eyes, the tall shadows of wandering European ships roaming these surrounding seas, mapping the colonial conquests of these islands. There, at the center of my children's universe, as they swam and played water polo with their brothers and sisters, I listened to Bob Marley, wrote this book, and counted my blessings.

I wrote the final pages while on sabbatical from Columbia, visiting Doha Institute for Graduate Studies in Doha, Qatar, where I am surrounded by my dearest and closest friends and colleagues from across the Arab world, teaching students from Morocco and Tunisia to Palestine and Iraq, some from the war-torn Syria and Yemen. We are all here thanks to the visionary institution-building tenacity of a towering Palestinian intellectual Azmi Bishara. I call this place *Hadiqah al-Ulama*, Garden of Learned People. Under our watchful eyes, they just planted 80 olive trees in this garden. It is in the middle of nowhere and for us homeless minds, the center of universe.

Ocho Rios, Jamaica
Jamaica, New York
Doha, Qatar
Summer–Fall 2018

Introduction
What's in a Word: "Europe"?

Aftabi dar miyan-e Sayeh-'i ...
Like a sun in the midst of a shade ...

Rumi, *Masnavi* (1273)

What's in a word: "Europe"? A continent, a global culture, a massive civilization, a state of being, a planetary imperial design, a nasty colonial concoction? Here, I look at Europe as a sign, a symbol, an allegory. I am far more concerned with Europe as a name rather than what it names. I am primarily looking at the sign "Europe" as a formalist—like a poet looking at a bridge, rather than an engineer looking at the same bridge. I am far more concerned with the form of the thing than the thing itself—of where it came from or where it is going. I don't think Europe *is* a thing in itself. Europe is a sign—like a red light or a cross—and I wish to read this sign through its signals, its affects, effects, affectations, echoes, reflections, resonances, shades, and shadows.

Europe is a mobile army of mixed metaphors. I borrow this phrase from Nietzsche about truth, and run with it toward and away from Europe, wondering what in the world it signals. We postcolonial folks around the globe are both victims and victors of this thing that calls itself Europe. We love it and we hate it—we are intimate enemies. We own it and are owned by it. We play with it, and it plays us. It disables us, and it enables us. We enable it and disable it. Because of Europe we have lost the worlds we knew as our own. Because of Europe we yearn to retrieve the worlds of our own. And because of Europe we oscillate between the world Europe has enabled and the world we wish to enable after-Europe.

Yes, Europe means imperialism, colonialism, militarism, conquest, and racism. Yes, Europe means science, technology, art, architecture, literature, and poetry, all concomitant with those nasty trajectories. Europe is good; Europe is evil. Europe is the strange case of Dr. Jekyll and Mr. Hyde. If he be Mr. Hyde, I say in this book, I shall be Mr. Seek.

Europe has never been just itself. Europe also lives and thrives and hides and resurfaces in its shadows—somewhere in between "Europe and non-Europe," in between "the West and the Rest." European colonialism may have ended here and there, but the condition of coloniality continues—not just economically, but also culturally, epistemically, morally, imaginatively. Imperialism may have morphed, but the empire sustains its relations of power—with a decidedly Euro-American signature. Nietzsche considered what he called *ressentiment* as the origin of Christian morality. In his gloss on Nietzsche, Max Scheler took issue with that characterization and proposed ressentiment not at the core of Christianity but at the roots of bourgeois morality that, in Scheler's estimation, had begun taking shape from the thirteenth century forward.

But the condition of coloniality that European colonialism begat from almost the same time was always already transnational, global, planetary. Neither Nietzsche nor Scheler thought this part worth considering. Whether in Christian or in bourgeois moralities, or the transmutation of one into the other, and whether spread globally through the proselytizing missionaries of the former or the colonial conquests of the latter, ressentiment became translational "transvaluation of values," as Nietzsche called it, and this mapped the moral fabric of a bourgeois Christian imperialism in which "good Christians" went around the world and did pretty nasty things, hanged twelve Native Americans to burn upside down, as Bartolomé de las Casas tells us in *A Short Account of the Destruction of the Indies* (1542–1552), in honor of the Twelve Apostles of Jesus Christ. The Sermon on the Mount did not mean much to them at such moments—nor did those Christian bourgeois mass murderers wait for Nietzsche and Scheler to psychopathologize their sense of ressentiment. The shadow of Christianity, or the shadow of bourgeois morality at the roots of European empires, unbeknownst to both European philosophers, turned that ressentiment upside down, where the power of the Roman emperor was no longer coveted and thus transvalued, but where an even darker force faced the power of the emperor. We postcolonials noticed no celebration of weakness, no sense of ressentiment, no transvaluation of values, from our Christian conquerors, and we were all born and raised in the shade and shadow of that darkness.

Let me put it plainly: Europe has always been looking over our shoulders when we write. In this book I am going to look over the shoulder of Europe and write back. For centuries Europe has been staring at us—in its dehumanizing anthropology of our strangeness to it. It is long overdue we started staring back at and staring down Europe—both in and of itself, and in its transmutations in the rest of the world. In this book, I am also trying to think the world beyond Europe, after Europe, not against Europe, but despite Europe.

One
Europe: A Mobile Army of Metaphors

What then is truth? A mobile army of metaphors, metonyms, and anthropomorphisms—in short, a sum of human relations which have been enhanced, transposed, and embellished poetically and rhetorically, and which after long use seem firm, canonical, and obligatory to a people: truths are illusions about which one has forgotten that this is what they are; metaphors which are worn out and without sensuous power; coins which have lost their pictures and now matter only as metal, no longer as coins. We still do not know where the urge for truth comes from; for as yet we have heard only of the obligation imposed by society that it should exist: to be truthful means using the customary metaphors—in moral terms: the obligation to lie according to a fixed convention, to lie herd-like in a style obligatory for all.[1]

> Friedrich Nietzsche, *On Truth and Lie in an*
> *Extra-Moral Sense* (1873)

On August 13, 1976, when I had just turned 25, the rather haphazard course of my life saw me seated inside an airplane leaving Mehrabad Airport in Tehran for Geneva, Switzerland. After two weeks around Lac Léman, on the stretch between Geneva and Montreux, I flew to Philadelphia, USA, for what would be the American extension of my Iranian life. Ever since that inaugural August 1976, I have traveled back and forth from one end of Europe to another, from London and elsewhere in the United Kingdom, to Saint Petersburg, Russia, and many more European destinations in between. While I lived in Iran, and long before I was based on the Eastern Seaboard of the United States between Washington, DC, and Boston, with Philadelphia and New York as my successive homes, the idea of "Europe" was an elusive abstraction, something everlastingly new, solid, permanent, irreducible, historic, prevailing. Soon after I began my frequent flights back and forth to Europe from the United States, "Europe" became a fixated and total visual and mental abstraction, something to behold, consolidating my earlier vision of it formed by my fascination with Italian neorealism and its echoes in German and French cinema, or else in Hitchcock's films, or Truffaut's, and before that in the fiction of Dickens, Zola, or Ignazio Silone, the artwork of impressionism and cubism, or else classical music from Handel to Brahms. With every trip to Europe—England, France, Germany, Switzerland, Holland, Belgium, Sweden, Norway, Finland ... all the way to Greece—Europe kept consolidating itself as the measure of meaning, a total and undiluted abstraction. It was strange: Europe was both very old, like the Parthenon ruins in Athens, and yet very new, like the most recent film of Ingmar Bergman. Once in Oslo, Norway, I saw Henrik Ibsen's play *An Enemy of the People* in the original Norwegian in their major city theater. I could not understand a word of the original. But I knew the play almost sentence by sentence and recited it in my mind in Persian. For a minute there I forgot if I was watching a Persian play in Norwegian or a Norwegian play in Persian.

My visits to Europe were regular but haphazard: a family visit to London, a vacation in Italy, or else a drive between Switzerland and Germany on another occasion. Eventually these trips became more professional: as a member of a film jury in Locarno or Saint Petersburg, delivering a keynote in Amsterdam or Berlin, a few more in Brussels, France, UK, or all the way to the imaginative edge of Europe in Turkey. I soon was no stranger to Europe. I knew people there, and people there knew me: friends, family, colleagues, comrades, students. Once even in a train station in Bologna a young couple approached me and the man introduced himself as one of my "fans" who read my work regularly!

I entered Europe in my twenties a wide-eyed stranger. I grew up to my sixties a familiar foreigner to its physical, moral, and imaginative landscape. I was twice attacked and robbed in Europe—once in Paris, once in London, both times by colored immigrants who looked just like me. After each incident, almost a decade apart, at the moment that I was being robbed, I felt strangely at home in Europe. I was not harmed in either of those two incidents. My two immigrant brothers just wanted their fair share of my wallet. After the second time, I went and reread George Orwell's *Down and Out in Paris and London* (1933), happily smiling to myself from cover to cover.

Strangers in a Familiar Land

From the very onset, Europe had an allegorical presence in the lives and thoughts of my generation of Iranians. We were only too consciously aware that this allegorical presence was global, universal, transnational, shared by all people drawn to and yet critical of the very idea of "Europe." Europe was the epicenter of "the West," and in a seminal text definitive to the moral and intellectual composition of my generation, by the towering Iranian intellectual Jalal Al-e Ahmad's *Gharbzadegi* (*Westoxication*, 1962), we were exposed to the knotted paradox of this allegory: Europe as an occasion for critical thinking, a space of drawing into and pulling out of the term as a colonial concoction. In later abusive takes on this transformative text, Islamists pushed it one way, while those uncritically enamored by "the West" and sold to its project capitalist modernity pulled it in the opposite direction—as the former lionized it, the latter vilified it. Some even went so far as to identify it as the very definition of what Nietzsche had called *ressentiment*, a sour grape attitude, of envying. We were really envious of "the West," these what Al-e Ahmad would call "Westoxicated" intellectuals charged, wanted to be part of it but resented the fact that we were not! It was quite a circus. In an utterly miserable misreading of the text, a book that had gathered an entire generation to think critically about our place in the world had become a talisman of reactionary politics. It was nothing of the sort. Quite to the contrary: with all its limitations, it enabled an epistemic shift in our critical thinking. Suddenly we realized we were part of a larger conversation from the global south. Against all such systemically abusive misreading, however, Al-e Ahmad's text was an act of liberation, a site of defiance, a rebellious narrative of rejecting self-alienation and reconfiguring a renewed sense of moral imagination, of political awareness, and above all, of historical agency.

Gharbzadegi was neither for nor against "the West," nor was it against modernity. It was a critique of colonialism and the colonized mind, one among scores of similar texts published across the colonial world at the time. Al-e Ahmad's essay was later falsely assimilated backward to an obscure professor of philosophy at Tehran University named Ahmad Fardid (1912–1994) and his fascination with the German philosopher Martin Heidegger. Al-e Ahmad scarcely knew of Heidegger, let alone enough to be fascinated by him. Al-e Ahmad knew no German, nor Heidegger was still translated into Persian at the time. Al-e Ahmad tells us Fardid had read his *Gharbzadegi* and subsequently introduced Al-e Ahmad to the German philosopher Ernst Jünger's book *Über die Linie* (*Crossing the Line*, 1949), and helped him translate it into Persian. Al-e Ahmad lacked any serious university education. He was enamored by the fact that a professor of philosophy at Tehran University had taken him seriously—and did as Fardid had suggested and they jointly translated *Über die Linie* and published it as *Ubur-e Az Khat*. But *Über die Linie* is a book on nihilism and has absolutely nothing to do with Al-e Ahmad's *Gharbzadegi*. Fardid was wrong thinking it did. The fact that Heidegger was attracted to another book by Jünger, *Der Arbeiter* (1932), and reported it influential on his own major essay *Die Frage nach der Technik* (*The Question Concerning Technology*, 1954) is entirely irrelevant to Al-e Ahmad's *Gharbzadegi*. This was and remains a comedy of errors in reading Iranian intellectual history backward and thinking Al-e Ahmad had apathy toward "the machine" or to modernity. But later historians of ideas, rightly angry with the Islamic republic, wrongly went all the way from Al-e Ahmad to Fardid and from Fardid to Heidegger and given Heidegger's notorious Nazism, from him to the Holocaust ... to denounce Al-e Ahmad and see him as the forerunner of the notorious Iranian president Mahmoud Ahmadinejad! It was (and it remains) quite a bizarre and surreal scene. *Gharbzadegi*, the seminal essay of its time, has thus been so systematically abused that scarcely anyone remembers or cares to read it for what it was. No doubt, Al-e Ahmad's own rhetoric and defiant prose, occasionally bordering with what Theodor Adorno in his magnificent essay *Jargon der Eigentlichkeit: Zur deutschen Ideologie* (*The Jargon of Authenticity*, 1964) would call "jargon of authenticity" sounded nostalgic for a nonexistent "self," and was partially responsible for such abusive readings, but the thrust and spirit of his essay were lost in and to the fury of the post-Islamic republic battle of historiography of who to blame for the calamity of the theocracy.[2]

Jalal Al-e Ahmad was our Aimé Césaire, Léopold Sédar Senghor, Frantz Fanon, and Edward Said all wrapped in one, though we did not know this at the time. It would take me a very long time to realize that Al-e Ahmad's liberating act had its own drawbacks, not in the sense that his ultra-Euro-modernist critiques would portray and object, but in a far more serious way. At the time we were reading him in the 1960s and 1970s, however, we could breathe more confidently in his emancipatory prose. In *Gharbzadegi*, which was Fanon's *Black Skin, White Masks* (1952) and Said's *Orientalism* (1978) in one, Al-e Ahmad had a very simple thought: that we as a people, a culture, a political consciousness were what he termed "Westoxicated," hit by a fixation with "the West"—that this figment of our imagination had become the measure of universal truth, and he meant it as in a disease, a malady, a distorted scheme of things, an ability to think critically outside the European frames of references, as such it was by no means a dismissal of modernity, but an epistemic change to the Eurocentricity of that modernity. Because this was a disease, as Al-e Ahmad understood it, then we needed to be cured of it and recuperate our own "self"-consciousness. Like anyone else in my generation, I was of course deeply drawn to Al-e Ahmad and his theory, and seriously disagreed with those who opposed him among his own cohorts (mostly the uncritical admirers of "Western modernity"). But I still remained, as I am today, quite skeptical of the idea of a "return to the self," which I think is a bogus proposition. We have no clue where this "self" is and what it means—except as an escape route away from "the West." I could not imagine any "self" to which to return without the simultaneous constitution of an "other" that is ipso facto an alienating force. But at the time the idea of this "return," which after Al-e Ahmad, Ali Shari'ati also elaborated even in more details, appeared quite compelling to us. With the same token, and just like Edward Said in *Orientalism*, Al-e Ahmad had in effect fetishized this West beyond history and right into allegorical terms. Today, I look at those youthful years with a sense of nostalgic affection but seasoned critical distance. To me, today, Europe, and a fortiori, the West, is not a reality sui generis. It is a delusional fantasy, a false consciousness, at the full service of an imperial hegemony. The objective is not to run away from it. The objective is to dismantle and overcome it—and in that act of deconstruction, postcolonial critics with a fetishized fixation on the West are as much an impediment as those promoting and celebrating it.

It would take decades of my life, my doctoral work with Philip Rieff (1922–2006)—the eminent Freudian cultural theorist at the University of Pennsylvania, staunchly conservative in his political culture—and my more serious exposure to seminal thinkers from Fanon to Césaire to Said, Gayatri Spivak, Ashis Nandy, V. Y.

Mudimbe, and Enrique Dussel, to eventually map out the details of this allegorical paradox between what Europe had enabled and what Europe had disabled at one and the same time, and plant and place me somewhere where I could begin to ask the questions I now wish to share in this book: Where is Europe? What is Europe? Where and what is this towering metaphor of time and space, of sense and sensibility, that has imagined itself the center of the universe, and by defiance or acknowledgment the world at large has reciprocated and acquiesced, revolted or reversed? Is it a geography or a civilization, a continent or a culture, an imaginative universe or an emotive register? In *We, the People of Europe?* (2003), the eminent philosopher Étienne Balibar addresses the idea of "transnational citizenship" from the vantage point of what he solidly establishes as "a European perspective." From theories of state to sovereignty of nations, or when the prospect of multiculturalism is unleashing deepest layers of racism, Balibar intends to right some serious wrongs in the manner Europe sees itself, and yet like any other European critical thinker, he ends up positively consolidating the very idea of Europe—however dialectically. But to me here in this book, "Europe" is a metaphoric moment that has exhausted its epistemic possibilities and has now positively imploded onto itself—and we need to move beyond it—but not before bidding it a proper farewell.

Foreign to its familiarities, a stranger at home, I stand in front of Europe and ask Europe please to introduce itself not with an accusatory finger, or to be sure with an extended hand of false friendship, neither with a raised fist of anticolonial anger, nor indeed with the affected forgiveness of a postcolonial reason. We have all been there and done that. Our time faces a different challenge: the challenge of overcoming Europe, bringing it to the fold of a different world it left in ruins. I stand in front of Europe as a metaphoric mystery— aware of the sustained course of its racist colonial and imperial atrocities, conscious of its false familiarities—basking in the sun of its recognizable shores as a mixed metaphor. I am neither Eurocentric nor Europhobic. Europhobia, I often say, is the worst kind of Eurocentrism. Between Europhilia and Europhobia dwells the space of our proverbial self as their other, or more bluntly in Nietzschean terms their good that cannot see us but their evil. We are at a point that we must join Nietzsche and see how we can go beyond that good versus evil by first recognizing their contingencies. "How could anything originate out of its opposite?" I still remember the joyous bewilderment I felt the first time I read that sentence in Nietzsche's *Jenseits von Gut und Böse: Vorspiel einer Philosophie der Zukunft* (*Beyond Good and Evil: Prelude to a Philosophy of the Future*, 1886) in a seminar with Philip Rieff at the University of Pennsylvania in the late 1970s. "Truth from error, for instance? Or the will to truth from the will to deception? Or selfless action from self-interest? Or the pure, sun-bright gaze of wisdom from a covetous leer?" How in the world did we miss that? I wondered out loud at the seminar. How did we fail to see that good and evil were not opposites but coterminous? The rest of that bold, brilliant, sarcastic passage has stayed consistently with me:

> Such origins are impossible, and people who dream about such things are fools—at best. Things of the highest value must have another, separate origin of their own—they cannot be derived from this ephemeral, seductive, deceptive, lowly world, from this mad chaos of confusion and desire.... It has not occurred to even the most cautious of them to start doubting right here at the threshold, where it is actually needed the most. ... But we can doubt, first, whether opposites even exist and, second, whether the popular valuations and value oppositions that have earned the metaphysicians' seal of approval might not only be foreground appraisals. Perhaps they are merely provisional perspectives, perhaps they are not even viewed head-on;.... It could even be possible that whatever gives value to those good and honorable things has an incriminating link, bond, or tie to the very things that look like their evil opposites; perhaps they are even essentially the same. Perhaps! But who is willing to take charge of such a dangerous Perhaps! For this we must await the arrival of a new breed of philosophers, ones whose taste and inclination are somehow the reverse of those we have seen so far— philosophers of the dangerous Perhaps in every sense. And in all seriousness: I see these new philosophers approaching.[3]

That Nietzschean dialectic remains at the core of my concern in this book—between one and the next, between good and evil, between self and the other, between now and the deferment— between Europe and its shadows: Islam and the West, the West and the Rest, one contingent on the other. Europe is not just Europe. Europe is a contingency. Europe is the mother of the other towering metaphor of our time called "the West," and the West is nothing without the Rest. "The West," as the offspring of Europe, grew more as an abbreviation for "Western Europe" rather than being on "the Western" side of the European "Eastern" fantasies. From "Western Europe," in turn "the West" emerged, somewhere between the West of the Danube River and the East of English Channel. Eastern Europe was always external, or the internal other, of Europe as a master trope, more in the domain of the Ottoman Empire, and precisely for that reason "European" philosophers and critical thinkers ranging from Slavoj Žižek (Slovenia) to Yanis Varoufakis (Greece) are more Catholic than the Pope when speaking of their "Europe" with the chip of the European "other" on their shoulders. The forced manufacturing of the European Union (EU), economically to counterbalance the United States, has always been contested by the Eurozone crisis dominant from Greece to Spain and Portugal, until with their xenophobic Brexit the British delivered the very idea of it a coup de grâce. As a trope, Europe is neither here nor there, both here and there—either way corroborating Europe as the cornerstone of merely being in the world. In eliciting all such similar or contradictory sentiments, Europe is ethereal, unreal, metaphoric, not material. What would the world do without Europe? It will reinvent itself. Nietzsche in effect anticipated that eventuality—for "whatever gives value to those good and honorable things has an incriminating link, bond, or tie to the very things that look like their evil opposites; perhaps they are even essentially same."

Truths Are Illusions

In *On Truth and Lies in an Extra-Moral Sense* (1873), Nietzsche proposes: "We still do not know where the urge for truth comes from; for as yet we have heard only of the obligation imposed by society that it should exist: to be truthful means using the customary metaphors in moral terms: the obligation to lie according to a fixed convention, to lie herd-like in a style obligatory for all...."[4] Suppose we take Nietzsche on face value—and suppose we extended his iconic definition of truth not as given but as an army of metaphor to his home and habitat as a European. What then? Would Europe not be the supreme truth of his and perhaps still our time—the measure of all measures, the location of all locations, the truth against which all other variations are assayed? Isn't that what Europe meant even to him? Is there any material evidence to the truth of Europe, or is it all "metaphors, metonyms, and anthropomorphism"? Isn't Europe like any other truth claim, really an "illusion" that has forgotten that it is an illusion? What will happen to this Europe, to this compelling illusion, if we were to remember it is an illusion? What a powerful illusion this Europe has been! It has cast the whole world, the entire universe, the entire course of human history, the very cast of any language we speak, in its own image, awaiting its fulfillment. But suppose we non-Europeans, and precisely as that—"non"-European—were to kidnap Nietzsche from Europe and cast his sardonic gaze back at Europe, at his own homeland, at his own blind spot.

In an equally famous passage in his now classic book, *Wretched of the Earth* (1961), Frantz Fanon wrote one of his most iconic phrases: "Europe is literally the creation of the Third World." Why would he say that, and what could that phrase actually mean today? Here is the context in which Fanon wrote that famous phrase:

> In concrete terms Europe has been bloated out of all proportions by the gold and raw materials from such colonial countries as Latin America, China, and Africa. Today Europe's tower of opulence faces these continents, for centuries the point of departure of their shipments of diamonds, oil, silk and cotton, timber, and exotic produce to this very same Europe. Europe is literally the creation of the Third World. The riches which are choking it are those plundered from the underdeveloped peoples. The ports of Holland, the docks in Bordeaux and Liverpool owe their importance to the trade and deportation of millions of slaves. And when we hear the head of a European nation declare with hand on heart that he must come to the aid of the unfortunate peoples of the underdeveloped world, we do not tremble with gratitude. On the contrary, we say among ourselves, "it is a just reparation we are getting."[5]

So Fanon clearly meant it in material terms, in the manner in which Europe was made rich and prosperous by the systematic theft of other people's resources—from Asia and Africa to Latin America and Oceania. Fanon's voice is angry and vindictive, though just and balanced. But today we no longer hear any European head of state say they want "to come to the aid of the unfortunate peoples of the underdeveloped world." Today we see European states building barbed-wires fences not to allow Syrian and other refugees to pour into their countries. Today we see people from Africa and the Arab and Muslim world risking their lives, drowning in the Mediterranean, trying to reach Europe. What about now? What would Fanon's words mean today? Today is the payback time, when "the Third World" has come to cash in what Europe took from it over a sustained course of colonial thievery. You might think well these Europeans are not those Europeans anymore. History has moved on. Suppose you are right thinking so. These Europeans may no longer be those Europeans. But Europe—their Europe and their forefathers' Europe—has remained the same: a mobile army of mixed metaphors. Today it might be the United Nations (UN), the World Bank, and the International Monetary Fund (IMF) that regulate the predatory capitalism that continues apace with its deranged logic, but the circumambulatory cycle of capital, labor, and raw material stays the same. Today Russia, China, and the United States may have stolen the show from Europe, but the heart of them all still remains what Europe signaled, and that Europe set in motion. Geert Wilders and Marine Le Pen and the neo-Nazis from Greece to the UK are the standard bearers of what Europe longs to regain.

Let's put Nietzsche's and Fanon's insights together, take Europe both metaphorically and concretely and answer these related questions with another more recent, perhaps more urgent, question: Why would Dalai Lama, evidently a kind, gentle, caring man, a winner of the Nobel Peace Prize, loved by millions around the world, Buddhist or otherwise, the very definition of tolerance and gentility say: "Europe, for example Germany, cannot become an Arab country. Germany is Germany."[6] Although finding his own remark entertaining, the Dalai Lama laughingly adds during his conversation with *Frankfurter Allgemeine Zeitung:* "There are so many." That is right: "Deutschland," he is reported to have said, "könne kein arabisches Land werden."[7] This is not a neo-Nazi skinhead sharing these sentiments with a leading German newspaper.

This is His Holiness Dalai Lama: "Germany cannot become an Arab country." Germany is not an Arab country, nor is it even "in danger" of becoming an Arab country. But why would Dalai Lama say such a thing—be so dismissive, derisive even, nervously sardonic of the very idea? What is it to him? He is neither a European nor an Arab—or is he not?

The answer to this question rests on Fanon's insight ("Europe is literally the creation of the Third World") and on Nietzsche's ("Truth … is a mobile army of metaphors … truths are illusions about which one has forgotten that this is what they are."). We have to bring the European iconoclastic philosopher and the anticolonial theorist from Martinique together. We must transgress the fictive psychological barrier between Europe and non-Europe to get down to the truth of the matter.

To be sure, while Nietzsche meant it metaphorically, Fanon meant it literally, as he puts it bluntly: "Latin America, China, and Africa. From all these continents, under whose eyes Europe today raises up her tower of opulence, there has flowed out for centuries toward that same Europe diamonds and oil, silk and cotton, wood and exotic products. Europe is literally the creation of the Third World." But there is also an even more potent, metaphoric (if we were to bring Nietzsche to the table) aspect to his iconic phrase, that the Third World has been definitive and instrumental in manufacturing the very idea, the metaphoric normativity, of "Europe," and with it the myth of "the West." Without "the Rest," "the West" did not even know itself let alone wonder what to do with itself. The world, not just the Third World, was the other of the same that became "the West." If we, the world, pulled ourselves out, "the West" would melt. We have been the metaphoric raw material with which Europe imagined itself. From the Egyptians and Persians down to the Chinese and the Indians, we have been the civilizational other of the Western self, of the European identity. We were reduced to a mere mirror into which Europe asked itself: Mirror, mirror on the wall, who is the fairest of them all? It made no difference if we, the mirror, agreed or disagreed, said aye or nay, the illusion in the mirror saw itself as real.

Dalai Lama and the rest of the Eurocentric universe around the world are conditioned to this idea of Europe as the figment of their own captured imagination, the whitewashed epicenter of their own metaphoric cosmos. Europe is on autopilot on colonized minds. It has nothing to do with any European philosopher, statesman, politician, or mass murderer. His Holiness cannot imagine this metaphor of "Europe," which in his mind is all white, all Christian, all therefore the civilized measures of our humanity, tinted with the presence of non-Europeans, Arab or otherwise. He in effect partakes freely and is categorically invested in the unexamined metaphor of Europe as the invisible army of truth beyond all reality and geography. In that assumption he is not a racist at all, for his mental makeup is already racialized, a normative entrapment he can never decode. This figment of imagination has nothing to do with the reality of Europe: like any country or continent fragmented along race, gender, and class, some welcoming, many resentful of the new immigrants and refugees. Not just the reality of this wave of migration, or even the reality of European Muslims long before these waves came to shore, but the reality of Europe as fractured in its layered composition opens to much different horizons. Put them together, these varied realities map out a vastly different Europe, composed beyond its own illusions, than the one Dalai Lama imagines. Europe as metaphor trumps the truth of even Europe itself as a fragmented reality even before, much longer and deeper before, these Arab refuges came ashore. Our dearly beloved Dalai Lama is trapped inside that metaphor.

In 2016, the city of London elected its first Muslim mayor, just before the UK opted to exit the EU. Yes, there was UK Prime Minister David Cameron who, to prevent this from happening, tried to re-create sectarian hostility in London on the model of British colonial practices in India. Yes, the new mayor had to shift to the right and denounce BDS (Boycott, Divestment, Sanctions movement of the Israeli settler colony) before he could get elected. But elected he was—and on merely symbolic and demographic registers, this was an indication of what is dawning on the opening horizons of Europe. With Brexit, UK has now opted for xenophobic nativism. Cameron soon announced his resignation. Yes, there are nervous "European" philosophers (as they continue to insist in thus designating themselves) like Slavoj Žižek, or even more zealous Zionists like Bernard-Henri Lévy and Alain Finkielkraut, or mass murderers like Anders Breivik, or politicians like Marine Le Pen, Islamophobe New Atheists like Richard Dawkins, who fume and fumble and philosophize at the sight of new Muslim immigrants. But there are also other defiant voices like Alain Badiou's who catch these retrogrades red-handed, and whose visions are far more embracing of the newcomers. But the newcomers will continue to come—welcomed or not, and they will turn Europe against itself, upside down, the metaphor of Europe running for cover from the truth of the changing Europe, with or without His Holy Highness Dalai Lama's approval.

Europe is changing, slowly but surely, self-imploding much quicker than the new immigrants and refugees would warrant it. The anti-immigrant hysteria in Europe is the subterfuge for something far closer at home—insecurity and exhaustion of the trope itself. Muslim refugees are awakening Europe to its own central paradox: both its racist foregrounding and its liberal illusions, and the force of this dialectic will forever alter the repressed memories of the thing that has called itself "Europe," and even more so "the West." Look at them closely: These refugees are liberators. They are liberating Europe from the deadpan myth of "the West." The reaction of nervous philosophers like Žižek, Lévy, and Finkielkraut, as indeed the rise of xenophobic nativism in the UK, France, Germany, or elsewhere in Europe, are symptomatic of a futile resistance to the full dimensions of a seismic change they are unable to see yet. But change is inevitable, not so much under the pressure of refugees but because of the bursting bubble of the myth of Europe itself that has long since exhausted its enabling emotive universe. Do you remember that racist Hungarian camera operator for a Hungarian nationalist television channel, Petra László was her name, who was filmed kicking and tripping refugees at the Hungarian border to prevent them from entering Europe? The idea of Europe resisting its self-implosion is as futile in its resistances László was in hers.

Suppose sooner than later, Syrians and other refuges entered and lived and procreated in Europe—then what? What will replace Europe as a self-centering metaphor of the world at large? Can Europe itself, the fragmented truth and layered realities of the Europeans, overcome the coagulated, frozen, fetishized sign of Europe? Will Europe fetishize even deeper its allegorical grip on reality, or will reality overcome it?

The Center Cannot Hold

Today, the Dalai Lama and millions of other troubled cartographers of our changing world will be disoriented and dizzy if they were to be denied "the European" figment of their own captured imagination. They will chuckle in nervousness at the very thought. But tomorrow the creative consciousness of a radically different geography will inform and people our fragile Earth—of that I am convinced. The bursting of the myth of Europe and its contingent metaphor of "the West" does not bode well for "the Rest" either, for it spells out the end of all the binary illusions this "West" has manufactured to believe itself more ardently. Chief among them is "the Islam" it has colonially manufactured to digest and rule it better, aided and abetted, to be sure, by Muslims themselves, who continue to denounce or celebrate "the West" as the cause or cure of all their ills. Not just Europeans in the West, but Muslims too will have to figure out what to do with themselves without "the West," without "Europe."

When in *The Wretched of the Earth*, Frantz Fanon wrote, "Europe is literally the creation of the Third World," he was in the throes of Algerian anticolonial uprising (1954–1962) against the French domination. More than half a century has now passed since he wrote those iconic words. What would they mean today, how would they resonate, what have they taught us, where do we go from where those words have long since located and left us? Today, millions of people from the former colonies of Europe are rushing to the major cosmopolitan epicenters of their former colonizers seeking refuge, as Europe closes its borders with barbed wire, bribes little tyrant Sultan wannabes like Recep Tayyip Erdoğan to keep them away from Europe, and as it self-implodes with the UK declaring its Brexit in the aftermath of the austerity measures ripping its very assumptions apart from Greece to Spain, with Germany and France standing up on the rubble of the mirage of once a Holy Roman Empire. "The wretched of the Earth" were never exclusively in Asia and Africa or Latin America. Europe had plenty of its own blue-blooded "wretched of the Earth" too. But these massive migrations have mixed and matched them all from one side of the globe to the next, pitting them against one another. The "wretched of the Earth" are now those 850 million human beings (according to a UN estimate) who go to sleep hungry every night—and they are right in your Berlin,

Paris, and London, and not just in our Cairo, Delhi, or Johannesburg. There is therefore no longer any "your" or "our."

Fanon's material and concrete declaration almost half a century ago had a hidden metaphoric dimension, that the very idea of Europe was the invention of the Third World, or indeed conversely the very idea of "the Third World" was the invention of "Europe." All these binaries go together, hand in hand—"Islam and the West," "the West and the Rest"—in dividing the simple logic of capital and its abused labor along fictive geographical and ideological boundaries to rule the world better. We need to place Fanon's concrete observation next to Edward Said's metaphoric reading—to see the wisdom of both better. "Orient," Said proposed,

> is not an inert fact of nature. It is not merely there, just as the Occident itself is not just there either. We must take seriously Vico's great observation that men make their own history, that what they can know is what they have made, and extend it to geography: as both geographical and cultural entities—to say nothing of historical entities—such locales, regions, geographical sectors as "Orient" and "Occident" are man-made. Therefore, as much as the West itself, the Orient is an idea that has a history and a tradition of thought, imagery, and vocabulary that have given it reality and presence in and for the West. The two geographical entities thus support and to an extent reflect each other.[8]

What can and must now be added to both Fanon's and Said's pathbreaking critical thinking is the fact that not just people in Europe or "the West" but in fact those in non-Europe and "the East" of that very "West," thus located and thus coding and locating themselves, contribute and corroborate in the making of that auto-normativity of "Europe" and the aggressive alienation of the Rest. The very phrase, "we Europeans," posits the "non-European," as in fact today the very phrase, "we Muslims," "we Arabs," "we Indians," "we Latin Americans," and so on are all, without a single exception, uttered as the mirror images of whatever it is when others assay "We in the West." That forced and fictive binary needs once and for all to collapse—for us to be able to see the world better. As evident in both Fanon and Said, with varied degrees of articulation, this "Europe" needs the "non-Europe" to even begin to locate and understand itself, and that non-Europe corroborates the very (fictive) reality of Europe anytime it affirms or negates "Europe." Europhobia is the worst kind of Eurocentricism—we must never forget that.

Where do we stand today—half a century after *The Wretched of the Earth* and decades after *Orientalism*? The rapid globalization of transnational capital, the decentered operation of labor and capital chasing after each other's East and West, North and South, massive refugee and labor migrations, dwindling accumulated capital return resulting in massive militarization of international relations, endemic Eurozone crisis, and formation of alternative economic blocks such as BRICS (Brazil, Russia, India, China and South Africa) are chief among the global indications that the kind of material or metaphoric bifurcations Fanon and Said, chief among many others in their generations, had sketched for us have long since ceased to exist and have rapidly dissolved into an amorphous operation of a decentered capital and desperate labor. This, of course, is not an entirely new or sudden development, and signs of a globalized capital and its systemic abuse of labor around the world were evident even at the time that Fanon and Said were theorizing our conditions of coloniality. But over the last quarter of a century, because of digital revolution and the rapidity of transcontinental means and modes of labor migration, we have witnessed a sudden exposure to cultural dissonance of the binary supposition between the colonial and the capital, between any East or any West, between the cosmopolitan centers and tropical peripheries that have all systematically collapsed. "World Trade Center" was and remains a misnomer. There is no center to globalized capital—and therefore no East or West to it. "Islam and the West" (an offshoot of the West and the Rest) has been the most potent ideological fabrication of our generation, of continued uses to neocons, Islamophobes, and white supremacists alike.

The influx of so-called "Syrian refugees" in the aftermath of the bloody consequences of militarization of the Arab revolutions (2010–2015) by the United States and its regional allies, which is in fact nothing more than a slight intensification of labor migration of war-torn refugees roaming around the globe in search of a decent life, is the most recent index of this massive transmutation of the intense circulation of labor and capital. It is now very clear that what we have for the longest time called "colonialism" was nothing more than the global abuse of labor by capital times geography. The fact and phenomenon of coloniality were the replica of the fact and phenomenon of governmentality, a political condition of domination to disguise and facilitate this endemic, systemic, and enduring abuse. Although the racialized condition of coloniality was quite unique and must be understood as such, colonialism as an economic force was integral to the global operation of capital, and thus one must not over-fetishize it at the cost of misreading the pernicious operation of capital.

Based on this premise, my principal proposition is very simple: the condition of coloniality that Fanon and Said had fully understood and theorized—with the European "West" on one side and the colonized "Rest" on the other—has now metastasized and entered a whole new phase where the colonizer and the colonized are no longer divided along any national, regional, or continental divide, that the colonial has always been embedded in the capital, and the capital in the colonial, that imperialism was never anything other than predatory capitalism writ geographically large, and that as Michael Hardt and Antonio Negri have successfully demonstrated in their Empire trilogy (*Empire, Multitude,* and *Commonwealth,* 2000–2009), the condition of "Empire" requires a synergetic reading of the current condition of class struggles that overrides fictive national and civilizational boundaries. If that were the case, as I believe it is, then how do we measure our worldly, global, and epistemological whereabouts—when and where Europe is effectively decentered, de-authorized, de-universalized, overcome?

A more immediate and critical understanding of the metaphor of Europe and its corollary extension into "the West" will enable a necessary grasp of how their contemporary transmutations have morphed into a site-specific understanding of our world affairs. Without the metaphor of "Europe," the world as we know it will conceptually collapse—and for all the right reasons. There is no "Asia, Africa, or Latin America" without this particular Europe that has occasioned and signified them all. Consider how a volatile bifurcation between Europe as a self-centering metaphor and all its manufactured others ("Asia, Africa, and Latin America") has historically been conducive to an epistemic conditions of knowledge production along hostile and mutually exclusive boundaries, with specific reference to Islam and Muslims, as now conceived to be the absolute other of "the West." Europe has been cast as the measure, the destination, and the destiny of our humanity. Based on this crucial epistemic formation, a mapping of the postcolonial subject the world over will reveal a steady streak of historical, political, and narrative defiance against this Eurocentric conception of the world, not just among Muslims but also in fact around the globe, from Asia to Africa to Latin America. By questioning Europe, I am questioning all its alterities, all its extended shadows—I am in effect questioning the epistemic paradigm at the epicenter of which stands Europe in its entirety. My sense is that the real world has moved far beyond this paradigm, but the false consciousness of Europe still thwarts our reading of the world.

But my objective here is not belaboring or mourning the demise of Europe as a metaphor. I have a different ambition. I am after finding out in what particular terms a renewed trust in our world would or could possibly emerge. My ultimate argument as a result is that an *aesthetic intuition of transcendence* has systematically built up in a decidedly non-Europeanized context to mark and register the manner in which the creative impulses to revolt have become critical in overcoming the very condition of coloniality we have inherited from our forebears. This *aesthetic intuition of transcendence* is rooted in generations and histories of protest arts—in film, fiction, drama, and poetry—from Asia to Africa to Latin America, and of course in Europe and the United States too. Without that intuition and the impulse it sustains, the world will never see itself liberated from the mixed metaphor of Europe—its colonialism and its modernity alike. Europe will never be defeated or overcome epistemically, even if it were politically—or perhaps particularly when it is politically. Europe will only be overcome aesthetically—by poets, filmmakers, novelists, dramatists, and so on—if they are not assimilated backward into the diabolic trap of "Third World literature." The volatile formation of the metaphor of "Europe," in its epistemic power of alienation, is evident in the modes of political and epistemic resistances it has created. We are witness to a seismic defiance beyond any epistemic control only in the varied forms of aesthetic formations. By the end of this book, I intend to place the world we live in on a far different register than the one suggested by "the West and the Rest," or alternatively by "Europe and non-Europe."[9] In the thrust of my arguments, I do not intend either to "provincialize Europe" (as the false premise now puts it), or to strengthen by opposing Europe. I intend to bring Europe into the larger domain of its own contradictions and thus open it up to the world at large, the world it has conquered and concealed. By way of showing how against protesting too much, the metaphor of Europe has long since exhausted itself, the serious demographic changes within Europe contextualize the even more massive forces of labor migrations from and into Europe. The rapid globalization of the public sphere on which we live, where the extended links of cyberspace and outer space have all come together, posit a whole different liberation geography. I wish to read and theorize that geography.

The Dangers of "Western Liberal Democracies"

Let me now turn to a very simple and straightforward acid test: the fact that what we call "Western liberal democracy" is decidedly inimical to world peace—that it is in fact a danger to world peace. This innate paradoxical composition of Western liberal democracy is a fine specimen of how the very idea of "the West" (or "Europe") is in fact a contradiction in terms, a mixed metaphor, for in effect it negates its own ideals of democratic liberalism. It could only boast of its exclusivity to the degree that its colonial shadows were hidden, as in when the mother of parliaments (UK) and children of Thomas Jefferson (the United States) conspired to rob a nation (Iran or Guatemala) of the mere possibility of democracy by waging a military coup against it.

But let us use a more recent example. Who elected Tony Blair as the prime minister of the United Kingdom for more than a decade (May 2, 1997 to June 27, 2007)? Did Iraqis vote for him—anyone in the Arab or Muslim world? Which UK political party did he represent? The retrograde Conservative or the progressive Labour Parties—in fact, as the leader of the Labour Party between 1997 and 2007? How many votes did he receive as the leader of the Labour Party? How many blue-blooded British and UK citizens freely and fairly and willingly voted for Tony Blair during the election? With major victories in 1997, 2001, and 2005, Tony Blair was the longest-serving UK prime minister from the Labour Party, leading his party to three consecutive general election victories. Was any Iraqi man or woman among those who so enthusiastically voted for him in such historic victories in the finest specimen of Western liberal democracy for the very "mother of parliaments"?

Now, when this very democratically elected UK prime minister cheated, lied, fabricated false evidence, engaged in massive propaganda, went on a rampage about "terrorism" to join the United States in invading and occupying Iraq, was Blair "the military strongman of a Third World dictatorship," as they habitually say, or was he in fact the democratically elected prime minister of a Western liberal democracy? One more question: They say that the free press is a pillar of these Western democracies. Fair enough. Did this press perform its critical task in the course of preparatory stage of the U.S./UK-led invasion of Iraq? Did the press in either the United States or the United Kingdom beat the drums of war and become effective propaganda tools for the Bush-Blair war on Iraq and Iraqis, or did they engage in investigative journalism exposing the lies of their elected officials?

Based on the definitive Chilcot Report, we have at long last learned for a fact that Tony Blair is a war criminal, that this man as the prime minister of a Western democracy is the cause of more murder and mayhem in the world than the entire gang of subterranean creatures called ISIS and all other Islamist militant groups put together.[10] Hundreds of thousands of Iraqi men, women, and children, innocent of any crime against anyone, were murdered, and Tony Blair is one among a handful of democratically elected officials in Western liberal democracies who is chiefly, personally, and singularly responsible for their murder. He and his ringmaster, the U.S. president George W. Bush, yet another two-term democratically elected specimen of Western democracy and his own constitutionally appointed officials like his Vice President Dick Cheney and Defense Secretary Donald Rumsfeld are all war criminals and must be arrested, put in a cage, and tried for that and perhaps even for crimes against humanity.

The Chilcot Report has detailed the misbegotten path to the U.S./UK-led invasion and occupation of Iraq predicated on barefaced lies and propaganda dismantling a sovereign nation-state and wreaking havoc on the entirety of the Arab and Muslim world—contributing in part to the creation of the murderous ISIS. In short, Western liberal democracies, as they call themselves, spell out disaster for the world at large. Some 1.6 billion Muslims are held accountable for the criminal gang of ISIS and their likes by Islamophobic crowds in the United States and EU, ranging from widely popular comedians like Bill Maher to mass murderers like Anders Breivik. Did any one of these Muslims vote for ISIS or al-Qaeda to be their democratically elected officials? If Islam is to be held accountable for a small gang of Muslim criminals whom no one elected as their representatives, then why should Western liberal democracies not be held accountable for mass murderers like Tony Blair and George W. Bush who were in fact fairly and freely elected by UK and U.S. citizens as their representatives?

Soon after Tony Blair's Great Britain, the selfsame Western liberal democracy was in full gear in the United States and had resulted in the election of an avowedly racist, white supremacist, xenophobic carpetbagger called Donald Trump as the president of "the oldest democracy in the world." Did the world have any say in the matter? Did a Palestinian child, an Iraqi mother, an Afghan widow, have anything to say about the matter? Can they speak? Can they vote in these sorts of elections? Is this democracy a model for the world to emulate—when a constituency in the UK or United States decides the fate of human beings in Asia, Africa, or Latin America? The Israeli settler colony built on the broken but defiant back of Palestinians by a gang of European militant adventurists also calls itself a "democracy"—in fact "the only democracy in the Middle East." Is that apartheid garrison state, built on the prototype of the apartheid South Africa, a model for the rest of the region? Zionism is the latest vestige of European colonialism—of the very trope of Europe—in the heart of the Arab world—and has nothing to do with Jews having a homeland in Palestine. Jews have always had a homeland in Palestine, and should always have a homeland in Palestine, along with their Muslim and Christian neighbors, in a free and democratic Palestine for all its citizens. But that is not what Zionism is. A European settler colonial project has demanded and exacted from Palestinians. What has that emblematic of European colonialism brought to our world—peace, prosperity, security? How can any decent human being in the world look a Palestinian in the eye and mention the word *Europe*?

We do not have liberal democracies anywhere in the world except in the imaginative geography that calls itself "the West," the emblematic extension of the trope of "Europe." We have tyrannies, dictatorships, and military juntas—most of them supported and sustained by Europe and its U.S. extensions—two prime examples of them are Saudi Arabia and Egypt. We have deep states, narco-states, supreme leaders for life, neoliberal Communist Party loonies—all of them demonized on the lunatic fringes of civilized polity. We have perpetual presidents, divine emissaries, and clerical theocracies— Turkey and Iran are best examples here. Even in India, which is called "the largest democracy in the world," it is really a Hindu fundamentalist fanaticism in which Muslim, Christian, and other non-Hindu citizens are less equals than others, even when they are not slaughtered and their intestines skewered and served as Muslim kebabs. So we mortals around the world neither have any claims on this Western liberal democracies (except through their colonial gun barrels) nor should harbor any delusion that it constitutes a promised land where when we reach all will be hunky-dory. Are we to work hard so one day we may have the rare privilege of producing a Muslim Donald Trump, an Iranian George W. Bush, an Egyptian Tony Blair, a Syrian Silvio Berlusconi? The internal implosion and narrative crisis of Europe have fortunately liberated the world from any such delusions. Francisco Franco in Spain, Benito Mussolini in Italy, and Adolf Hitler in Germany were vintage European pieces of jewelries that emerged from the very bosoms of these Western liberal democracies. So we need not remind Europe of their beloved Winston Churchill's nasty racism and genocide in India and elsewhere to believe that this cherished thing they call Western liberal democracy has been an existential threat to the world, including to Europe itself.

The question, however, is not personal, or specific to any democratically elected official here and there in the United States or EU. The question is the normative allegory that has branded itself Europe and is now self-imploding: European democracies, European values, European principles of human rights (shattered by the first arms sales to an Arab potentate with a fat bank account who walks on a red carpet on the tarmac of any European airport). The world at large is liberated from this illusion. In opposing the tyrants who rule over the world at large—including the long shadow of European tyrants from Hitler, Mussolini, and Franco to U.S. tyrant wannabes like Trump and all the other turns around the world Europe consistently supports—the world is entirely on its own—back to the drawing board. I write as an Iranian who was born in 1951, and two years into my birth, the United Kingdom and United States conspired and toppled a democratically elected government of my homeland. I am the living testimony that

Europe, the United States, and "the West" a fortiori are paragons of hypocrisy from which to learn anything about democracy. I will read as I have read Plato and Aristotle entirely independent of the false claim this Europe has laid on them. The world does not have any model, any blueprint, any ideal, any aspiration coming to it from anywhere, least of all from the chimera that calls itself "the West," or the allegory that stages itself as "Europe." One quick look around the globe and it becomes clear this Europe has been the singular source of calamity anywhere and everywhere it has fathomed to Westernize. People around the world are collectively liberated from the delusion of Western liberal democracies and must now build their own conceptions of liberty and freedom from ground up, from lived experiences to theoretical articulation, freed from the mixed metaphors that had reached them from the calamity of European colonialism to the imperial thuggery of the United States.

"A European Buddhism"?

"I understood the ever spreading morality of pity," Nietzsche says in *The Genealogy of Morals* (1887), "that had seized even on philosophers and made them ill, as the most sinister symptom of a European culture that had itself become sinister, perhaps as its by-pass to a new Buddhism? to a European Buddhism? To nihilism?"[11]

How so—I wonder. European Buddhism? Really? Why is it that when European philosophers and politicians, the best and the worst of them, look for a foreign referent as a metaphor for what is worse in them? Nietzsche would, of course, not be around when the Buddhist monks in Myanmar went slaughtering Muslims to figure out how accurate a metaphor of nihilism his "European Buddhism" would be. But still alluding to a non-European metaphor to understand the worst of Europe remained constant to generations of philosophers and even critical thinkers who thought "Oriental despotism" was something inbred and ingrained, as they wrote from the heart of the European colonial savagery around the world.

Beyond the reach of even the sublime sarcasm of Nietzsche, "Europe," as a mobile army of mixed metaphors, is dichotomous. Europe means non-Europe too. Europe cannot be Europe without non-Europe. As staged by Joseph Keppler, European Civilization will be annulled and void without non-Europe putting a barbarian

Coinciding with the British reconquest of the Sudan was this cartoon drawn by Joseph Keppler, a frequent contributor to the American political satire and humor magazine, Puck. Keppler portrays the conflict between the British and Sudanese as a struggle of the representatives of "civilization" against the forces of "barbarism." Although the imagery used to depict the 'barbarians' is not specifically evocative of the Middle East, it is a reflection of the predominant Western attitude toward the enterprise of colonialism and imperialism at the dawn of the twentieth century. (Source: http://teachmiddleeast .lib.uchicago.edu/historical-perspectives/middle-east-seen-through-foreign-eyes /islamic-period/image-resource-bank/image-07.html).

wall of resistance to its delusional fancies. The color codification stages the binary. Europe is the white female, triumphant; the non-European is male, colored, barbaric. Here and elsewhere, Europe is the defining metaphor of colonial modernity—world conquering, defiant, self-centered. It violently exploited the world and beautifully staged itself. It constituted, alienated, and made strange and barbaric the others to know, recognize, identify, discover, and celebrate itself. As such, that metaphor is now exposed and has imploded. Upon the metaphoric depletion of its power, Europe is reaching back to its fascistic roots—its claws widely opened and sharpened in its neo-Nazi skinheads. Such visual staging of the European "self" and all its "others" has now reached its allegorical ends. The barrier and the boundary between Europe and non-Europe, that triumphant arch that separates the white civilization from the colorful barbarians it manufactured to rule, have been metaphorically crossed. Upon the moment when Europe is effectively decentered, de-authorized, and de-universalized, the non-Europe is released from its binary entrapment and liberated to discover itself for itself beyond Europe, before Europe, no longer in the shadow of Europe—and with that worldly liberation will also be liberated Europe itself.

Two
Europe, Shadows, Coloniality, Empire

Only through forgetfulness can man ever achieve the illusion of
possessing a "truth" ... What is a word? The image of a nerve stimulus in sounds. But to infer from the nerve stimulus, a cause outside
us, that is already the result of a false and unjustified application of
the principle of reason. ... The different languages, set side by side,
show that what matters with words is never the truth.... The "thing
in itself" (for that is what pure truth, without consequences, would
be) is quite incomprehensible to the creators of language and not at
all worth aiming for. One designates only the relations of things to
man and to express them one calls on the boldest metaphors.[1]

Friedrich Nietzsche, *On Truth and Lie in*
an Extra-Moral Sense (1873)

On July 22, 2011, a fertilizer bomb was detonated outside the office
of Prime Minister Jens Stoltenberg in Oslo. Shortly after this deadly
explosion, in which eight people were killed, a heavily armed man
posing as a police officer—with white skin, blonde hair, fierce and
determined in his disposition—landed on Utøya island from a ferry
and for more than an hour fired his automatic rifles randomly and
intermittently at campers at a Workers' Youth League, killing
scores of youngsters, some as young as 14 years old. When security
forces finally arrived at the scene, the mass murderer surrendered
without any resistance. The man was later identified as the
31-year-old Norwegian national named Anders Behring Breivik.
Upon his surrender, Breivik confessed to authorities that the
purpose of his deed was to save western Europe, Norway in particular, from a Muslim takeover.

Before launching his attack, Breivik had electronically distrib-
uted a manifesto he had written and published and entitled *2083:*
A European Declaration of Independence, in which he had detailed
the ideological foregrounding of his massacre.[2] In this manifesto,

he identifies Islam, cultural Marxism, and feminism as the three-fold sources of European decline and decay. He calls for ideological confrontation with all these three targets, and advocated for the mass expulsion of Muslims from Europe. Before he engaged in his mass murder, it is doubtful anyone except his few supporters and interlocutors knew of this text—though he extensively cites the racist pronouncements of leading U.S. Islamophobes as his inspirations. He succeeded in his stated purpose, and as a result of his notoriety, a massive global readership came to know about and some even to read his manifesto. Europe and European civilization was in danger, he told his readers. Muslims were the key factor infesting the purity of European culture, and cultural Marxists and feminists were chief collaborators of Muslims in this conspiracy against Europe.

Anders Breivik: The European

No one other than Breivik himself was or is responsible for his heinous crime. His action does not represent Europe, Christianity, or even those who may consider themselves "white Europeans." Millions of European Christians might even racially identify as "white" but are entirely innocent of any shared responsibility or complacency with what Breivik did. His action was and remains as representative of millions of Christian Europeans as the action of Islamic State (IS) represents Muslims. Muslims are as innocent of the Islamic State, and Jews of Zionism, as European Christians are of the Breivik mass murder and the hateful ideology he and his ilk have fathomed.

We need to read and understand Breivik's manifesto the same way that we read and understand Molla Omar, Osama bin Laden, or Abu Bakr al-Baghdadi's proclamations, or read and understand the ideological convictions of Zionism that insist on the systematic European colonization of Palestine, expulsion of its native inhabitants, and the establishment of a garrison state in cahoots with the imperial designs of the United States in the region.

The significance of the Breivik document is limited to what it actually says, to factors it identifies as the enemy of Europe, of the vision of a "pure Europe" it projects, of the enemies of Europe it identifies: what the Norwegian mass murderer calls Islam, cultural Marxism, or feminism are all figments of his own troubled imagination. Much has been correctly written about the sources of his Islamophobic imagination having in fact originated in the United States, from a pathological gang of rabid Islamophobes (many of them hard-core Zionists) chiefly responsible for fomenting hatred toward Muslims by way of manufacturing a delusional enemy to their favorite settler colony. We need to examine Breivik's manifesto as we examine the symptoms of a disease in a body that is otherwise perfectly capable of health and happiness. The text of the manifesto is important because we hear its echoes in the range of racist ideologues and politicians from one end of Europe to another, politicians like Marine Le Pen in France, Geert Wilders in Holland, many other similar figures in UK responsible for the xenophobia of the Brexit campaign, and then of course the sort of Islamophobes across the Atlantic that eagerly anticipated the rise of Donald Trump. In short, the significance of the manifesto is in the wider white supremacist racism it reflects in the most blatant prose, a good portion of it cited from Zionists across the Atlantic and that in turn echoes among political parties in Europe and now in the Republican Party in the United States, as refashioned into a xenophobic white nationalism by Donald Trump and the ideology of Trumpism he promotes.

Anders Breivik's document is the antithesis and thus the fulfillment of Nietzsche's prophetic soul. Breivik is the result, and his manifesto the fulfillment of what Nietzsche feared would be the result of the absolutist metaphysics of the word *Europe*. Today, about a century and a half after Nietzsche's prescient words, there is no understating of what the European iconoclastic philosopher meant without reading the delusional drivel of Breivik, or seeing his nightmare fulfilled. When Nietzsche asked, "What is a word?" he may or may not have had the word *Europe* in mind. But that seminal word, definitive to his philosophy of presence, could not have been too far from his mind. When Nietzsche said, "Only through forgetfulness can man ever achieve the illusion of possessing a 'truth,'" he meant a historical forgetfulness of the delusion called "Europe" that if left unchecked would result, as it did, in monsters like Hitler soon after him and then Breivik who more than 150 years after Nietzsche declared:

Most Europeans look back on the 1950s as a good time. Our homes were safe, to the point where many people did not bother to lock their doors. Public schools were generally excellent, and their problems were things like talking in class and running in the halls. Most men treated women like ladies, and most ladies devoted their time and effort to making good homes, rearing their children well and helping their communities through volunteer work. Children grew up in two-parent households, and the mother was there to meet the child when he came home from school. Entertainment was something the whole family could enjoy. What happened?[3]

There is a vast difference between what Hitler did with the word *Aryan* and what Breivik did with the word *Europe*, but Nietzsche's reflections on the conceptual foregrounding of both these atrocities before they actually happened capture the quintessence of Europe where it matters most: where the thing collapses upon itself. Hitler did to Europeans, and Breivik to his victims, what King Leopold II of Belgium did to Congo or the British to India, or the French to Algeria—all in the name of Europe and their colonial possessions.

"Europe" Is a Recent Invention

For the longest time, we in their "Orient" have been the subjects of the European incessant, debilitating gaze. They made us just stand there and they watched us, robbed us, studied us, slaughtered us, museumized us. We were their *objet de curiosité*, the source of their wealth, the matter of their amusements, the subject of their social sciences. They have kept looking at us, collecting us, placing us in their galleries and universities, studying us into nullity as if we were dead meat. Their anthropology of us requires an anthropology of them, a criminology of their motives. It is long overdue we returned the gaze and started looking at them—our conquerors and tormentors—and we have been looking back at them for quite some time. Who are these people who call themselves "Europeans" and who keep studying the world to nullity? What is this thing that holds them together and they call it "Europe?" We will be far gentler with them than they were with us, far more humane, far more considerate and understanding. We will bring the best of them to bear on the worst of them—we are not vindictive, we are merely curious. But we will have to look, and as we look they will get nervous. We will look at their mass murderers and colonialists, at their artists and their poets, their philosophers and their critical thinkers, with equal gentility and horror, and with utmost consideration of their worries and wonders. From Césaire to Fanon to Said, we have done a lot of complaining—as we must have. We are done complaining. We no longer wish to complain. But we need to explain them to themselves and to us. We need to put this thing that calls itself "Europe" on the pedestal. We will be gentle.

Our consideration of Europe will not be the task of just pointing fingers at its faults. That would be too easy. The task is to go after the link, the pathological mirroring of "the West and the Rest," of Europe and non-Europe. Europe is not just in the light of its own name but hiding in the shadows of its colonial images. The Breivik document is the most grotesque manifestation of something serious—that Europe is in trouble, that Europe is in demise, and that these pathological symptoms of its decline and fall are the psychotic symptoms of a serious ailment that has far less dramatic, far calmer and composed political manifestations in electoral politics, in ideological foregrounding of xenophobic hatred of immigrants, with Muslims as the primary target of this revulsion and enmity. Too much attention to the target of this enmity, namely Muslims and other immigrants, distracts from a far more serious aspect of the ailment, that Europe itself, even without such delusional enemies is in trouble, that these delusional enemies Europe is inventing for itself are in fact the subterfuge for the mere allegory to give itself a sustained cause of existence.

When Europeans say "man" or "person," they mean "European man" or "European person." This is precisely what Michel Foucault, the groundbreaking European philosopher, meant when he famously wrote:

As the archaeology of our thought easily shows, man is an invention of recent date. And one perhaps nearing its end. If those arrangements were to disappear as they appeared, if some event of which we can at the moment do no more than sense the possibility—without knowing either what its form will be or what it promises—were to cause them to crumble, as the ground of Classical thought did, at the end of the eighteenth century, then one can certainly wager that man would be erased, like a face drawn in sand at the edge of the sea.[4]

Here and elsewhere, what Foucault and all other European phi-losophers like him before or after, meant by "man" was and remains "the European man," the man as it was conceived by European mo-dernity, and his prophetic declaration that this man was about to disappear rings true to the colonial ear too if we were to translate it into our sensibilities that what the French philosopher meant was the European man, not the African, Asian, Latin American man, or person. In a typical Euro-universalism, Foucault said "man" but meant "European man," though he thought the European man was just man. The European man, just like Europe itself, was the recent invention of European capitalist modernity. Foucault's prognosis that this conceptual construct would soon disappear is a fortiori ap-plicable to the Europe that has been coinvented in the selfsame course of historical developments. European man and Europe were twins, the products of the same capitalist modernity. We in the colonial world know this for we have been the playing field of both.

Let us now add to Foucault's wisdom Fanon's insight, and things become a bit clearer. In his *The Wretched of the Earth*, Fanon wrote: "Today Europe's tower of opulence faces these continents, for cen-turies the point of departure of their shipments of diamonds, oil, silk and cotton, timber, and exotic produce to this very same Eu-rope. Europe is literally the creation of the Third World."[5] The relationship between Foucault and Fanon, unbeknownst to them-selves, is underwritten by the organic clink between globalized capitalism and colonialism, between Europe and its colonial shadows, between the invention of the European man in the course of capitalist modernity and the cross-invention of Europe by the colonial condition of production. Much to his theoretical limita-tions, Foucault was entirely blinded, except for a generic political commitment, to the colonial consequences of the modernity he ably critiqued.

Historically, Europe has cast a long shadow over the Earth—at once economic and cultural, political and epistemic. Europe and its shadows still define and bewilder the world. Let us think of the Eu-ropean *shadows* in Jungian terms, the dark side of the European character, its projected primitive, negative, boycotted side of its soul. The shadow is forbidden but desired, and thus Europe and its shadows are the zone of the forbidden and the denied intertwined. Let us think of the European shadow as its colonial extensions, where the European daddy goes to work, and leaves mommy and the babies back home in peace and comfort, safely tucked away from the barbaric site of their daddy's daily chores, so at night mummy and babies can dwell in civilized peace. The colonial shadow is the evil side of the European self-consciousness, its damned repressed, where it does not want to remember what it has done, and dislikes those who remind it of its atrocities. It is the darker side that makes the lighter side of the European persona (again in Jungian terms) possible, plausible, cultivated. With its colonial shadow, the European persona would be like Dr. Jekyll who has not exorcized its Mr. Hyde from himself. The colonial shadow of Europe is its historical expression of the far deeper archetypal (Jungian) persona—where the shadow and the persona cohabit—uneasily.

Europe has always been contingent on its shadows, predicated on its negations, conditioned by its protesting too much against the Rest of its West—the non-Europe to its Europe. Take the Rest away from the West and Europe does not know what it is and will dissolve unto itself. Europe is more by omission than by commission. There are two principal omissions contingent on Europe, one is *temporal* to Europe's conception of itself and the other *spatial* and adjacent to it. Europe invented a dark age in its own past to see itself enlightened in its present modernity. Europe invented ancient and medieval stages for itself to believe in its own longevity and therefore modernity. Europe invented a Greco-Roman heritage for itself to retrieve it in what it considers its renaissance. These were all in epistemologically temporal terms. Then Europe invented a spatial distance from itself—an Asia, Africa, and Latin America, a vast and expansive Orient to authenticate its Occidentality. Take the Orient away from the Occident, and it disappears into the thin air. Europe is not affirmative. It is always contingent on a negative dialectic, on a negation, on an omission, on lack—Europe is what its others are not. There is no Jungian persona to Europe without its multiple shadows. Its multiple shadows are now coming back to haunt it. They trouble its illusion of itself.

In the course of the World Cup 2018 in Russia, the African striker Kylian Mbappé at once thrilled and troubled the French and by extension the European perception of themselves. He was testing the very notion of the European—of Europe. Who was he—African or French or both or neither? Could an African be a European? He was too good a footballer to be made alien; he was too black to be a white French conception of "French." "The French" just like "the American" and just like "the European" was always white. It had been color-coded. The 19-year-old kid, the "new Pelé," as they called him, was dashing, expensive, committed to helping disadvantaged children, and he played football like a dream. He had become a public figure. France wanted him, but did not know how. Europe wanted to claim him, but in what terms? Mbappé and other black French footballers such as Paul Pogba and N'Golo Kanté complicated the white French delusion of themselves. After the semifinals, when France defeated Belgium, Marine Le Pen, the proto-fascist French far-right National Front racist leader chuckled: "When I look at Les Bleus, I don't recognize France or myself." Of course, she did not. They were mostly black. She was white. The twain—the persona and the shadow—shall never meet.

To the world at large, Europe was an allegory of empire; "civilizing" this empire, as it fancied itself doing from one end to another, was its ideology, capitalist modernity its modus operandi, the United States its first extended persona, when they both become the centerpiece of what they now called "the West," while Israel is today its last colonial legacy—its embarrassing insignia in the world for things it wished the world could forget but of which the Zionist project reminds them on a daily brutal routine. The rest of the world, thus "rested," became the colonial shadow of what this Europe had thought itself to be. Europe and its American, Israeli, and Australian extensions were all white. By America, they did not mean the First Nations, or African slaves, or the colored immigrants. They meant only the white settlers, as they did in Israel, to the exclusion of the native Palestinians, or Australia in which their First Nations do not figure. The same is true about Canada. Europe and all its extensions were, and were to remain, white.

Today, we are catching Europe at its dying day when as an idea, as a metaphor inseparable from the colonial relations it initiated and sustained, it no longer convinces or commands attention—it is a relic of what it used to be, an aging racist gentleman just like Prince Philip of England. It is quite charming. Those colonial relations that produced the binary of Europe and non-Europe persist in a new form today that does not anymore follow the national, state-centric, or civilizational lines. The colony is already in the metropole as the metropole has always been in the colony. Just look at the four "national" football teams that made it to the World Cup 2018: France, England, Belgium, and Croatia. Three of these four flags were the flags that robbed the world blind in Asia, Africa, and Latin America, and as they have retreated to their home turfs, toward them have come throngs of their former colonies, some of them great footballers, who are Algerian, Cameroonian, or Iranian when they fail to score but French, English, and Belgians when they do. Europe is not feeling well.

The historic course of colonialism that had created Europe has ended but the condition of coloniality continues. Why? The normative basis of colonial domination has ended under the myth of the postcolonial state. But the illusion, the false consciousness, the phantom feel of Europe still continues. The civilizational othering of the gestation of Samuel Huntington and Francis Fukuyama has now yielded to the more vulgar versions of Niall Ferguson, Donald Trump, the Brexiters, or the Steve Bannons, Stephen Millers, and Anders Breiviks of the world.

In the Colonial Shadows of Europe

It is not "man" that is a recent epistemological invention. It is the "European man" that is so recently conceived. This is not to suggest that the African, Asian, or Latin American man had already been invented, or cared to be invented. It is simply to say the invention of "European man" was coterminous with the invention of Europe as the locus classicus of capitalist modernity over which globalized imperial project this European man presided. The autonomy, agency, power, the sense of self-entitlement, and audacity to conquer this European man was built on the broken back of non-European men and women. What Foucault diagnosed as the epistemic condition of the knowing subject in his European context has entirely different dimensions in it colonial contexts, which I have spent more than two decades of my scholarship trying to map out in details. The rise of human sciences in the sixteenth century coincides with the colonial ascendency of European empires around the globe, particularly in Asia, Africa, and Latin America. We colonials were denied agency because we were the subjects of those sciences. The modern European formation of the very idea of "humanity" (etymologically rooted as it was in the Latin *humanitas* and the Greek *philanthrôpía*) was coterminous with their colonial conquest of the world, with the disciplines of anthropology, economics, and biology squarely rooted in their colonial conquests. Darwin's theories of natural selection, even before giving birth and legitimacy to the imperial arrogance of conquest and domination, were coterminous with British colonies and his scholarship in fact entirely contingent on the five-year expedition of the second voyage of HMS *Beagle* to South American coasts and beyond. The same holds true of the disciplines of economics and linguistics that were equally contingent on the colonial conquests that European imperialism had enabled. By the time the three Foucauldian seminal sciences (biology, economics, and linguistics) were thoroughly established in the nineteenth century, so was the vast spread of European colonialism from which resources the material and theoretical foregrounding of these disciplines were formed.

"Man" was a "European man," and the "European man" was invented and then dis-invented in Europe, by the Europeans, for the Europeans—and on that scheme the rest of us were just bystanders, too nonhuman to be man or woman. The pride and joy of European philosophy in the nineteenth century, Immanuel Kant's (1724–1804) three seminal critiques were instrumental in manufacturing an autonomous European subject presiding over these sciences, and the knowing subject of Kant was a European subject, and we, the world, were delegated to the knowable world, objects of Kant's and his European subject's knowledge and curiosity, and he personally and philosophically considered us Asian, African, and Latin American people "completely black from head to foot, a distinct proof" that what we say is "stupid." This not because of what we said, which "might be something worth considering," but just because we were not white Europeans. As he once put it succinctly:

> Father Labat reports that a Negro carpenter, whom he reproached for haughty treatment of his wives, replied: You whites are real fools, for first you concede so much to your wives, and then you complain when they drive you crazy. There might be something here worth considering, except for the fact that this scoundrel was completely black from head to foot, a distinct proof that what he said was stupid.[6]

It is imperative to keep in mind that this was not a mere passing racism. This was definitive to his philosophy. We the non-European colored folks were part of the knowable world, we could not possibly be any knowing subject. That would have completely dismantled his philosophical system.

Kant, of course, was not alone in such lofty opinions of the non-Europeans. On more than one occasion, Emmanuel Levinas (1906–1995), the distinguished Lithuanian phenomenologist—went out of his way to dismiss the non-European as nonhuman. "When I speak of Europe," he wrote, "I think about the gathering of humanity. Only in the European sense can the world be gathered together ... in this sense Buddhism can be said just as well in Greek."[7] Staying with what and who they are, how they were born, the non-Europeans are not humans—in the eye of the ethical philosopher who famously sought the sight of the (European) knowing subject in an encounter with "the face of the other." "I often say," Levinas said (not once or twice, but "often"), "although it is a dangerous thing to say publicly, that humanity consists of the Bible and the Greeks. All the rest can be translated: all the rest—all the exotic—is dance."[8]

The object of the three Foucauldian disciplines was not man but the European man, thus invented in shadowy contradistinction with the non-European person. The object of European psychology were the black and brown and yellow and red shadows of the European man (thus invented and color-coded to cross-authenticate "the white man"), who were all beyond the realm and reach of psychology, for we were all colored and dark and dancing with ourselves to the tunes of Levinas's real philosophical musings and in the shadow of that psychology. But the European man was dis-invented as fast as it was invented—and thus the whole project of "alternative modernities" crumbled like a house of cards. By the time Freud, Jung, and Lacan were done with this "European man" and handed him over to Heidegger, Derrida, and Foucault, nothing was left of him to be the sovereign subject of any knowable world. By the time Noam Chomsky was done with his structural linguistics, this man was there as a mere vehicle that had inherited a grammar. Europe was undoing itself. European man was just a ghost in his colonial domains. The European interlocutor had died, but "religious intellectuals" in Iran (as they called themselves) were still busy talking to him, trying to convince him he was wrong. Jürgen Habermas did his Teutonic best to reserve the European project of modernity, and with it the European, before Syrian refugees began banging at his door and he did not know where to run.

What was left was no man, but a European subject under ~~erasure~~ and in deep crisis. By the time Heidegger had published his *Letter on Humanism* (1947), the European man had already ceased to exist. By the time Barthes published his "Death of the Author" (1967), even the European author was dead. By the time Ferdinand de Saussure was done with his *Course in General Linguistics* (1916), the European knowing subject was already dismantled. All of these announced the birth of the European post-humans, the death of the European man, all within the high philosophical theorization of the European crisis—particularly pronounced in the aftermath of the Jewish Holocaust. Maurice Blanchot was the last European author to be able to say "I"—sarcastically and under ~~erasure~~—at the moment when the postcolonial "I" had just begun speaking. The Cartesian *cogito* had started the "I," and Blanchot effectively ended it—precisely at the moment when in the words of Enrique Dussel, we had come to realize: "before the *ego cogito* there is an *ego conquiro;* 'I conquer' is the practical foundation of 'I think.'"⁹

Let me get back to this notion of "shadow" at the heart of my take on "the European man" here. In Akira Kurosawa's *Kagemusha (Shadow Warrior,* 1980), we are introduced to a lower-class criminal who is recruited to impersonate an ailing emperor to dissuade the enemies of the clan from invading and conquering them. By the end of the film, we cannot tell the difference between the original and the fake, between the emperor and his shadows. That's the story of Europe and its colonial shadows—the emperor is hiding in its own shadows, in its own colonial impersonators. As the shadow of Europe, the colonized world was its unconscious, the dungeon of its hidden and repressed desires, the place where it was being ideologically incubated. Somewhere between Freud and Jung, the shadowy unconscious, neither personal nor archetypal but entirely historical, became colonial. The European "Orient" was the shadow unconscious of Europe, its repressed desires, where its repressed would return. The more the Orient was demonized, the more it was desired to be conquered and the more Victorian became the bourgeois morality. The map of the European shadow unconscious is a colonial territory of its erotic desires to conquer and possess. We postcolonial theorists are all the illegitimate children of that desire, born out of wedlock, disrespectful to bourgeois morality of all the legitimate children of the emperor. In the words of our brother Edmund in King Lear (Act 1, Scene 2):

Thou, nature, art my goddess. To thy law
My services are bound. Wherefore should I
Stand in the plague of custom and permit
The curiosity of nations to deprive me
For that I am some twelve or fourteen moonshines
Lag of a brother? Why "bastard"? Wherefore "base"?
When my dimensions are as well compact,
My mind as generous, and my shape as true
As honest madam's issue? Why brand they us
With "base," with "baseness," "bastardy," "base," "base"—
Who in the lusty stealth of nature take
More composition and fierce quality
Than doth within a dull, stale, tirèd bed
Go to th' creating a whole tribe of fops
Got 'tween a sleep and wake? Well then,
Legitimate Edgar, I must have your land.
Our father's love is to the bastard Edmund
As to the legitimate. Fine word, "legitimate!"
Well, my legitimate, if this letter speed
And my invention thrives, Edmund the base
Shall top th' legitimate. I grow, I prosper.
Now, gods, stand up for bastards!

"The West and the Rest": A Confounded Delusion

The idea of Europe, I propose, is defunct because it has now hit its most central paradox. It was built by robbing the world and building its moral and imaginative confidence—and now the world is coming back to rob it of its delusions of power and authority, refusing to tickle its fancies anymore. Europe colonized the world *territorially*, while at the same time manufactured a periodization in its own history *temporally*. It narrated itself backward to Plato and Aristotle, as it conquered for itself a planet to rob of its own multiple worlds. Europe was an illusion that soon made itself forget of what it was, and now the refugees are bringing back its own repressed memories. Europe is aging and it needs young labor—but does not like the laborer. It likes them to stay where they are—in Asia, Africa, Latin America, at the mercy of its superior sense of mercy and generosity. Swedish mothers are sending their young children to Caribbean vacations, there to procreate and make more white babies. The British royalty is staging their young princes' virilities, constantly showing them young and cute and kissing and cuddling and begetting children. But it is a losing battle—demographic changes are against them. Look at Lars von Trier's films like *Dogville* (2003) to see how Europe (and its image of the United States) is morally self-imploding. Europe began dissolving much faster than it took to manufacture itself. This is not a creative crisis. This is an existential crisis.

As a potent allegory, Europe has lost its luster but lives a de-feated life with Donald Trump at one side and waves of immigrants on the other, and Anders Breivik and Brexit and Le Pen and the like in the middle. Europe is petrified by Trump, and by extension by the monster created to protect against its Russian nightmare, and yet the same Confederate racism that once ripped this country apart is coming back to haunt it. The United States emerged as the imperial extension of the very logic of Europe as a colonial project. But the globalized monstrosity of the empire has made Europe redundant and burdensome to the United States. At least since World War II, Europe has been an appendix to the United States—a burn to its military and an asset to its imperialism. During the Cold War, NATO was an extension of U.S. military might to offset the Warsaw Pact and now beyond. It is not accidental that soon after its foundation in 1948, the European settler colony of Israel shifted its reliance and alliance away from Europe and toward the United States, facilitating its domination of the region. By the time of the Gulf War (2003), and particularly the French opposition to it, Secretary of Defense Donald Rumsfeld began to speak of "the new Europe," by which he meant the recently de-Sovietized eastern European states beholden to U.S. economic aids. There is no differentiating between the old and the new Europe when the very idea of Europe is in jeopardy.

The end of Europe as a towering metaphor is nothing to celebrate or to mourn—it is a phase in our collective history—colonizers and colonized. Muslim empires ended, but Muslims survived, as did Arab empires, and before them the Romans, the Spanish, the Chinese, the Persians. The condition of coloniality occasioned by Europe is now amorphous, with no commanding or convincing culture to sustain it in any hegemony. The Europeans' Enlightenment ended with the Holocaust, its modernity in its own postmodernity, its post-structuralism in postcoloniality. Today, Europe can only exist vicariously as a proto-fascist politics of the neo-Nazis in

Europe and the KKK-inspired Trumpism in the United States, or similar politics in Australia, or a racist apartheid state of Israel, without any convincing philosophical, moral, or cultural claim to any one of them. Europe's towering philosopher Heidegger was a Nazi, its most exquisite artist Paul Gauguin was an abusive racist, its anthropology rooted in colonial criminality, its political science on political domination of the globe. There is nothing in "Western" science and technology, culture and literature without a long and nasty colonial shadow. What will emerge from the ruins and relics of Europe and all its shadows are the ruins and relics of once a glorious but flawed claim on our credulities that must now come together in writing a new chapter of post-European, post-Western, entirely real and worldly, awareness of who and what we are.

Europe continues with its precarious life by creating false enemies like Islam, immigrants, Syrians, Africans, and so on—as the United States does with a similar cast of Mexicans, Muslims, immigrants, blacks, all from places President Donald Trump has collectively called "shitholes." Today, three crucial events mark and expose the vulnerable origins and limitations of Europe as an allegory: (1) Trump elected as the head of a racist, xenophobic country and with full executive power, (2) the racist apartheid state of Israel and its European origins in both colonialism and anti-Semitism, and (3) the xenophobic reactions to waves of migrants and the rise of neo-Nazis. Islamophobia marks the Christian disposition of Europe as an idea. It exposes the faultiness of Europe as the quintessential condition of coloniality that had created it in the first place. All its sciences have now ended up in the nuclear calamity that hovers all of us on this Earth, all its moral philosophy ended in and at the Holocaust, all its glorious literary masterpieces ended in Donald Trump's tweets, all its artistic achievements museumized into no organic relevance to the rest of its cyberspace distraction. Its music is abandoned in the mothball opera houses serving nothing but vacuous status symbols of a bored and boring bourgeoisie. Its cinema is today overshadowed by masters from Asia, Africa, and Latin America. Where Europe reigned supreme now competes for the slightest attention in Cannes, Venice, or Berlin.

At this stage, as a result, we need to go beyond a cliché criticism of Eurocentricism—for we have all been there and done that. We must see Europe for what it is, what it has always been: a once potent cluster of metaphors that have now been depleted of meaning

except for the dangerous nostalgia it invokes in its racist, xenophobic rise of the neo-Nazis and the far right. My concern in this
book is no longer with the truism of Eurocentricism—it was once
but no longer insightful. It has become a truism. Of course, Europe
is Eurocentric. Every village anywhere else in the world thinks it is
the center of universes. We need to think upstream and down-
stream. My concern is with the consequences of the full recognition
that Europe was nothing more than a colonial delusion with potent
allegorical powers, and now that it is exhausted, where are we (humanity at large) headed? The endless attempts to find meaning
either in Europe or in the national identities within Europe are in
fact desperate goose chases, all protesting too much to save what is
no longer there. The rise of nationalist and fascist movements
throughout Europe—from Greece to Spain—is in fact the strongest indication that the old allegory no longer signifies, no longer
convinces, even to its own true believers. Europe was like a religion,
with capitalist modernity its theology, and universal emancipation
of humanity its eschatology, its false consciousness, the "opium of
its bourgeoisie." All of this it borrowed from Christianity and secularized as "Europe." That is the reason the only binary match for
"the West" was of course "Islam," a universal religion. We never
hear of "Buddhism and the West," or "Judaism and the West." We
only hear of "Islam and the West"—for Islam too had an imperial
cast to its religious convictions. Its *Adab* ("literary humanism"), you
might say, was its "secularism." "Islam and the West" is the recent
vintage of the old hostility between Islam and Christianity. The
more universal the claim of Europe qua Christianity secularized,
the more universal had to be its principal adversary. Judaism thought
it had dissolved into itself—and thus its incurable anti-Semitism.
Islam was insoluble—and thus its Islamophobia.

With the false binary of "the West and the Rest" now rendered
completely meaningless, for "the Rest" is already in "the West," and
"the West" has always been in "the Rest," the condition of postcolonial paradox in which we now live can only fuel hatred and enmity
where no convincing ideas or even ideologies and therefore no he-
gemonies exist to hold any empire together. Militant xenophobia
and violent Islamism mirror each other and are in fact the insignia
of a failing phase of the history of "the West." The vicious expansion
of Islamophobia as the most potent political animus of European
politics is the clearest indication of the collapse of all highfalutin

European ideals of tolerance and pluralism into the most twisted fanatical zealotry that the collapse of the metaphor of Europe has accessioned. The crisis of the European self-delusion culminated in its endemic anti-Semitism and ultimately the horrors of the Holocaust, and is now seeing its final demise in Islamophobia.

Piercing Gaze, Longest Shadows

Through a monumental imperial hegemony that had the whole planet as its playing field, the world at large has been forced to think itself in relation to Europe, mostly that it is far behind Europe, or that it is catching up with Europe, or at best that it is against Europe, but perforce distorting, self-inflicting, multiple and various cultures and civilizations in terms domestic to the self-assured primacy of this thing that has called itself "the West" or "Europe." The end of Europe is not an ideological proposition. I say so not gleefully or mournfully. The end of Europe is a historical process finally coming to an end, like the conjugation of a verb, or the exhaustion of a paradigm that no longer has any room to spell itself out. It was good in many respects while it lasted, and it was murderous in many other respects at its zenith. Today, that moral and imaginative power of Europe and perforce "the West" it begat have given way to barbed wires, fortified borders, fascist xenophobia, mass murderers on the loose, lunatic U.S. presidents. With Trump, the rise of racist ideologues like Marine Le Pen in France or Geert Wilders in Holland, and their racist counterparts in the rest of Europe—all as the last-gasp futile efforts to project epistemic certainty via imperial control over a planetary condition in which "the West and the Rest"—Europe and all its various shadows are deeply fragmented under the pressure of global capital. The world at large has now morally and imaginatively given up on Europe, with its crowning achievement, Donald Trump, an existential threat to the globe, with "liberal democracy" the most hypocritical proposition in modern political history. In this book I propose to be "an aesthetic intuition of transcendence"; I will argue the world at large has finally and happily transcended any reliance on European forms, arguments, and audience. "The Syrian refugees," as they are called, are coming to Europe not in search of moral philosophers or art galleries. They are just running away from wars Europe is partially responsible for creating.

In my *Islamic Liberation Theology: Resisting the Empire* (2008), I have already argued in some detail that dialogical delusion of "Islam and the West" has historically been the most potent subterfuge under which Europe has sustained itself and cross-corroborated its manufactured enemies. That delusion has long since collapsed upon itself into a caricature of its former potency. My proposition was and remains decidedly epistemic and cultural but predicated on principally material and political foregrounding. The binary of Europe and non-Europe corresponded to an assumption of the operation of capital that was center-periphery, which no longer holds—in fact, it never did. The polylocality of capital and labor was always there but concealed under the ideological subterfuge of "the West and the Rest." The manufacturing of Europe as a mobile army of mixed metaphors was definitive to the false binary. The material foregrounding of that binary no longer exists—in circulation of labor, capital, and market. But the mobile army of metaphors keeps marching on, spinning around its own tail.

There was a time we could speak of a European project—we knew what they thought it was: to rob the world and call it "Western civilization." But is there any longer such a thing? The condition we call "postcoloniality" has implicated the West and the Rest into each other's bosoms. Liberal democracy, human rights, universal brotherhood of mankind—does any one of much highfalutin phrases mean anything anymore? What human rights when a rich Saudi prince with a fat checkbook to buy military arms to drop bombs on Yemeni children can have the red carpet rolled for him all the way to Buckingham Palace? Do the British really not see their Buckingham Palace takes the backseat to Disney World in Florida? Europe has both imploded and exploded. Europe has imploded by virtue of the moral and philosophical crisis it has faced since the Jewish Holocaust, and exploded by losing any semblance of power and hegemony its liberal institutions may have once held for the world at large. The crisis in the Eurozone, racist uprisings against the entry of refugees and migrants, Brexit, geopolitical challenges posed by Russia reclaiming its regional and global power have all thrown a monkey wrench at any global claim to moral authority to Europe. There are underlying similarities between the views of thinkers as apparently dissimilar as Slavoj Žižek and Niall Ferguson—they both (one from Left and the other from Right) think that Europe is the measure of truth. They are both delusional.

When I propose Europe has ended, do I mean for Europe itself or for the world at large? Europe has always been a dialectical proposition, a dialogical utterance. It has never been self-contained. It has always been a contingency. It is neither a pure conjecture on part of Europeans, nor an entirely fictitious fabrication by all its Others. As an ideological trope, Europe has always been an imperial allegory predicated on the material foregrounding of capitalist modernity. The terms "medieval Europe" or "ancient Europe" are recent historiographical fabrications. Europe is the ultimate sign of capitalist modernity—its signature definition. It is a combination of both its self-projections and others buying into it by the force of its imperial hegemony. It is therefore neither here nor there, neither in Paris nor in Cairo, neither in London nor in Tehran. It is somewhere, in an imaginative geography of the in-between—for it is both here and there, neither here nor there. It is a two-faced mirror, in which two adversaries are posited to see each other in their reflections. You take Europe from the non-Europe, it does not know what to do with itself. You take Europe from Europeans, they will look like that proverbial cat with their whiskers cut off. My reflections as a result are located precisely in the space in between, where "Islam and the West" as a potent example of "the West and the Rest" has been posited, placed, and perpetuated. I wish to lift his two-faced mirror in between—for us to be able to see the naked reality with its own rhyme and reasons but without the smoke and mirror of this allegory. That Europe has ended is most evident therefore neither in Europe nor in non-Europe but precisely in the liminal space where "the West and the Rest" has crafted a comfortable delusional location for itself. We must start adjusting our eyes to see beyond this two-faced mirror.

If we were to offer a material explanation for this ending of Europe, we might, as I have already suggested, point to how Europe began its long and illustrious history as the towering metaphor of capitalist modernity, and with the epicenter of that capitalism now effectively moving to cyberspace, that metaphor has lost not just the material foundations of its might but also the ideological foregrounding of its sustainability. This heuristic disjunction between metaphor and materiality, between Europe and cyberspace, is only to place my proposal in contemporary history, where time and narrative have both become amorphous. Europe as a metaphor remains still evident despite the failure of Europe as materiality. The phantom mantle of Europe has historically been invested in other cultures and climes sometime without even knowing it as such. In the case of the United States, it is the cultural heritage of Europe in its vastest colonial consequences in the enduring myth of its white supremacist consciousness. The United States is Europe times global history. The United States picked up where Europe lost its breath. Europe in short is not just in Europe. It is now mainly in the United States, and it is in every elite structure of postcolonial power that helps in the global foregrounding of Eurocentric imagination and power. Europe is in Asia, Africa, the Americas—Europe is in the double space of the mirror that it has fancied itself beautiful. We will then gather the European shadows in the face of its own historic powers, now miasmatic, metaphoric, metamorphic.

As both metaphoric and metamorphic, Europe is nowhere and everywhere—and that is where we will have to locate and liberate it from its allegorical incarcerations in all the colonizing and colonized minds—so that it can join the rest of humanity in peace. To go to the root conditions of Europe and see it dismantled epistemically, morally, and imaginatively, is to see its varied global gestations as its last dying breaths. The task is not to "provincialize" Europe. The task is to dismantle its illusion. The notorious white supremacist ideologue Steve Bannon, the former Trump adviser, is the best example of trying to sustain this European origin of his version of race supremacy. His ethnonationalism, reminiscent of Hitler and the Nazis, is a metamorphic vintage of European fascism. At least since the events of 9/11, I have proposed that the collapse of the twin towers of the World Trade Center was the collapse of the "Islam and the West" as two opposing metaphors that have kept themselves in power. This I proposed and still maintain as a sign of the end of the materiality of center-periphery in the global operation of capital, which is no longer Eurocentric, nor is it Asia-centric or any other centric. It has just exacerbated its always amorphous operation. Today, that amorphous operation has completely dissolved both materially and symbolically the centrality of Europe and perforce "the West." Although European philosophers like Slavoj Žižek and Alain Finkielkraut are now the leading ideologues of this delusion of "the West and the Rest," or of "Europe and non-Europe," generations of obsessive over-reading of Said and Fanon have also in their Europhobia in fact exacerbated this Eurocentric fixation. To overcome Europe and see the widening world open its horizons, we need to de-fetishize, de-allegorize, consistently historicize its rise and demise.

Europe in the Mirror of Others

Art historians tell us the West Indian paintings of London-based Italian painter Agostino Brunias (circa 1730–1796) depict images of slavery in refined and sanitized brushes, representing the manner in which European colonialists wished to imagine themselves in other people's homeland.[10] As Mia L. Bagneris demonstrates in her excellent recent study of Agostino Brunias, *Colouring the Caribbean: Race and the Art of Agostino Brunias*, there is something about these pictures far more important than a mere ethnography of how to read race relations—but in fact how to manufacture them visually. Here, the latest European fashion becomes the public image of Europeanization of the colonized, marking them from their own brothers and sisters in bondage. European clothing thus becomes an insignia of power and status, a regalia of difference and distinction. The naked body of the natives is the base of all the other clothed bodies, the ground from which all the other fashionable dresses emerge. What is crucial here is the adaptation of the African

Agostino Brunias, Linen Day, Roseau, Dominica—A Market Scene *(circa 1780).*

headgears into the European fashion in a manner that embraces and nativizes the heritage of the colonized cultures and peoples. The headgear is assimilated upward to the European fashion, while at the same time marking its difference and locality. Europe and its shadows are both staged and harmonized here, in a manner that a forced singularity is manufactured from the truth of two divergent facts.

We need such careful historicizations of Europe and its shadows in European and non-European arts and literatures to see how the end of Europe is morphing into something after-Europe, something occasioned by the European fall but transcending it without despair, and toward that end, what manufactured legacies continue to resist it. What that after-Europe is remains to be seen. Our task today is not prognostication of that future form in or out of Europe. Our task today is theorization of the vanishing presence of our own history from the allegorical ruins we have inherited. The only way for Europe to survive is to cease to be Europe and join the world against its nastiest enduring shadow, the Trumpism at the heart of American Empire. Only by dissolving itself into the world it once robbed blind and murdered en masse can Europe cast its best profile against its ugliest shadows spread from one end of the Earth to another.

Three

Whence and Wherefore "Europe"?

There is no document of culture which is not at the same time a document of barbarism. And just as such a document is never free of barbarism, so barbarism taints the manner in which it was transmitted from one hand to another. The historical materialist therefore dissociates himself from this process of transmission as far as possible. He regards it as his task to brush history against the grain.[1]

Walter Benjamin, *On the Concept of History,* 1940

A specter is haunting Europe. The specter of Islam. Muslims are coming by the thousands—by the hundreds of thousands, by the millions. Europe is becoming "Eurabia," a portmanteau of Europe and Arabia, conspiring to Islamize and Arabize Europe. "Most European Muslims," Niall Ferguson reassured himself and his fellow racist white supremacists back in 2004, "are, of course, law-abiding citizens with little sympathy for terrorist attacks on European cities. Moreover, they are drawn from a wide range of countries and of Islamic traditions, few of them close to Arabian Wahhabism. Nevertheless, there is no question that the continent is experiencing fundamental demographic and cultural changes whose long-term consequences no one can foresee." He called that state "Eurabia."[2] But he had borrowed the term from a conspiracy theorist named Bat Ye'or who had written a book called *Eurabia: The Euro-Arab Axis,* in which she had looked into some darkly shining crystal ball and saw the coming alliance that would be by definition "anti-Christian, anti-Western, anti-American, and anti-Semitic." The *New York Times* had considered Ferguson's regurgitation of such hallucinatory gibberish worthy of its readers' attention.

Such hallucinatory soothsaying banks on the European memories of their Ottoman nightmares now coming back to haunt them. I just read in the news the Netherlands counterterrorism police (NCTb) had arrested a man suspected of threatening an attack on anti-Islam, anti-Muslim, right-wing lawmaker Geert Wilders, the organizer of a Prophet Muhammad cartoon competition. As the head of the right-wing Party for Freedom, or PVV, Geert Wilders is notorious throughout Europe for promising to ban the Koran and close down mosques. It is quite a mess—a self-fulfilling prophecy of lunatic fringe coming to pass in real-time narratives. Europe feels threatened—by a small portion of Syrian and other Arab and Muslim refugees coming to its frightened and wired borders from wars and mayhems Europe is in part responsible for waging against Muslims in their homelands, ravaged as they already are by local and regional tyrants that European leaders are happy to sell arms to so they can murder Muslims en masse in places like Yemen, where millions of human beings are on the verge of starvation by the Saudi bombing—courtesy of European and U.S. arms manufacturers with official political blessing and enthusiastic support of multinational corporations. There is always a funny moment when a Saudi "prince" comes calling on European capitals to buy arms and sell gibberish and suddenly you start reading European editorials wondering "What about the human rights?" At such moments you need a hammer or a pillow near you, whichever is handier. All it takes is a Mohammad bin Salman and his fat checkbook to expose the undaunted hypocrisy that is sold as "European civilization." Europe is not becoming Eurabia. But the fanciful fear of such a transmutation has both deep-rooted anxieties and bigoted contemporary politics of fear and loathing. We need to clear the air, however, and stay focused on the very word: "Europe."

Redrawing the Coffeehouse Map of Europe

Whence and wherefore this endangered Europe—this overanxious, conflicted metaphor of abnormal normativity? How did Europe universalize its particularities, particularized other people's universalities, and made itself normative to others' abnormativity? Before we even turn to how Césaire, Fanon, Said, or any other critical thinker from the colonized world understood "Europe," and then in turn how I propose to push forward, update, and overcome it, we need to think ourselves in the minds of leading European thinkers (not phony fear-mongers and conspiracy theorists like Niall Ferguson or Bat Ye'or, but serious thinkers) and how they have seen their metaphoric continent. Is Europe an idea sui generis, or is it always contingent on the cultural construction of an Other against which the idea of Europe can bounce and understand itself? Can there be a "European civilization" without an "Islamic, Chinese, Persian, or Indian civilization" counter-essentializing and corroborating it? These Others can be fancied as benign as Hindu or Buddhist civilizations or as dangerous as Islamic and Chinese. But varied shades of difference are quintessential in positing Europe as normative. That I and many other critical thinkers believe Europe is indeed the creation of its normative encounter with its changing alterities, its manufactured Others, that it is a mixed metaphor of power and domination, negation and abnegation, does not negate the fact that Europeans themselves have a different conception of themselves, and it is crucial for us to think through such conceptions. "Europe is made up of coffee houses, of cafés," declares the eminent Franco-American literary scholar George Steiner, in a piece cowritten with Benjamin Ramm, who then further add:

> These extend from Pessoa's favorite coffee house in Lisbon to the Odessa cafés haunted by Isaac Babel's gangsters. They stretch from the Copenhagen cafés which Kierkegaard passed on his concentrated walks, to the counters of Palermo. No early or defining cafés in Moscow, which is already a suburb of Asia. Very few in England after a brief fashion in the eighteenth century. None in North America outside the gallican outpost of New Orleans. Draw the coffee-house map and you have one of the essential markers of the "idea of Europe."[3]

The key point in this exquisite conception of Europe is when Steiner and Ramm say, "No early or defining cafés in Moscow, which is already a suburb of Asia." Why conceptually and territorially implant a dismissal of Asia from this refined and eloquent reading of the "idea of Europe"? The "suburb of Asia" is also the suburb of Europe—Russia as the purgatorial space where the paradise of Europe is saved from the hell of the rest of the world. Fair enough. Europeans are entitled to their illusions too. But seriously? There were no cafés in Asia, Africa, and Latin America, when the very word for the coffee Europeans enjoyed in their cafés came from Turkish *qahveh*, from Arabic *qahwa*, probably via Dutch *koffie*. Where did the very beans for coffee come from? From Austria or Norway or from Ethiopia and Yemen? On what planet is this Europe? What are these European thinkers smoking when they think of their Europe? Hashish? Well that too comes from India and Iran.

Whether smoking hashish or drinking coffee, these Asians, Africans, or Latin Americans must have occasionally done it outside their cots and igloos and in some public square with their fellow cave dwellers.

When exactly did these markers of "Europe" appear in Europe? I remember one lovely evening in Vienna, an Austrian colleague was explaining to me why they offer you a small glass of water when you order a coffee in cafés in Vienna and elsewhere. I naively answered, "to wash the coffee down?" No, my Viennese friend said. Coffeehouses in Vienna, he told me, were the remnants of the Ottoman period. When they left, the water in Vienna was very dirty. Putting a clean glass of water next to your coffee was a sign that particular coffee was made with that clean water. This may or may not be an apocryphal story. But I share it because in the Ottoman Empire, you already have a territorial link between Asia and Africa, overriding Steiner and Ramm's dismissal: "No early or defining cafés in Moscow, which is already a suburb of Asia." The moral of the story is not to mark folkloric or even literary sources to the origin of coffee and coffeehouses. If Europeans enjoy their coffees and think it fell from sky on their continent, let them enjoy the grass they are smoking. The moral of the story is to mark the origin of coffeehouses not in Europe but in the always already global context of the bourgeois revolutions that had occasioned the formation of both public spaces and public spheres upon which coffeehouses now emerged. Coffee- or teahouses as spaces for public gatherings popped up in Paris, Vienna, Istanbul, Cairo, Mumbai, Tokyo, Johannesburg, Cape Town, San Francisco, or New York when the rise of the bourgeois public sphere (Jürgen Habermas's conception of it) appeared. The same is with the rise of novels as a literary form, or the publication of the first newspapers. Just like coffeehouses, novels are not European phenomena, as the Eurocentric version of the story would have it. Novels are bourgeois phenomena. They appeared in French, English, German, Arabic, Russian, Chinese, or Persian, when the transnational public spheres contingent on the formation of the transnational bourgeoisie appears. There is nothing "European" that is not already contingent on the planetary operations of the promiscuous and predatory capital and its colonial consequences around the globe.

Who gets to think, read, and write "Europe"? "You know, Hamid, you must understand I am really a Europeanist," a prominent Bengali postcolonial theorist colleague of mine once told me—and she meant it seriously. This, I have always thought to be true not just because this colleague with a PhD from an Ivy League university teaches in the Department of English and Comparative Literature at another major Ivy League university. All major theorists of the condition of postcoloniality are indeed Europeanist. The whole world in one way or another is Europeanist. We have learned Europe the hard way. We also get to write (about) Europe from the shadow of Europe, for it stands too much in its own sun. My writing Europe is therefore neither from a position of power nor from a position weakness. As all other postcolonial thinkers meditating the condition beyond postcoloniality, I too am writing from inside Europe—for there is no outside Europe, anywhere, on this planet—for the sun never set on the union Jack. There is therefore a history, a historicity, a self-consciousness, an agitated awareness of who is and who is not a European, about the writing of this book, at this particular time, when Europe is being pulled asunder from inside and the outside—by mass murderers and barbed wires, by neo-Nazi rallies and xenophobic politicians, by philosophers and Nobel laureates alike. We are the colonizer and the colonized, witness to our own undoing. I write Europe therefore neither with vengeance nor with glee. We have crossed those divisive borders a long time ago. The fate of Europe is the fate of Syrians, Iraqis, Afghans, Somalis, and Palestinian refugees, in or out of their homelands. It is not just Europe that planted Israel as a settler colony like a thorn in the side of Asia—as a penance for its Holocaust sins. We too have planted ourselves inside Europe—and not just territorially. Read any racist European philosopher and see how the nightmares of "Syrian refugees" haunt their dreams.

There is, to be sure, an urgency to such questions whoever asks them—the urgency of a Syrian couple and their defenseless children crossing dangerous seas to get to *their Europe*. As I write these lines, Spain is in turmoil after the October 1, 2017 referendum in Catalonia, and can scarce hold itself democratically together. The British have already voted for their Brexit, the Scottish want to secede, as do the Venetian from Italy. Similar separatist sentiments or movements are evident from one end of Europe to another to another. The center of Europe—its metaphoric core—cannot hold. Europe is internally and externally falling apart. What could hold this continent, this metaphor, together beyond its racist neo-Nazi conspiracy theorists? There is no separating the fate of the colonizer and the colonized from each other anymore. As guest workers and suicidal bombers, the colonized are here, and they are there. There is nowhere to run. This is the moment when the continual divide can no longer hold. We are too late defining Europe by its coffeehouses, and we are too late in contesting that definition too. Europe is being de-defined by the disposable coffee cups of "Syrian refugees" following the GPS on their mobile phones for the quickest ways to bypass eastern European barbed wires to get to Germany—and Europe is being nervously redefined by racist philosophers imagining fundamental differences between Europeans and non-Europeans. The task of critical thinking today is not to de- or redefine Europe. It is to think beyond its perils and promises.

Orientalism Is Occidentalism

By accident (certainly not by design) over the last decade or so, I have been thinking, reading, writing, and publishing a number of books with my UK-based publishers that I might as well call them "my European books," even after Brexit. They do not deal with Europe as such until the very last put them in a new light. My book *Iran, the Green Movement and the USA: The Fox and the Paradox* (2010) partook in Habermas's theory of public sphere as much as it did Hannah Arendt's take on the French and American Revolutions and her notion of public space. But the main impetus behind my theoretical concerns in that book was, of course, taken from the American civil rights movement, and its transnational disposition in solidarity with the antiwar movement targeting U.S. imperial operations in Vietnam. By now, my idea of this public sphere was entirely transnational, and though rooted in Habermas's conception of the European bourgeois public sphere, had seen it through its global unfolding, a theme I then pursued even more vigorously in *Persophilia: Persian Culture on the Global Scene* (2015).[4] In this book, I mapped out a transnational public sphere upon which the social and intellectual histories of Europe and Iran were interwoven. If you were to read these two books together, you'd see I have systematically de-fetishized Europe and began reading it into global history. As a metaphor, Europe was the product of a colonial environment when European empires had focused their colonial consciousness on this term. That imperial project was ipso facto global, and so was the transnational public sphere on which Europe was crafted as an overriding allegory of domination. Like the multiple empires it served, Europe was a global mascot signaling and symbolizing the transnational public sphere that sustained and celebrated it.

My *Brown Skin, White Masks* (2011) was decidedly and obviously a take on Fanon's *Black Skin, White Masks* (1952) and his critical thinking under the French colonial domination in Africa. Here, my concern was not merely to update Fanon's psychoanalytic of colonial domination from North Africa around the globe, but to see how the inner dynamics of Eurocentric imagination sustains an organic hold on our humanity—and the manner in which white supremacy is internalized. My site of critical thinking had by now shifted from Iran to western Europe to North America, and to the inner working of American imperialism as the extended historical shadow of "Europe." But I had kept a firm foot on Fanon's critique of Europe, for this theoretical link nourished an umbilical cord between me and Fanon that extended his historic insights into a larger frame of political references. Europe was by now morphing from one continent to another as the normative catalyst of undersetting postcolonial history. Fanon was rightly focused on Europe, and perforce had fetishized it beyond its historicity. For me now, the truth of Europe was a historical fiction.

My book *The Arab Spring: The End of Postcolonialism* (2012) went decidedly against the grain of the epistemic foregrounding of European colonialism and read the Arab revolutions in an emancipatory "post-Western" mode. By now I was completely liberated from the colonial geography of "the West and the Rest" and spent a good number of pages on what I called the "liberation geography" of the Arab uprisings—where the Tahrir Square in Cairo had become the epicenter of a whole new planetary politics. My theorization of a phase in revolutionary uprising where the postcolonial condition of knowledge production had exhausted itself opened new horizons into thinking beyond the limited topography of a Eurocentric imagination. The end of postcoloniality here meant Europe as a metaphor had effectively lost its colonial power of self-centering itself even beyond its military power to dominate and dictate the terms of revolt. Throughout that book, I looked at the condition of European coloniality as an exhausted episteme, and thus the emancipatory terms of the Arab revolutions I articulated in decidedly regional terms—regional in the sense of retrieving a worldliness beyond the European political imagination.

In *Can Non-Europeans Think?* (2015), I zeroed in on the metaphor of Europe and the manner in which it enables and disables thinking—privileging itself as the site of "philosophy" and dismissing the world as incapable of any serious critical thinking. Ethno-philosophizing other modes of thinking—Chinese philosophy, Islamic philosophy, African philosophy, and so on—were all cross-authenticating what was "philosophy" and kept exclusively for Europe. Why?, I wondered. This seemed quite odd to me that the continent that had ruled the world with wanton cruelty could assign itself the privilege of critical thinking but deny it to the world that was the subject of its savagery. How could that be? This monorail theory of history that Hegel had fathomed for "the West" where philosophy began in Athens and came westward until it reached his neighborhood in Berlin seemed quite delusional to me—a deliberate epistemic violence on the world at large and its capacities for thinking. Indians, Chinese, Arabs, Persians, Africans, people in Latin America had no philosophy? Then there must be something weird about the very notion of "philosophy." Even ants and bees are capable of reflections about their habitat. How could human beings be denied that privilege? What disease was this "European" self-assurance that thought only itself of such thinking they call "philosophy"? The more I thought about this, the stranger the whole proposition of "Western metaphysics" appeared to me—that it was made possible by drawing a wall and denying it to others. No spot on planet Earth is self-contained. Everything comes from somewhere else—moves around. The Egyptians, Hebrews, Indians, Chinese, Persians, people in other parts of Asia, Africa, Latin America—they had thought too, and their thoughts circulated, traveled, came to, and then went from Europe. Why, by what authority or ignorance, did Levinas think what people around the world did was "dancing," not philosophy? To the degree that European imperial thuggery around the globe—from the Roman Empire until Donald Trump—had generated a condition of imperial philosophizing, so had the sites subject to such imperial power created moral and imaginative sites of resistance to it. To the degree, also, that European empires had enabled and empowered agential audacity to think the globe the playfield of its philosophers, so had other empires—those in China, Japan, India, Persia, and the rest of the Islamic world or anywhere else for that matter. If knowledge and power were coterminous, there were other imperial powers around the globe, equally conducive to the epistemic audacity to think the world one's playground. Europe as a metaphor was at once enabling and disabling, full of no doubt crucial insights into who we were and where we lived, but all of it contingent on a structural blindness to worlds it by nature denigrated and denied to rule and subjugate. These were some of the thoughts preoccupying me while writing that book.

This book, *Europe and Its Shadows,* is integral to the theoretical topography of the critical thinking that was narrowing in on Europe over the last couple of decades—beginning from its colonial edges and eventually coming toward the very mythic center of it. It is perhaps in the course of writing the latter two books, *Can Non-Europeans Think?* and *Persophilia,* that I began to see the clear points of demarcation between my generation of critical thinking from that which we had inherited from Frantz Fanon, Edward Said, and Jalal Al-e Ahmad as its main hallmarks. Europe was no longer a singularly fetishized object of criticism for me, but a site of worldly diagnosis, where we could start thinking where the epistemic origins of our entrapment had inaugurated. Europe was not unique for me—in positive or negative terms. Europe was part of a larger world, integral to multiple worlds, that needed a fresh reading—needed de-mythologizing. I was no longer interested in the manner in which Europeans had manufactured a body of knowledge they called "Orientalism," but in the manner in which this Orientalism had informed us about the psychopathology of Europe as a historical incident. All empires manufacture knowledge in a manner that best fits their imperial will to power. The entire course of "Islamic law" was one such ideological formation of the Arab/Muslim empires. Persians, Chinese, and Mongols too had their own respective modes of knowledge production about the world, compatible with their will to power. From Fanon to Said to Al-e Ahmad, Europe was singled out, fetishized, criticized (and of course rightly so)—but above all, metamorphosed into a myth. But at this point I considered such fetishization outdated, counterproductive, obscuring to further insights. We needed to historicize, de-mythologize, and not continue to fetishize. I considered that fetishizing inimical to critical thinking, to the necessity of cultivating a historical imagination that began long before and extended long after the incident called "the West." We needed to study "Orientalism," not to get angry why these Europeans so systematically misrepresented us this way. We needed to study "Orientalism" as a psychotherapist would study the nightmares of a patient, or a sociologist the sociopathological symptoms of social malaise, or a literary theorist the tropes of prose, or a historian the passing fixation of an empire with domination and hegemony. We needed to return the gaze, using the evidence of European political and ideological domination to understand how this particular imperial adventure had mapped itself out. Orientalism, in short, was in fact Occidentalism. We had been misreading Orientalism. We thought it was about us. No: It was about them.

From Al-e Ahmad to Fanon to Said and After

At this point Al-e Ahmad's iconic essay, *Gharbzadegi* (1962, variedly translated as "Westoxication," "West-struck-ness," "Westitis," "Euromania," or "Occidentosis"—all relatively correct), prepared the fertile ground on which Fanon's *Wretched of the Earth* (1966) could happen and to anticipate Edward Said's *Orientalism* (1978). I think Al-e Ahmad has been unfairly and damagingly left out of this postcolonial conversation. The fact the Al-e Ahmad wrote his essay in Persian and Fanon in French kept the two seminal texts relatively obscure in the larger colonial world until the publication of Edward Said's text in the dominant colonial language of English gathered momentum in bringing a more global attention to them all—far more to Fanon than to Al-e Ahmad. It is important for the world outside the Iranian intellectual history of time to know that Léopold Sédar Senghor (1906–2001), Aimé Césaire (1913–2008), and Patrice Lumumba (1925–1961) were integral to the critical contours of the generation of Al-e Ahmad at the time that he wrote *Gharbzadegi*. I have been repeatedly surprised and saddened in conversation with the leading Arab, Turkish, Indian, African, and Latin American critical thinkers (with very rare exceptions) to be so utterly oblivious to the intellectual scene in Iran of this crucial period. It is impossible to discount or disregard the monumental significance of Edward Said's *Orientalism*. But the wide-ranging trajectory of his critical thinking was deeply rooted in rich soils of the total topography of which even he was not fully aware. The fact that the Egyptian sociologist Anouar Abdel-Malek (1924–2012) had long before Edward Said and simultaneously with Al-e Ahmad articulated a critical stand vis-à-vis "the West" and its mode of knowledge production about the world further places Said's seminal work in a proper historical context—how in the Orient itself, as it were, critical thinkers were not waiting for Edward Said to announce the colonial rootedness of "Orientalism." None of this is to detract an iota of significance from Said's magisterial achievement that changed the shape of scholarship for an entire generation of critical thinkers, but simply to take stock of a genealogy that preceded and succeeded his work in a trajectory of crucial epistemological consequences. At this point, I could clearly see how Orientalism was in fact paradoxically Occidentalism—that what we were reading in Orientalism was not as much about us but about them. This recognition changed the map of Eurocentricism beyond Europhobia and brought Europe into the fold of our common critical thinking—neither privileged nor demonized.

Edward Said was a crucial transitional figure, a potent catalyst, and eventually lost his political vigor next to Fanon, Césaire, and Sangrur, while DuBois, Malcolm X, and James Baldwin became far more pronouncedly significant—for by now the internal and external abuses of power by white supremacy had brought Fanon and Malcolm X, Césaire and Baldwin, together. Said had separated the East and the West (however inadvertently) to make the case for the way Orientalism worked. It was now time to bring them decidedly together to overcome them both—and here the wide tapestry of critical thinkers that went from Asia and Africa to Latin America became more important. At this point, I could clearly see how Edward Said's *Orientalism* had blinded us by its insights, distracted us by its eloquence. It had concealed more than it revealed. It discovered an island and mistook it for a continent. It is just like Michel Foucault's *Madness and Civilization* that took European asylum houses (in the grip of his provincialism) and thought these tiny spaces were sufficient enough to house the European Un-reason, whereas the enormity of the colonizing Reason of the Enlightenment modernity needed the continental vastness of "the Orient" to house its Unreason. The real house of European un-Reason was its "Orient." Said de-historicized Orientalism. He took a snapshot of a running river and called it "Orientalism." This was a necessary blindness to make his insights possible. Forever we are indebted to Said, as we move beyond him.

Edward Said took the colonialism that was always already contingent on capitalist modernity and fetishized it as a reality sui generis. This was the major point of Aijaz Ahmad's severe critique of Said's *Orientalism*.[5] They were both right. Said had to do a surgical removal of the colonial from its capitalist foregrounding to see its pathology. Ahmad was right to bring the wound and the body together. Because he was a brilliant literary theorist of English literature and knew very little of history or culture of other climes, Said cast his insights upon the entirety of world history with little historical sensibility to the manner in which the globalized capital creates both its culture of domination and modalities of residences to it. He soon engaged in a fistfight with the notorious Orientalist Bernard Lewis, and his utterly brilliant epistemic insights were derailed into a political boxing match over the Israeli-Palestinian politics (noble as that battle was in its own right). His destabilization of Orientalism had a fatal flaw in which he confused and conflated the mixed metaphor of Orientalism as Pharmakon, as both poison and panacea, as kill and cure. He did not see how Orientalism was in fact Occidentalism—the symptom of a pathology of power and knowledge. He never asked himself why did the most subversive European philosophers, poets, and artists turn to what they called "Persia," which was after all placed at the very heart of Said's "Orient." This Orient was not the same Orient that Said's Orientalists used for colonial domination. Quite to the contrary. This was the Orient European philosophers, poets, and literati used to subvert the rising prison house of Reason the Enlightenment was building— that generations later Michel Foucault detected and theorized. This Orient was instrumental in the making of German Romanticism and American Transcendentalism. This Orientalism was no ideology of colonialism. That Orientalism was compromising the very philosophical foregrounding of capitalist modernity and its Enlightenment project. Said was too Arab-centric in his critique of Orientalism to see this. The Persia, India, China, and pre-Islamic Egypt of that Orientalism was of a different vintage.

Edward Said paid little to no attention to Persophilia, or to the European turn to India or China because he was fixated with the Arab nationalist revolt against European colonialism—particularly in the case of Palestine. Orientalism was very much a post-1967 Arab-Israeli war product. This was a noble political cause but seriously detrimental to his theoretical insights. The world for him was "the West" where he lived and the Arab world where he ironically romanticized in the heart of his own Palestinian politics. India, China, Japan, Persia, and the Ottoman Empire were far more present and important in the European imagination than the Arab world ever was, which scarce existed except in the framework of early Islamic history until the rise of Arab nationalism against the Ottomans. Arabs scarce even existed in the European imagination until the rise of Islam in the seventh century, and that was limited to Christian Orientalism of hatred and loathing of all Muslims. Not until the decline of the Ottoman Empire did the Europeans pay any serious attention to Arabs in order to agitate Arab nationalism to mobilize them against the Ottomans. For much of the European history of encounters with Muslims, Turks were the object of hatred and hostility and not the Arabs. Arabs had lost any imperial claim on world history since the collapse of the Abbasid Empire, and in fact long before that with the rise of the Turkic Seljuqid Empire. The most significant episode of the Crusades was an encounter with the Ayyubids led by the Kurdish general Salah al-Din al-Ayyubi. Much of this history was lost to Said, fixated as he was with the Arab cause (again—a perfectly legitimate political position but theoretically detrimental to his insights).

In the heat of his own intense Arab nationalism, into which he had falsely translated his commitment to the Palestinian cause, Edward Said ignored all these facts and took Europeans' entirely negligible encounters with Arabs for a much longer and diversified history of Orientalism. His synecdoche was false and flawed. From the biblical age to classical antiquity, Persia loomed largely over European imagination—in fact, making that imagination "European" by virtue of the encounter with its non-Greek alterity. The Achaemenid Empire towered over both the biblical and the classical antiquity—as the forerunners of the very idea of "the West." It was Xenophon's *Cyropaedia* that competed with Plato's *Republic* for universal attention. It was Aeschylus's *Persians* that captured the horizons of classical antiquity. India, China, and Japan were far more crucial in the European encounter with their Orient—as best evident in European visual and performing arts, particularly opera. The Ottomans were dominant when Mozart was composing his *Abduction from the Seraglio* (1782). Nietzsche called his revolutionary prophet Zoroaster not Muhammad. In the Christian European fixation that dates back to Dante's *Divine Comedy* (1308–1320),

Arabs—the way post-Ottoman European Orientalism later understood the term—had no presence whatsoever in the whole history
of European Orientalism until much later when it served their colonial interests in the Ottoman territories. For Europeans, Arabs
were a much later colonial concoction—compared with Persians,
Chinese, or Indians. In a bizarre way, Edward Said's conception of
"the Arabs" in his *Orientalism* was Orientalist!

If Said paid closer attention to these facts and therefore expanded
his over-Arabized conception of Orientalism, he would have noted a
much more serious paradox—that Orientalism is in fact Occidentalism.[6]
He would have done so if he had paid closer attention to Raymond
Schwab's *Oriental Renaissance* (1957), a text that foreshadowed, anticipated, and seriously compromised Said's *Orientalism* (1978) by decades.
Schwab had demonstrated the significance of European encounter
with the Orient as tantamount to a second, Oriental renaissance, and
the point of analysis for Schwab was almost exclusively Indian, not
Arab. He was an Indologist, the subject of his investigation into the
heart of British colonial encounter in India that had facilitated a much
wider European encounter with the subcontinent.[7] If Said had broad-
ened his post-Ottoman fixation with the mis/representation of Arabs
and started where Schwab left off, he would have asked himself why
the most iconoclastic European philosophers, poets, composers, and
artists were so fixated with China, India, or Persia. Why did Hegel go
back to India, Egypt (pre-Islamic and non-Arab), and Persia to map
out his philosophy of history? Why did Nietzsche choose a Persian
prophet in his most subversive philosophical treatise? Was Nietzsche
a colonialist too? Why did Montesquieu, Handel, Mozart, and in fact
all other European philosophers, artists, and composers down to
Wagner choose Persian themes in their most revolutionary works?
What had Matisse seen in Persian themes? As I have shown in
Persophilia, the devil of Orientalism was in the detail of Persophilia.

In the capable hands of Edward Said—and before him Frantz
Fanon and before him Jalal Al-e Ahmad—the necessary critique of
Europe had paradoxically fetishized Europe, as the critique of
Orientalism had de-historicized Orientalism. Fixation with "the
West" had turned it from a historical phenomenon to a mythic icon.
Dismantling the myth of Europe requires a simultaneous over-
coming of the manner in which our elders have fetishized Europe to
shoot it down. We need to overcome Europe by bringing it back to
the leveled playing field of history. The critique of Europe has been

instrumental in cross-authenticating it as a metahistorical myth. That was a necessary fetishization then, as is our de-fetishization today. From Al-e Ahmad to Fanon to Said, and generations of post-colonial thinkers before and after them, they set a crucial discourse in motion. We must push it forward even beyond their horizons.

The Historical Is Epistemological

This wider and more politically generous attention to Europe and its Orientalism is not merely a matter of a more enabling historical or geographical frame of reference. It is also epistemologically emancipatory. It prevents any false demonization of Europeans, as a people; it brings them back into the fold of humanity at large and allows for the most critical European thinkers to be placed next to Asians, Africans, and Latin Americans to rethink the world anew. The invention of Europe as a civilizational category is tantamount to the inventing of "the white people" as the normative measure of our humanity—and that invention must be reverse-engineered. It is imperative to keep in mind that hostility toward Muslims in the United States today (as the ideological extension of Europe) is part and parcel of hostility to African Americans and Latino Americans—all from the mythic epicenter of "the white people." Indian Sikhs living in the United States or Canada are systematically subjected to racism not just because they look Muslim but because they look foreign and they wear a turban—as opposed to a red baseball cap with the logo "Make America Great Again" written on it. The hostility against Africans in Israel is no less vicious than against Palestinians. This xenophobia makes no distinction among Asian, African, or Latin Americans—for it is focused on cross-authenticating "the white people." As a European colonial project, Zionism is conditioned to see Palestinians as subhumans. "We look at them like donkeys," the earliest generation of Zionists thought of native Palestinians.[8] "White people," thus ideologically manufactured, hate nonwhites as a negation all at the same time. This renewed rise of racism, neo-Nazism, fascism, and white supremacy, in both Europe and the United States, is a symptom of a changing demography of a delusional metaphor called "white people" as an ancillary category of "Europe."

There are no white people. It is all an illusion. There are no black people. There are no red, yellow, brown, blue, purple, crimson, or any other colored people. These are all socially constructed delusions to cross-authenticate "the white people" as a metaphor of power. Delusions though with real, frightful, murderous, and genocidal consequences. None of these facts have been hidden from us. There is a vast body of scholarly literature on the social construction of race, gender, and ethnicity. In his monumental two-volume study, *The Invention of the White Race* (rev. ed., 2012), Theodore W. Allen as early as in the 1960s had documented the mannerssssss in which the ruling elite in the United States had devised the category of "white people" by way of economic exploitation of African slaves and the social control of the emerging polities. More recently, in her *Birth of a White Nation: The Invention of White People and Its Relevance Today* (2013), Jacqueline Battalora has offered an examination of the enduring issue of race in the United States, tracing it back to when "white people" were invented through legislations and enactment of laws. The invention of the "white people" as the simulacrum of Europe was the cancerous cell of racism metastasizing in the United States.

The problem with this scholarly body of literature is not only the fact that its erudite messages do not get through to racists like Donald Trump's white supremacist supporters. The problem is that such archaeology of hatred does not erase the fact that a massive body of humanity has suffered precisely because they have been branded as "black" or "red" or "yellow" or "brown"—in short "non-European." Racially constituted to divide and rule, those colorful delusions have become social facts. Central to all such socially constructed delusions are the relations of power they entail and sustain—whether color-coded, classed, racialized, or gendered. "One is not born, but rather becomes a woman," Simone de Beauvoir declared in her pathbreaking book *The Second Sex* (1949). In later, critical expansion of this idea, scholars like Judith Butler have shown how varied social practices are definitive to the formative constitution of gender. The same is true about race or ethnicity. One is not born, we may extend de Beauvoir's insight, but rather becomes white, or black, and so on. One, a fortiori, is not born "non-European." One is made "non-European."

The gross spectacle of racist terrorists in August 2017 parading with power in Charlottesville, Virginia, USA, and President Trump's unabashedly siding with proto-fascist white supremacists brought this solid streak in American politics to global attention.

However limited or extensive this "base" of Donald Trump's presidency might be, the politics of white supremacy became openly integral to the racial imagination of U.S. politics. Taking cues from their president and his chief advisers like Steve Bannon, Stephen Miller, and Sebastian Gorka in the White House, a small but increasingly vocal armed militia calling themselves "white nationalists" (a euphemism for white supremacists) marched with torches like the KKK, saluting like Nazis, and chanted xenophobic and anti-Semitic slogans through Charlottesville, Virginia. These are the driest and deepest layers of racial hatred from the time of the first European slaughter of Native Americans, from the time of mass slavery of African Americans, now finding the right environment to surface for air. Every shred of this racist legacy—the very idea of it—is traceable to Europe.

As a society and a polity, and as an extended shadow of Europe, the United States has never been cured, never been treated, and it has never resolved its racist history. It has just kept shoving it under a thin veneer of liberal hypocrisy and bourgeois etiquette at home, and projected it outward in the form of warmongering abroad. From the Korean, to Vietnam, to Afghan and Iraq wars, the U.S. invasions and occupations of other countries are underwritten by racial hatred, by an assumption of racial superiority, and the white man's mission. That racialized politics is today most evident in Israel, the European settler colony in the heart of Palestine. The affinity of neo-Nazi white supremacists for Zionism and for Israel is a match made in the racists' heaven. Self-delusional liberal Zionists act surprised that a nefarious white supremacist like Richard Spencer has openly admitted on an Israeli TV show that Israelis "should respect him" for he is "a white Zionist." But the world at large is not surprised at all.[9] Of course, he and his ilk are all "white Zionists." That the liberal Zionists do not wish to admit (for it exposes their own racism) is that the white supremacists' Zionism is integral to their anti-Semitism and vice versa. Nothing exposes the racialized origin of European colonialism better than Israel does today.

The roots of Zionism as the dominant ideology of a European settler colony are in European white supremacy, evident in the much more universal colonial culture Europeans have left behind in Asia, Africa, and Latin America—to all of which Israel is now a last bastion. Israel today is a perfect model, an aspiration in fact, for neo-Nazi white supremacists in the United States and Europe. That these neo-Nazis are also violently and unabashedly anti-Semitic and Zionist is exactly the recognition that now stares European and American Jews in the eye. Today, European and American Jews find themselves at a momentous crossroads where their historic struggles against racism, xenophobia, and anti-Semitism place them face-to-face with Israel and the racist ideology on the basis of which it was founded. Because of the history of their own sufferings at the receiving end of European racist bigotry, Jews have always been at the forefront of fighting for justice. Scarce anyone has suffered more racist injustice in Europe than have Jews—from the widespread pogroms, through the Crusades, and down to the Holocaust. Today, they are put in the unfair position to defend Israel—very much like Muslims being put in a position to defend ISIS, or Hindus to defend Hindu fundamentalism of Bharatiya Janata Party (BJP) in India, or Buddhists to defend the Buddhist nationalist slaughter and genocide of Muslims in Rohingya. All of these expectations to explain or defend or apologize or even to denounce are categorically unfair.

We must therefore categorically distinguish between Judaism and Jews on one hand and Zionism and the Zionist project on the other—as we do between Muslims and militant Islamism, or between Hindus and Hindu fundamentalism, and so on. Judaism is a world religion. Zionism is a European settler colonial project, and as such a militant ideology of state formation. Islam is a world religion. Islamic ideology is a militant project at the roots of Islamic Republic of Iran. Islamic Republic in Iran and the House of Saud in Saudi Arabia do to Islam what Zionism is doing to Judaism. One can extend these examples to Christianity in the United States, Hinduism in India, or Buddhism in Myanmar. Such comparative consideration will make the issue quite clear that Israel is not singled out for an unfair critical assessment of its systematic theft of Palestine and "incremental genocide of Palestinians" (as the distinguished Israeli historian Ilan Pappé has put it).[10] To disengage the fabricated collapsing of Judaism and Zionism, we can simply point out that all Jews are not Zionists, and not all Zionists are Jews. There are more Christian, and now even Muslim and Hindu Zionists than there are Jewish Zionists—and that is the end of conversation about the matter.

Benjamin Netanyahu's son openly calling Black Lives Matter and the Antifa "thugs" and "scum" and dismissing the significance of neo-Nazis marching in Charlottesville, Virginia, speaks voluminously of the racist sentiments at the ideological roots of Israel.[11] How could that heinous position be explained by any decent human being, let alone by survivors of one of the most wicked crimes against humanity in history as perpetrated by the Nazis against European Jews? The young Mr. Yair Netanyahu speaks openly and without the diplomatic finesse of liberal Zionists or the intellectual sophistication of a *New York Times* columnist. He says it as it is: the structural hostility of Zionism to any emancipatory civil rights movement, and its equally foundational affinity with xenophobic anti-Semites. Today, Israelis have absolutely no moral authority, not an iota, to denounce the neo-Nazis in Charlottesville, Virginia, for the neo-Nazis intend to do in the United States what the Zionists have already done in Israel: the ethnic cleansing of Palestine is a model for white supremacists in the United States. Mass expulsion of Palestinians, the massacre of Palestinians in Deir Yasin and elsewhere—those are the Zionist trademarks the neo-Nazis hope and wish and strive to replicate in the United States. "Charlottesville," as a result, "is moment of truth for empowered U.S. Zionists," as it has been pointedly suggested, especially for those boldfaced conquerors of Palestine "who name their children after Israeli generals."[12] The militant nexus of U.S./Israel is today the transatlantic prototype of racist white supremacy that sustains and advances the murderous myth of white people civilizing the world. Europe is the origin of this myth. Israel is the patent evidence of the settler colonial consequences of that myth. Never should any Jew anywhere in the world be in a position to explain, or defend, or account for what Zionists are doing in Palestine—or a Muslim to explain the atrocities of ISIS, or a Buddhist the genocide of Muslims in Myanmar.

The distinguished novelist and Nobel Prize laureate Toni Morrison has observed: "All immigrants to the United States know (and knew) that if they want to become real, authentic Americans they must reduce their fealty to their native country and regard it as secondary, subordinate, in order to emphasize their whiteness."[13] But the question is not fealty to any "native country." The question is rather the systematic subordination of all immigrants, regardless of how they have been color-coded, to the myth of the "white people" and the violent fantasies of their civilizing missions. No brown, black, or any other thus colored person can ever be completely "white." But their trying to pass as white is a mechanism of humiliation and denigration they willingly play to presume they are part of the power structure and a more "normal" human being. This psychopathology came to the United States with European settler colonialists and informed their slaughter of Native Americans, and it was exacerbated in the course of transatlantic African slavery. With every new wave of immigrants, this racist European pedigree keeps repeating and consolidating itself.

In *How Jews Became White Folks and What That Says About Race in America* (1998), Karen Brodkin has put forward one line of argument as to how American Jews began to pose and perform themselves as "white" since World War II. The practice is not peculiar to American Jews, of course. Upon their arrivals and one generation into a successful economic status, other recent immigrants, Muslims and Hindus alike, Iranians and Indians in particular, have also sought to posit and pass themselves as (almost) white. Becoming white has always been the most potent way for racialized "minorities" to overcome their violently alienated personhood in order to become something they could (and should) never be. Whiteness is the most solid European legacy left behind as the very idea of "America" began to racialize its domination of the continent. Struggle for racial justice must therefore commence and continue with the full knowledge of how racial divides were socially manufactured and politically sustained before we can learn how to overcome them. The full acknowledgment of the murderous history of racism in the United States and Europe is the first step toward dismantling it. No postmodern or post-structuralist deconstruction of race can disregard the sustained history of racism as coterminous with capitalist modernity. It must acknowledge and sublate to overcome it.

Here, we need a "double consciousness" of a different sort than the one W. E. B. DuBois famously theorized. This "double consciousness" is not between a universalized white and a reified black consciousness. It is between the false "colored" consciousness on one hand and the liberated consciousness for a democratic uprising on the other. The vast, beautiful, and ennobling consciousness of all racialized people—black, brown, yellow, red, or else the Jew, Muslim, and so on—must here come together to empower a new liberation *Farbenlehre* that no longer partakes in but dismantles and overcomes the false consciousness of the racialized minorities. The invention of "white people" was a blatant mechanism of European and Europeanized power and domination. Dismantling that murderous myth will break down the backbone of a racist ideology that has kept a settler colonial consciousness in power for too long—from the earliest European settler colonies in the "New World" to Israel. Here, the historical becomes epistemological, and an active retrieving of the vanishing power of presence enables a more enabling retrieval of the past.

Europe: A Fragmented Allegory

To dismantle Europe as an idea, we must understand the manner of its undue prolongation. The postcolonial theorists are as much responsible for this prolongation as the fact and phenomenon they were rightly criticizing. Frantz Fanon's groundbreaking *Wretched of the Earth* enabled a body of critical thinking beyond his immediate horizons. More than half a century after its original publication, much has changed and much has remained the same. As we think Fanon, we think the world around us—from Europe and beyond Europe into worlds that Europe has read and misread, enabled and disabled all at one and the same time. If we are to transcend Eurocentricism and Europhobia and bring the very idea of Europe and the very assumption of "Europeans" into the world at large, we must begin by overcoming the colonial conditioning of this metaphor. With every turn of my arguments in this book, I am pushing Fanon forward to a renewed recognition of our lived experiences—from within and now beyond our notions of coloniality. Europe is a depleted metaphor, clinging to its remaining energy like a drowning survivor of a shipwreck. The rise of far right from one end of Europe to another, Brexit, the eastern European zeal to be more Catholic than the pope in their insistence they are "Europeans" are all signs of this desperation. Fanon said Europe is the creation of "the Third World." Said suggested "the Orient" is the invention of "the West." We now know they were both right but also limited by their own time lines: both Europe and the Third World are each other's inventions. This is how knowledge reproduces and procures itself. We need to discover the new worlds (real and possible) around us: the pending environmental calamities, the massive population movements, degenerative sectarianism, rampant xenophobia—these are the indices of the emerging worlds—all rooted in the conditions of our coloniality but now fragmented into the particles of multiple and possible worlds.

The world we live in today is the logical consequence of the colonial savagery of Europe around the globe—not just in material, environmental, and human terms, but also in terms of the critical apparatus of thinking about Europe we have inherited. The idea of Europe in and of itself has never been as fragmented and volatile as it is today—and yet we need critically to catch up with the current condition of the world in which Europe finds itself dissolving. The current post-Brexit world in Europe, coinciding with the Trump presidency in the United States, comes at the tail end of the Thatcher/Reagan romance with a deregulation bonanza, with neoliberal free fall, with neoconservative "Project for the New American Century." The year 2016 pronouncedly changed the landscape of the very idea of "the liberal democratic West," for "the West" itself, to be sure, was never an ideal for the world at large, and in fact brought it nothing but gut-wrenching colonial catastrophe and unending misery, whether championed by UK under Thatcher or crusaded by Reagan and his progenies. Labor under Blair consolidated Thatcherism and added to it even more global warmongering, as the United States under Obama wreaked havoc on the world precisely on the model of Reagan who was one of Obama's heroes and role models. The Conservative/Labour or Republican/Democratic bifurcation means very little to the world at large. The liberals on both sides of the Atlantic are now lamenting the "illiterate white working class" who they believe have robbed them of their lofty illusions about "Western liberal democracy." People around the world are only laughing bitterly at this self-pitying charade.

The overriding assumption of Europe is being pulled and pushed from its edges and its inner core. Brexit was and remains a clear indication that the illusion of Europe as a unified idea or coherent polity, economy, and culture is coming to pieces. It is not just the majority of the British who have voted to exit Europe and resorted back to their own xenophobic anxieties. The very same sentiments are evident throughout the rest of Europe, whatever that means anymore—from Greece to Spain, and from France to Scandinavia. From France, Austria, and the Netherlands at the heart of the continent to Greece and Denmark on its farthest ends, the rise of the xenophobic right is a clear sign of dismantling of the very idea of Europe as the epicenter of its own imaginative geography. It is quite telling that the only adamant voices to keep talking about Europe on *BBC World News* are in fact eastern European post-Soviet republics who were never considered "the real Europeans" to begin with. Germany is holding them all together for they offer the necessary cheap labor and potential market to sustain its economy. The hostility toward Angela Merkel, the German chancellor, for her welcoming "Syrian refugees" points the rivalry now evident between native cheap labor and their transnational rivalries. It is an internal colonization of cheap labor by transnational capital to which the Syrian and other refuges are now an external factor. These unfolding realities have both confirmed Fanon and Said's insights and yet have superseded them. "Europe" has lost its metaphoric power of othering anything anymore. It has become even more internally convoluted than before. The task at hand is to build on Fanon and Said's insights and move forward beyond their respective Eurocentricism, which has been conducive to the Europhobic manner in which they have been read. Governmentality in Europe is coloniality elsewhere, and vice versa. Conditions of coloniality have transcended any binary of national, regional, or continental divide. Cheap and dispensable labor facing transnational amorphous capital— that basic and fundamental fact knows no Europe or non-Europe, no self or other. The conditions of governmentality and coloniality have become one and the same.

If Europe is thus internally convoluted and externally exposed, and if the world and Europe are finally collapsing onto each other, where do we go from here, how do we measure our worldly whereabouts? If the condition of coloniality mirrors the condition of governmentality, as I propose it does, then our modes of knowledge production on both sides of the divide are deeply flawed, compromising the very epistemic foregrounding of even critiquing the relations between knowledge and power. What Fanon and Said did was both materially and metaphorically positing the colonial (Oriental) and the capital (Orientalist) on two opposite camps. They no longer are. They are categorically separate but politically contingent, occupying the same space, woven onto each other, just like Israel and Palestine, the colonizer and the colonized. Within each falsely manufactured camp, you have both the colonizer and the colonized as Albert Memmi and Ashis Nandy realized a very long time ago. If so, then we need to unfurl that involute shape into a flat and democratically leveled plane. The collapse of the metaphor of Europe is the inaugural moment of remapping the world in freer, more democratic, fairer, more just, and more responsible terms. From the ruins of Europe as a fragmented allegory we must retrieve its most betrayed promises against its most terrorizing deeds.

Gauguin's Colonial Harem

As I write these words early in September 2018, the Swedish general election has left the two main political parties tied, with the anti-immigration nationalist Sweden Democrats (SD) winning about 18 percent of the vote, up from 12.9 percent in the previous election. This is not just in Sweden. Across Europe, xenophobic and far-right political parties have achieved significant electoral gains, some are already in office, others poised as the main opposition, forcing centrist positions to shift to the right. There is a sense of violent desperation in Europe today. There is a sense of exasperation outside Europe. A state of siege seems to have dawned on Europe and Europeans. Europeans feel threatened—their ways of life in danger of outsiders. They have all but forgotten or repressed the fact they went around the globe destroying other people's ways of life first. As the central metaphor of "modernity," Europe is self-destructing—for it is increasingly hypocritical, intolerant, racist, prone-to-fascistic uprisings. There is a prevailing sense of "après moi, le déluge" in and about Europe—in more than one sense. After Europe is gone, the deluge will follow—and let it follow. If Europe were to fall, let the world go to hell too. Europe sees itself as the last vestige of safety and civilization. If Europe is gone, all is gone. Europhilia is in mourning. Europhobia is rampant. Where and what and wherefore is this thing going: Europe?

To embrace Europe and gently whisper to it "let it go," we need to think through Europe's own supreme philosopher Nietzsche's proposition that truths are illusions that have forgotten what they really are, and work toward his point that truth is a mobile army of metaphors, metonyms, and anthropomorphisms. Europe is such a truth—the supreme example of that truth. In that sense, the truth of Europe as a mobile army of mixed metaphors needs to be understood and superseded. How did that mobile army of metaphors—or "mixed metaphors" as I propose—gather force, how can it be demobilized, and upon what leveled plane of common destiny can Europeans be brought back to the fold of a fragile humanity at large?

From material to metaphoric to normative—the abiding terms of European self-ascendency—we reach the artistic invention of Europe through aesthetic works of self-othering such as Paul Gauguin's colonial escapades in particular. Much debates have come to bear on Paul Gauguin's (1848–1903) work in recent exhibitions and scholarship, for despite his monumental significance in modern European art, his "lifestyle," as the critics call it, did not exactly follow a bourgeois morality of the Victorian age. It turns out the man was a syphilitic pedophile whose most famous body of work, "the Polynesian-babe paintings," were in fact the product of his wanton cruelty with underage sex slaves he had procured in the South Pacific islands of Tahiti and Hiva Oa, where he took three native teenage brides, infecting them and many others with syphilis, having sex with them while painting them in the hut he had called "La Maison du Jouir (The House of Orgasm)."[14] The obvious issue here is the fact that Gauguin cut a particularly nasty figure as a European colonial artist, savagely exploiting the subject of his art, while tickling the aesthetic fancies of his European audiences to this day. The systematic canonization of his body of work, definitive to the classics of Postimpressionism, could of course not care less about such acts of pure evil. As such, he was not a contradictory figure at all. He is contradictory only to the liberal bourgeois morality that loves his art but is uneasy about his openly partaking in the immoral savagery of colonialism. Was he the only European with syphilis having sex with underage children in a colonial "harem"? His art is therefore a Trojan horse—in its aesthetic appeal, it conceals the terror of European colonialism, and how the very idea of Europe was in fact contingent on this paradox, on this mixed metaphor. The issue boils down to this:

> To some, Paul Gauguin is one of Modernism's great bohemian renegades, a giant of Post-Impressionism who broke free from Europe's bourgeois shackles in a trailblazing, soulsearching quest for creative liberation in the South Seas. To others, he was a fraudulent cad, milking the myth of the noble savage to satisfy his exotic fantasies while boosting the market for his art back home. He is one of history's great dilemmas, and more than a century after he painted his controversial

compositions of nude, brown-skinned Tahitian girls—including several of his pubescent lovers—the art world continues to grapple with his legacy.[15]

Those "bourgeois shackles" were for domestic purposes only—to give Europe a false sense of moral superiority, borrowed from Christian triumphalism and made "secular" for the age of capitalist modernity. They had no place or currency on the pagan site—the colonial corner of European fantasies, through which they sent anthropologists, Christian missionaries, and pedophile artists spreading syphilis. Colonialism was the wet dream of European bourgeois morality.[16] Europe was the Dr. Jekyll to Mr. Hyde's colonialism. Mr. Hyde did things back in the colonies Dr. Jekyll did not reveal on the front home. Gauguin had breached that gap and made an artistic career out of it. To put it another way:

> But while there are plenty of white, male artists whose troubling lifestyles can be understood somewhat separately from their art, the difficulty with Gauguin is that his behavior is laid bare on his canvases. It doesn't take a politically minded scholar or critic to recognize that his representations of nude Tahitians reflect a sexual and racial fantasy forged from a position of patriarchal, colonialist power.[17]

Those "sexual and racial fantasies," as indeed "forged from a position of patriarchal, colonialist power," were the terms of Gauguin's European fantasies. But here we must be careful not to confuse Gauguin's "patriarchy" with the way European bourgeois feminism delimits it. This particular patriarchy is thickly accented in and by colonialism. It is a colonialist's patriarchy. It is a patriarchy perceived and practiced by a European specifically on a colonial site, on a colonial body, on colonized children he thinks are his to possess and to paint and to rape at the same time. The trouble with bourgeois feminism of the European vintage is that they confuse this "patriarchy" with the generic patriarchy they habitually and rightly criticize.

As "the father of modernist primitivism," Gauguin and his generation of revolutionary artists were instrumental in the invention of Europe as an abiding metaphor, a civilizational category, a unified culture—to which their art is indeed definitive. They made

Paul Gauguin, The Siesta, *(circa 1892–1894).*

Europe "Europe" by enabling a position of power and gaze for it. "Europe" was that which gazed—looked, leaned, depicted, staged, exhibited. "Non-Europe" was that which was gazed at and staged, owned, and possessed. In his magnificent art and ugly immorality, Gauguin exposed the high culture and the underbelly of that culture in an art that Europe much loved and celebrated and a life Europe had to publicly denounce but privately desire. Europe has always been a self-referential entity paradoxically contingent on the manufacturing of its alterity—Islam, Africa, Latin America, India, and so on. As a Christian proposition, Europe always needed its pagans, Jews, Muslims—but above all, its "primitive" to assure itself of its advancements and progress. As a self-centering story, it always needed its peripheral anecdotes. As a self-raising allegory, it always procured its pariah to define them by negation, by exclusion. It was white, so it needed its blacks, browns, yellows, and reds. It was masculinist, so it needed a weaker sex—internal and external to it. The weaker sex and the Jews have been the internal others of this Europe—but blacks, browns, Muslims, and the primitives were the external threats, now banging at their gates. Almost all its major monuments (aesthetic or otherwise) were there to posit its *modernity* as the dialectical outcome of its Hegelian Geist. Its Enlightenment needed Darkness. Its cubism sought its roots in African art. Its Gauguin needed his Tahitian slave girls. Even Kant could not define its sublime and beautiful before casting a long look at the Orient and dismissing it as "grotesque." As evident in Gauguin and Picasso, that totalizing gaze toward the other posits a danger zone at once attractive and repellent. But all of that as metaphor, not as reality, these realties are now coming back to haunt their own metaphors. The metaphors that were incorporated to conform the superior race as reality have now come back to haunt, to negate, those assumptions. Those subversions of the metaphors of alienation and domination of capital over labor, capital over the colonial, are what is deeply troubling to Europe and to Europeans. But that is also a moment of liberation, when the delusion of Europe is being liberated from its own internalized othering.

To reverse the European gaze, to begin to look at Gauguin with a probing postcolonial gaze, the world is now in a position to wonder and write back. It is imperative to keep in mind that we write and look back not for Europe to read or look away. Europe did not write for the world to read or to approve or even to acknowledge. Europe wrote out of its abiding colonial confidence of knowledge production. The world is now writing with a post-Western confidence and doesn't if Europe reads or does not read the world. The point here is neither antagonism nor indifference. The point is the confidence the world needs to cultivate to write from the heart of a condition of coloniality that is now to be overcome. On the colonial site, books like Jalal Al-e Ahmad's *Gharbzadeg/Occidentosis* paradoxically consolidated Europe as a reality sui generis by carving it out of the global cycle of capitalist modernity and arguing it had done the world wrong. Similarly, Edward Said's *Orientalism* had given Europe, or "the West," the power to create its own alterities. Fanon had already declared Europe literally the creation of the Third World. Today, however, the alterity of Europe is coming to a closure, seen for what it is—its identity convoluted. The proximity of European identity to its alterity, however, is anxiety provoking. Its fiction is catching up with its reality.

"To brush history against the grain," as Walter Benjamin proposed, demands the location of the postcolonial somewhere between

WHENCE AND WHEREFORE "EUROPE"? / 79

Europe and non-Europe, elbowing on both sides to keep the crucial hermeneutic edge sharp and meaningful. The intensity of the interface between Europhobia and Europhilia is the sign of the crisis of the metaphor of Europe exposing the rotten roots of its most glorious achievements. We need not uncritically adore nor blindly hate Gauguin and his art. We must recognize the rotten roots of its aesthetic sublimity—and live with it. The metaphor is therefore no longer self-evident—it's dialectical. It has become self-conscious. It is the moment of the return of all it had successfully repressed—that it was fake, manufactured, invented, created, as Fanon said, by what it called "the Orient," or later "the Third World." The Orient and the Occident, Europe and the Third World, cross-invented and thus corroborated each other—and we were caught in between. The Europe and non-Europe were creatively and critically coinvented, coterminous, co-contingent. They co-imagined each other—while Europe did it from a position of power and self-consciousness, non-Europe received it from a position of weakness and subsequent *ressentiment*. The metaphor of "the flood of refugees," now haunting the nightmares of European philosophers and laymen alike, is the moment of "après moi le deluge." The non-Europe is coming ashore Europe for safety and prosperity, while Europe is protecting its borders with fear and trembling. "The West" and "the Rest" are no longer worlds apart—they never were. "The West" has had to face the fact that it was in "the Rest" and "the Rest" is already in "the West"—not just as refugees but as the internal others—the Jews and the Roma, the poor, the disenfranchised, the gay, the lesbian, the transgender, anything and everything that threatens the masculinist potency of "the West" as a metaphor of conquest and domination. The refugees have opened the Pandora's box of "Europe." We, the world, are not here to dance on the grave of "Europe." We are here to mourn its elegance and remember its atrocities. "Friends, Romans, countrymen, lend me your ears," as Marc Antony put it in Shakespeare's *Julius Caesar:*

I come to bury Caesar, not to praise him.
The evil that men do lives after them;
The good is oft interred with their bones;
So, let it be with Caesar.

So let it be with Europe. Much of the evil in the world is because of Europe, but let the good in it not be interred with its bones.

All the alterities of the victorious masculinist self that was Europe are now coming back to haunt it. "Syrian refugees" as a metaphor is awakening Europe to its own internal anxieties—its Jews (now switched to Muslims), Turks, Roma, and homosexuals, all those the Nazis hated on behalf of Europe and sought to eliminate completely. Brexit has exacerbated this recognition and updated its provenance. The metaphor of Europe is therefore self-consciously fragile these days. It has lost its imperial virility and colonial vigor—and above all, its epistemic centrality to what we know about the world. We are on the verge of a new revelation, a new metaphor—what it is we don't know yet. It is neither Europe nor non-Europe. The moment is eschatological, triumphalist, and therefore dangerous. As its supreme Other, Islam is no longer to be understood. Islam is the enemy and Islam is to be destroyed. We are back to Christian fanaticism of the Crusaders vintage long before liberal Orientalism took over. Habermas's European public sphere has always been already transnational where the Orient has been part of the European idea of itself—though he never saw that. A full recognition of that fact opens up Europe in ways Habermas never imagined. Under these circumstances, revolutionary inauthenticity (exactly the opposite of the authenticity nativist resistance to Europe imagined) is the only way out of ethnic nationalism—whether in the East or in the West of the imaginary divide. "Islam hates us," says U.S. president Donald Trump. "Islam is cancer," said his first National Security Advisor Michael Flynn. Western Christianity is thus resuscitated and waged against the world in a neo-Crusade that has metamorphized its idea of "the Holy Land" onto Israel. "Islam is a disease" is the final reading of Islam—where Orientalism pointed but did not go. On the side of resistance, Muslims have only one path, solidarity with others, upon a transnational public sphere that is theirs but not theirs exclusively. When in Saudi Arabia, the holy sites of Islam are occupied territories; the Muslim *Qibla* cannot but become metaphoric too.

"A document," Benjamin surmised, "is never free of barbarism, so barbarism taints the manner in which it was transmitted from one hand to another." Europe, the metonymy, is one such document. Its barbarism has tainted the manner in which we have received it. As one such metonymy, Europe has always been a dialogical product. The more you hate its barbarism, the more you cross-authenticate it. The more you love its mystic air, the more you mythologize it. As a mixed metaphor, Europe banks and thrives on being in a state of flux.

In its Orientalism, it empowered itself by designating its nemesis as its object of knowledge. In our critique of its Orientalism, we have corroborated that power differential. The whence and wherefore of Europe are intersectional, cross-referential, mirror images of each other. The Achilles' heel of Europe is the deadly paradox dwelling in its philosophical and aesthetic self-assurances, when the world discovers that in its Heidegger, there is a Hitler, and in its Gauguin, a harem full of syphilis-ravaged slave girls in Haiti. The world too must turn to the poetic of its triumphant resistance to unpack, decode, dismantle, and overcome Europe with no rancor, with no vengeance, and with malice toward none—just to save itself.

Four
Europe and its Shadows

Spatially central, the ego cogito constituted the periphery and asked itself ... "Are the Amerindians human beings?" that is, Are they Europeans, and therefore rational animals? The theoretical response was of little importance. We are still suffering from the practical response. The Amerindians were suited to forced labor; if not irrational, then at least they were brutish, wild, underdeveloped, uncultured because they did not have the culture of the center. That ontology did not come from nowhere. It arose from a previous experience of domination over other persons, of cultural oppression over other worlds. Before the ego cogito there is an ego conquiro; "I conquer" is the practical foundation of "I think." The center has imposed itself on the periphery for more than five centuries. But for how much longer? Will the geopolitical preponderance of the center come to an end? Can we glimpse a process of liberation growing from the peoples of the periphery?[1]

Enrique Dussel, *Philosophy of Liberation,* 1980

In a timely and poignant piece on the rise of strongmen around the globe, half-way through the presidency of Donald Trump in 2018, the *New York Times* published a piece in which it argued "the surprise disclosure ... that the Communist Party was abolishing constitutional limits on presidential terms—effectively allowing President Xi Jinping to lead China indefinitely—was the latest and arguably the most significant sign of the world's decisive tilt toward authoritarian governance, often built on the highly personalized exercise of power."[2] The list of these powerful men reaching for increased power, according to the *New York Times,* included "Vladimir V. Putin of Russia, Abdel Fattah el-Sisi of Egypt and Recep Tayyip Erdogan of Turkey, all of whom have abandoned most pretenses that they rule according to the people's will." These samples indicated that there was now an "authoritarian reversion" around the globe—though the examples offered as evidence were all of the "Oriental despotism" vintage—with no reference to any European or U.S. examples of such "authorities reversions." Reading this piece, we were left to wonder: Were there no examples of frightful totalitarian regimes, dangerously powerful men, fascistic ideologies, undemocratic and in fact decidedly antidemocratic havoc that Europe and the United States have committed against themselves and against the world? Why opt for a territorial and not a temporal frame? Why is it that when they look for a metaphor of terror and tyranny, they look outside themselves, not in the light of their own deeds but in the extended shadows of their "West," their "Europe"?

The Discrete Charm of Oriental Despotism

The piece in the *New York Times*, in fact, refers to Francis Fukuyama's theory of "The End of History" as the measure of truth, to the effect that Western liberal democracy were meant to be "the final form of human government." Among these Oriental despots, Putin is singled out as an "illiberal international" par excellence that began all this terrible trend. To be sure, there is a reference to Donald Trump in this piece, though only as having failed to denounce such trends, giving him the credit that he is in a position to do so, and then although "President Trump's critics say that while he may not yet have eroded democracy in the United States, his populist appeals and nativist policies, his palpable aversion to the news media and traditional checks on power, and his stated admiration for some of the strongest of strongmen are cut from the same cloth." At stake was a comparative vision in which Trump was an anomaly in Western democracies and as such could only be understood in terms of non-Western and perforce Oriental despots.

To the degree that Trump could be considered "cut from the same cloth," it was only because he could be approximated to those "Oriental despots" who "greet him as one of their own." One observer was even quoted as having said, "liberal democracies in the United States and even in Europe no longer look like such an inspiring model for others to follow." This sad news for Western liberal democracy was therefore treated as an unfortunate aberration. Xi, Putin, Erdogan, and Sisi have simply welcomed Trump as one of their own—an Oriental in American disguise. If, the moral of the story therefore goes, Hillary Clinton had been elected, all would have been perfectly normal.

As fate would have it, within just a few days after this piece by the *New York Times* appeared, CNN reported how in a behind-closed-doors meeting, Donald Trump had expressed his darker wishes of maybe just like his Chinese counterpart he too could be a president for life. "He's now president for life. President for life," Trump is reported to have said with a certain sense of envy. "No, he's great. ... And look, he was able to do that. I think it's great. Maybe we'll have to give that a shot someday."[3] The CNN report further adds: "The remarks, delivered inside the ballroom at his Mar-a-Lago estate during a lunch and fundraiser, were upbeat, lengthy, and peppered with jokes and laughter. But Trump's words reflected his deeply felt resentment that his actions during the 2016 campaign remain under scrutiny while those of his former rival, Hillary Clinton, do not." The moral of the story was left up in the air—that the democratically elected U.S. president had tyrannical aspirations only if the nosy press were to leave him to his own wet dreams.

The day after the CNN revelation, the *New York Times* editorial board realized the piece they had published at the end of February exonerating Trump from the list of those Oriental despots was perhaps premature so they published an editorial in which they confessed, "Donald Trump Sure Has a Problem with Democracy."[4] "President Trump just doesn't get it," they now declared, "There's something in the man that impels him reflexively to celebrate the authoritarian model." But still the image of the world that the *New York Times* editorial board saw was one of foreign dictators abroad surrounding a vulnerable democratic home: "As for Mr. Trump's line about becoming president for life: His audience was said to respond with laughter, and let's hope it was nervous laughter. They and we have reason for anxiety. It's not too much to say that as the authoritarian model gathers strength abroad, democracy is under assault at home." Tyranny was thus considered a foreign disease threatening the otherwise perfectly happy and healthy body politics of the United States.

What was amiss here was how the prototype of fascism of the farcical Trump had exhibited ever since he began his bid for the White House needed no foreign model—that he was and had remained as American as that proverbial "apple pie." In this comparative fear of tyranny, no one cared to ask: Who pulled out of Paris climate accord—Xi, Putin, or Trump? Who dropped "the mother of bombs" on Syria—Xi, Putin, or Trump? Who competed with North Korean leader in nuclear rhetoric thuggery—Xi, Putin, or Trump? Who laid waste to Iraq? Successive U.S. presidents or Xi or Putin? Who is helping Israeli settler colony steal Palestine and slaughter Palestinians? Xi, Putin, or the last 20 successive U.S. presidents? Who dropped the first atom bombs, who presided over an entire history of slavery, who inherited a country built on the genocide of Native Americans? Who has waged war in every corner of this planet? Who has plotted and changed democratically elected officials? Who had helped assassinate? ... The absurdity of pointing fingers at the Egyptian general al-Sisi or the Turkish president Erdogan as a model for Trump points to a much deeper anxiety. Petty dictators incapable of even a proper slaughter U.S. or Israeli style in Iraq or Palestine, these wannabe dictators aspire to be a Hitler, a Mussolini, a Franco, or any U.S. president—but fail. In matter of political prototype, we must proceed from the most powerful to the most pathetic—from Trump to Sisi, ad not the other way around.

In another piece in the *Atlantic*, we read about a whole slew of despots for whom Trump has expressed some sort of admiration: the Chinese president Xi Jinping, the Russian president Vladimir Putin, the Philippines president Rodrigo Duterte, the Turkish president Recep Tayyip Erdogan, the Egyptian president Abdel Fattah el-Sisi, the late Iraqi leader Saddam Hussein, the deposed Libyan leader Muammar Gaddafi.[5] Do you see something common among them? They are all non-European and non-America. They are all Orientals—except for one quick mention of Mussolini at the end for whom Trump had also expressed one quick tweet and then retracted it.

As a deeply and thoroughly American powermonger, rooted in his European prototype, Trump is an improbable tyrant—a dangerous buffoon, a vulgar racist so outrageous that no decent American would ever want to admit he is one of them. With Trump at its helms, American democracy is an existential threat to the world—this is the issue hard for any North American or western European to admit or digest. Chinese or Russian or Turkish or Egyptian authoritarianisms put together is no such threat. All of those blatant aberrations from anything remotely democratic are ruled by pretty stable tyrants. The United States is governed by a dangerously delusional president, fairly and freely elected in the world's oldest democracy. The world is not afraid of Xi, Putin, Erdogan, or Sisi. At the writing of these lines, the world is not even as afraid of the North Korean strongman Kim Jong-un as it is of Donald Trump. As the most dangerous global threat to our safety and security, by virtue of the racist, insane, charlatan it has elected as its president, the United States is not in a position to warn us about authoritarianism in the world. There is no more serious threat to our global future than environmental catastrophes, and Americans have elected an opportunist charlatan ignoramus careerist who denies this global threat, considers it a Chinese plot, and pulls out of the meager measures of the Paris Accord. What chutzpah, what arrogant blindness would lead the *New York Times* to speculate about authoritarianism in China, Russia, or Turkey sitting in the heart of the foulest threat to our sanity and reason? Pinch yourself gently before you punch others, to paraphrase a splendid Persian proverb.

To be sure, neither Chinese nor Russian authoritarianism, nor American democracy, and of course a fortiori nor Turkish or Egyptian Sultanism, or indeed Iranian Mullahcracy is any model whatsoever for any nation in search of a political format for its future. Francis Fukuyama's notion of "the end of history" was delusional when it was first triumphantly theorized, but it was perhaps premonitory for the end of American history—the end of the European delusion of having theorized and practiced a form of liberal democracy unrivaled and exemplary in the world. The American neocons who included Fukuyama had cooked up something they called "the new American century"—but little did they know the world is forever cured of its American nightmare. We need to rethink Marx's famous phrase that history repeats itself once as tragedy and then as farce. Trump is a descendant of Mussolini via Berlusconi. From the former he gets his fascistic instincts and from the latter his businessman charlatanism. He does not have his Sturmabteilung brown shirts yet. But he has unleashed the white supremacist thugs all the way from the NRA to the KKK to frighten and intimidate people into silent complacency. No doubt millions of determined Americans are out in the street resisting Trump and Trumpism. But the backlash to them adds momentum to the fascistic segments of society. All of these frightful developments are of exclusively European and U.S. origin and vintage products of

Western civilization—which we must help bring out of scare quotes and let it face truth and reality.

Trump may never become a Mussolini—but the Berlusconi in him is sufficient to unleash the conditions of fascism in the United States that the liberal bewilderment is so adamant to exorcise out of Western liberal democracy and pin on some Arab, Russian, or Chinese character. Understanding the fascism of the farcical that Trump has inaugurated requires far more than one, two, or ten essays or articles and books on the subject. This is a phenomenon that requires extensive scholarship precisely because the existing disciplines of social sciences and even humanities are so constitutionally prejudicial against returning the anthropological gaze on others around. Neither Americans nor Europeans are completely qualified to study Trumpism—Americans because they are too close to the calamity they have occasioned and Europeans because he is a direct descendent of their vintage fascism. It is crucial that critical thinkers and scholars from Asia, Africa, and Latin America come together and study this American phenomenon and publish their findings in learned essays and books—in a kind of anthropology in reverse, or effectively reverse engineering the entire discipline of anthropology as European and then by extension North American anthropologists have perpetrated upon the world. The pathology of Trump and Trumpism is no isolated event. The devastating consequences of climate change, including hunger and loss of food security for millions, forced migrations, escalating conflicts over land and resources, rise of disease epidemics, accelerating extinction of animals, sinking coastlines and entire island nations will never be completely addressed or understood without a serious pathological study of the European origins of Trumpism. Meanwhile, consider the fact that even a mini-tyrant wannabe like Benjamin Netanyahu is approximated to a non-European fascist, in this case to the Argentinian Peron. "The Netanyahu regime is a populist, Peronist right," the liberal Zionist venues like *Haaretz* declare, "It's doubtful it can even be called fascist; fascism is an ideology with core values that can be challenged."[6] From its imperial heartland, the United States to its colonial coastlines in Israel, Europe faces an existential crisis and seeks to shift the thrust of self-understanding to its metaphysical others.

A Potent Binary

The discrete charm of Oriental despotism is a red herring, a subterfuge, so Trump is not seen in the direct line of descent from Hitler, Mussolini, and Franco (potentially capable of equal horrors)—for the allegory of "the West" cannot fathom itself the source of evil. It has successfully repressed the memories of both its colonial horrors and the slaughter of the European Jews. It looks for Oriental sources, its everlasting cause of evil, to exorcise itself of any such darker souls. Europe and its shadows complement each other—they need and corroborate each other. The most potent binary metaphor of our time, "Islam and the West," is the resourceful simile of this bifurcation. This very recent cognitive binary has been dangerously productive over the last two centuries—and it has finally lost its synergetic potency. So far as it has lasted, this binary has been definitive to the enduring centrality of "Europe." Islam is what the West is not. The West is what Islam can never be. To break this false binary, there is not more vulnerable fracture than the delusion of this self-othering machination. "Spatially central," as Enrique Dussel says, "the ego cogito constituted the periphery and asked itself ... 'Are the Amerindians human beings?' that is, Are they Europeans, and therefore rational animals?" This insight was necessary, but it is no longer sufficient. It is no longer sufficient to complain, or even to explain. We must start thinking from the day after tomorrow when the West, we realize, has rested in peace, that for the longest time the postcolonials have been talking to a dead interlocutor, kept mummy-like alive by virtue of this very delusional dialogue.

As the most potent binary metaphor of our time, "Islam and the West"—a specific version of "the West and the Rest," or "modernity versus tradition," or "progress versus backwardness"—has been dangerously productive over the last two centuries, pitting one imaginary entity against another, and now again revived ever since the traumatic events of 9/11 in 2001 in a new (desperate) gestation. The binary, however, has in fact lost its normative synergetic potency—and it is now sustained by the false force of a deeply flawed and compromised "Western media." That very designation, "Western media," is its own involuted machination. It feeds on itself, as it feeds politicians and pundits. This binary has been definitive to the enduring centrality of Europe as a repository of ideals and aspirations that are there not by affirmation but by negation, not by virtue of what this Europe actually is but by what others are believed to lack. They are not positive attributes of Europe but negative attributes of non-Europe. My intention in much of my scholarship over the years has been to break this false binary, expose its rotten roots, and liberate our language from its false consciousness.

When this Europe wants to distance itself from the Rest, it attaches itself to its "America," to the United States of America, its colonial offspring and now its imperial benefactor. The EU and United States have a symbiotic relationship: EU gives the United States its sense of a nostalgic past and normative continuity as "the West." The United States gives the EU a sense of wild madness of their misbehaving, ruffian cousins, who are there to protect their cultural heritage. The distinguished European philosopher, and the author of *Nous n'avons jamais été modernes* (*We have never been Modern*, 1991), Bruno Latour thinks "Europe alone, only Europe" can do it. Do what—you may wonder? Well of course, save the world, what else? The civilizing mission: The white man's burden—the burden of Gauguin's syphilis in Tahiti and King Leopold's greed in Congo. But why, if a non-European might be bold and impertinent enough to ask? Bruno Latour answers: Because Trump has abandoned Europe, he thinks. "In 2017," Latour believes, "just when France and Germany will have to vote in national elections, Europe has lost, because of Trump, the protection of what could be called the 'moral umbrella' under which it has lived since the war, an umbrella which is at least as important as the nuclear arms one."[7]

Really? Since World War II, Europe has lived under the "moral umbrella" of the United States? Good for Europe. But bad for the world. What "moral umbrella" is it exactly that the United States until Trump has offered Europe is for Europeans to tell. But has the United States offered any such "moral umbrella" to the rest of the world, too? How many vicious military coups has this "moral umbrella" of Europe staged around the globe, thwarted their democratic aspirations, and destroyed their confidence in their own political future. Let's just name a few: From Argentina to Zaire through Iran (1953)—including Guatemala (1954), Haiti (1959), Brazil (1964), Congo (1960), Dominican Republic (1961), South Vietnam

(1963), Uruguay (1969), Bolivia (1971), Chile (1973), Argentina (1976), El Salvador (1981), Panama (1989), Peru (1990)—just to name a few most notorious examples. Did the United States offer its "moral umbrella" to these countries too—or just its military coups and perpetuation of miseries for people living in these countries? Was the United States offering this "moral umbrella" to Afghanistan and Iraq and Libya when it leveled them to the ground? Was this "moral umbrella" extended to Palestinians being maimed and murdered with their land stolen by U.S.-armed and -enabled Israel? What will make a European philosopher so utterly blind to the world and speak of the "moral umbrella," no less, of the United States until Trump? Does any European philosopher have anything half-decent to say about anything at all outside Europe? Yes, indeed if that is the understanding of Europe, under the "moral umbrella" of the United States, then it must, then it better, go its way alone, for it is as much an existential threat to the world as its "moral umbrella" has been. European philosophers are philosophers of Europe, categorically irrelevant to the world at large.

Islam and the West

But no moral outrage—it is not good for clear thinking: On the thin line between Europhobia and Europhilia, "Europe," mummy-like, continues to imagine itself consolidated as the measure of truth, the very picture of the real, under "the moral umbrella" of one of the most violent empires in world history. The flood of refugees has threatened the European identity and successive waves of migration is transforming it, frightening its philosophers out of their wits. It is the Muslim heritage of these refugees that most bothers Europeans, and precisely this Islamic pedigree of victims of U.S. and European warmongering in other homelands that has triggered Europe upward toward its metaphorical upspring to "the West," where "Islam and the West" are cast as dramatic opposites, mortal enemies. With Enrique Dussel, we might rephrase the question, "Are Muslims human beings, that is Are they Europeans, and therefore rational animals?" The theoretical response to that question, as the Argentinian counter-philosopher has thought, is of little importance. Muslims will have to suffer the practical responses the question raises. These Muslims are suited for cheap labor; if not irrational, then at least they are brutish, wild, underdeveloped, uncultured because they did not have the culture of the center. Europe is aging. Europe needs a young *labor* force, and yet Europe does not like the *laborer* that has to deliver that labor. "Islam and the West" is the immoral umbrella of this paradox.

The fateful events of 9/11 and their aftermath have cast the twenty-first century into a presumed global encounter between "Islam and the West." We have been there and done that. A group of 19 individuals targeted a number of symbolic sites in the United States, most notably the World Trade Center in New York and the Pentagon in Washington, DC, and crashed passenger airlines they had hijacked into them with deadly results. Now a decade and a half into this century, "Islam and the West" seem to be everywhere at each other's throat. Not a single day passes without an urgent and frightful item of world news capturing headlines of the old and new media writing a new page or chapter on this seemingly fateful, civilizational confrontation. A battle of epic proportions seems to have been waged between two key components of humanity: "Islam and the West"—one an abstraction, the other a metaphor. Major news organizations, heads of state in Europe and North America, murderous militant outfits like ISIS, Boko Haram, and al-Qaeda, liberal and conservative pundits, all seem to agree that there is a war between "Islam and the West." This is a delusional war.

"Islam and the West at War" was the lead title of a column by the senior *New York Times* columnist Roger Cohen.[8] "Across a wide swath of territory," he proposed, "in Iraq, in Syria, in Afghanistan, in Pakistan, in Yemen, the West has been or is at war, or near-war, with the Muslim world, in a failed bid to eradicate a metastasizing Islamist movement of murderous hatred toward Western civilization." As evidence, Roger Cohen offered: "Over the more than 13 years since Al Qaeda attacked America on 9/11, we have seen trains blown up in Madrid, the Tube and a bus bombed in London, Western journalists beheaded, the staff of *Charlie Hebdo* slaughtered, Jews killed in France and Belgium and now Denmark." One, of course, need not cherry-pick any such abstracted number of items to argue the United States has been bombing the Muslim world from one end to another, slaughtered hundreds of thousands of innocent Muslims in Afghanistan, Iraq, and through its proxies in Yemen and Palestine—not to mention a calamitous role in the mayhem in Syria and Libya. But where would such tit-for-tat arguments take us—that the West is more at war with Islam than Islam with the West? But would that argument still not beg the question—the very assumption of "Islam and the West," at the heavy cost of ignoring any number of other more urgent economic, environmental, and political factors at work? Why this propensity to iconicity and allegorical thinking?

The Paris attack of November 13, 2015, and the subsequent San Bernardino attack of December 2 of the same year continued to mark a bloody bifurcation between "Islam and the West," deeply affecting the regional elections in France and presidential elections in the United States. Hate crimes against Muslims and even legislations targeting Muslim nationals were equally on the rise. The unfolding events seemed ripe for even more bloody incidents, even harsher anti-Muslim developments, with no end in sight. In the United States and Europe, Muslims were sitting ducks, their religion, culture, languages, dressing habits, facial identities subjects of disgust and ridicule. Islam is a disease, said Michael Flynn, then national security adviser to U.S. president Donald Trump, in the body of all Muslim and "must be excised."[9]

What does this presumed epic battle between "Islam and the West"—between a perfectly healthy and an utterly sick people— actually mean? Who is fighting whom? What is this "Islam," and where exactly is this "West"? Somewhere between western Europe, their Zionist settler colony in Palestine, and the apartheid South Africa before Mandela dismantled it is "the West." When did these binding abstractions and binary oppositional metaphors—"Islam and the West"—get hold of our critical thinking? Is Islam just a religion or a damning catchphrase for an estimated 1.8 billion human beings, and is this "West" just a geographical location somewhere on the globe or is it a civilizational identity, a coded cultural metaphor, built and bent on denying others their humanity? More than anything else, it is in the binary supposition of "Islam and the West," that the two sides are imbalanced, used and abused in a decidedly Pickwickian way, not in the ordinary and etymological sense of the words but in the pointedly loaded political parlance. In what particular way can the 1,400 years of civilizational unfolding of a world religion be summoned into just one word, "Islam"—placed next to the allegorical gathering of a recent imperial concoction called "the West" and offered as the towering binary of our time— be the explanatory frame of reference for the current events? Why are blatantly criminal acts politicized, as the patently political acts criminalized? How, when, and why did "Islam and the West" emerge as two radically, diametrically, and eternally opposite binaries? The metaphoric trap becomes real, the very condition of the colonized minds, on both sides of the divide, enable the West to rule, disabling the Rest to resist by its own terms.

The eventual rise of that binary has had a prolonged contemporary history. The Arab and Muslim identity of the assailants responsible for the attacks against the United States on September 11, 2001, and the subsequent U.S. military campaign against Afghanistan in the fall of 2001, Iraq in the spring of 2003, and then President Bush's declaration of an open-ended "War on Terror," have consistently given an extended lease on life to the hostile duality presumed as transhistorically waged and in full throttle between "Islam and the West." They corroborate the underlying assumption that these wars are varied examples of the enduring hostility and irreconcilable differences between two civilizations: one boasting the European Enlightenment at its core, the other suffering the predicament of Islamic fundamentalism at its roots. Why such bold and flat generalizations, wherefore their potency and penchant for headlines? What happens to historical accuracies, analytical nuances, judicious cultural comparatism when it comes to "Islam and the West"? The West is deeply invested to repress and ignore the long and lasting European imperial legacies. Islam is trapped inside a binary in which it must always remain reactive, robbed of any agency for Muslims as Muslims.

Though of a more distant origin, this binary assumes renewed significance with every turn of the screw in atrocious events in our daily lives. The train bomb attacks in Spain on March 11, 2004, and then the London underground bombing on July 7, 2005 (with the fact and fear of even more attacks around the globe) have further fueled a universal concern that we are indeed in the midst of a civilizational conflict. The militant attackers represent Islam in its entirety, and their targets, the West in full abstraction. The alleged plot to blow up passenger airplanes flying from the UK to the United States in August 2006 created even more unprecedented security measures and perhaps forever changed the face of international travel, all squarely blamed in what both then Prime Minister Tony Blair of England and then U.S. President George W. Bush called a civilizational conflict with "Islamic fascism." Terms were coined, sentiments soared, anger channeled. Arabs and Muslims, whether Asian or African, were all marked as moving targets of the West, determined to bring down Europe.

All of the earlier indications finally culminated in the rise of ISIS (aka ISIL, or Islamic State) as perhaps the most viciously violent proto-Islamist gang notoriously visual and decidedly graphic in their brutal acts of violence perpetrated on innocent victims, Muslims and non-Muslims alike. The rise of ISIS can be traced back to the early uprising against Bashar al-Assad in Syria, which in the aftermath of his bloody crackdown resulted in the formation of militant Sunni opposition to his Alavid rule. Predicated on the U.S.-led invasions of Afghanistan in 2001 and Iraq in 2003, this cycle of violence eventually connected to widespread disgruntle in Iraq by the forced process of de-Bathification in the course of the U.S.-led invasion, conquest, and occupation of Iraq. The Sunni reaction against the Shi'i domination of Iraq in the south and the aggressive militarization of the Syrian Revolution eventually came together and resulted in the formation of ISIS as a notoriously violent organization seeking to regain control against both the U.S. military and its regional allies. But the circumstances of the rise of ISIS soon faded back into an aggressive essentialization of the group into yet another militant Muslim outfit, which—combined with similar formations in Afghanistan and Yemen (al-Qaeda), or Africa (Boko Haram)—gave a solid momentum to the rise of a discourse of Islamic militancy and Islam as the categorical opposite of "the West." Such terrorizing acts as the murder of *Charlie Hebdo* cartoonists in Paris in January 2015, or attacks on synagogues in Holland added further momentum to these sentiments. Every single incident and development was taken out of its immediate context and essentialized. "Islam and the West" were now in full-fledged war against each other according to a widely globalized narrative of these events. No sense of sanity was in sight, no words of wisdom, no balanced argument, no text placed in any context, and above all no historical framing of the manufactured opposition to pave the way for disengaging the violent formation of two grand illusions scarcely in touch with reality.

Soon after the San Bernardino attack of December 2, 2015, on December 7, the Republican presidential front-runner Donald Trump called for "a total and complete shutdown of Muslims entering the United States." The future of the two dangerous delusions colliding against each other had now become deeply ingrained in the very fabric of American politics.

The Twain Tears Each Other Apart

More than ever in living memory, "Islam and the West" *appear* as two principal forces set on a permanent collision course, as if from time immemorial. Scholars and foreign affairs analysts ranging from Samuel Huntington, Francis Fukuyama, and Bernard Lewis to Gilles Kepel, Olivier Roy, and Niall Ferguson have written extensively on the historical and strategic encounters between "Islam and the West." Have they perhaps missed something? Are we not in need of a slightly different and more enabling perspective to disengage these two dangerous illusions clung on each other with no end in sight? Are they not all invested in manufacturing this deadly binary? This ontology, again to rethink Dussel, "did not come from nowhere. It arose from a previous experience of domination over other persons, of cultural oppression over other worlds. Before the ego cogito there is an ego conquiro; 'I conquer' is the practical foundation of 'I think.'" This binary is the trace of that foundation. We are catching "Islam and the West" at the tail end of "I conquer, therefore I think."

To cut to the chase: The assumption of this binary between "Islam and the West" is categorically wrong, analytically flawed, historically misconstrued, and yet politically so astonishingly potent. This binary opposition is fictitious, fabricated on two false premises, politically anchored on a pervasive ideological codification of prolonged battles over material resources and strategic advantages. This dangerous liaison has over two centuries wreaked havoc in modern history. The underlying material forces giving cause, poise, and posture to this binary opposition have now been historically exhausted, dismantled under the weight of their own categorical exhaustion—precisely at a moment when the world falsely takes its dying flame for a flamboyant resurrection. "Islam and the West" was and remains a potent colonial concoction.

I know what I propose here is entirely counterintuitive. Precisely at a time that the whole world testifies to a *rise* in Islamic militancy, I propose the *end* of "Islamic Ideology" as one of the most potent countercolonial and anti-imperial ideologies of the last 200 years. Exactly at a moment when there is a militant crescendo in defense of "the Western civilization" (particularly in the aftermath of 9/11), I suggest the final collapse of that coded ideological fabrication—and thus I argue a case for the end of the binary opposition colonially supposed and dangerously sustained between "Islam and the West." A full recognition of this conceptual and political end of civilizational binaries I believe to be definitive to a clearer and more enabling understanding of the current circumstances and of the path ahead. "Islam and the West" as two binary oppositions have ended their productive ideological formations—their cognitive associations, however false, productive to the point of exhaustion. This is the end of their respective illusions, the fictive frontiers they have respectively fabricated in and about each other.

What today is referred to with the iconic certitude of "9/11" was in fact the cataclysmic culmination of a Manichean opposition that was colonially manufactured and out to effective hegemonic use between "Islam and the West." The planes that were crashed into the twin towers of the World Trade Center also marked the collapse of the twin towers of "Islam and the West" as the mirror image of each other. At the moment of the last dying flame of an exhausted candle, I place it in front of the mirror that has reflected its illusion as if in perpetuity. What I therefore propose is a critical marking of a historic turning point when one of the most potent ideological fabrications of colonial modernity, its overriding false consciousness, marks its own demise. The "West" would not have been possible without the "Islam" it manufactured, nor this colonially manufactured "Islam" without that "West" it kept cross-corroborating. The twins have conceptually asphyxiated each other, themselves, to nullity.

Over the last quarter of a century, in a succession of best sellers, ranging from Francis Fukuyama's *The End of History and the Last Man* (1993) to Samuel Huntington's *The Clash of Civilizations and the Remaking of World Order* (1998) to Bernard Lewis' *What Went Wrong?: The Clash Between Islam and Modernity in the Middle East* (2002), the civilizational opposition presumed between "Islam and the West" has reached intensified and ominous proportions. Even in perhaps the most sober and levelheaded arguments among these sorts of highly popular books, a recent volume on the emergence of Islamist movements, *Jihad: The Trail of Political Islam* (2002), the French political scientist Gilles Kepel has joined the proponents of this argument, and disregarding a whole slew of colonial and imperial circumstances given a full account of the serious upsurge of militant uprising in much of the Muslim world as an indication of the cosmic battle between "Islam and the West" or "Islam and modernity." This particular episteme has been used and abused, milked and mutilated *ad absurdum.* There is belligerent illiteracy, a deliberate disregard for the criminal atrocities of European colonialism as the *condicio sine qua non* of the rise of Islamism among a whole slew of other forms of revolutionary nativism. Such reactionary ideological nativism, Islamism or otherwise, has of course added insult to injury in their own terms, and failed to deliver anything remotely resembling a democratic outcome of their postcolonial pedantry. But this is entirely contingent on the colonial condition of their political production. One should not have the slightest hesitation marking the deep-rooted racism of such consistent disregard for non-Europeans' histories, plucking them out of their geographical habitat and opting for an insanely ahistorical juxtaposition between Islam and the West. Non-Europeans, Muslims and blacks in particular, simply do not exist as agents of their own history, responding to the murderous record of European racist militancy in the course of their criminal colonialism. If as much as they open their mouths to say "ouch," and they will say so inevitably in Arabic, Persian, or Swahili, and so on, these European historians start screaming: "Islam and the West."

The Naked Lives of Muslims

In this series of highly influential and widely popular best sellers, Muslims are taken out of their colonial context, Europeans exonerated of all the terrors they have perpetrated, the generic epithet "Islam" is placed in the immediate vicinity of "the West," and then a quintessential malady is detected in it, right before a genealogy of its political degeneration is diagnosed. Facts are cherry-picked, historical episodes contracted, and sentiments set to override the devil of details. In Gilles Kepel's estimation, for example, representing a wide spectrum of sentiments in Europe and the United States, the principal purpose of these Islamist movements is toward the establishment of "a global Islamic state based solely on a strict interpretation of the Koran." Such assumptions, and indeed the generic sentiments that they represent, are wrong, in fact ludicrously ahistorical and inaccurate. The crescendo of Islamist movements over the last 200 years has in fact come to an end and we are at the commencement of an entirely different phase in the social history of

Muslims and their collective faith. Under the thick and disorienting smoke screen of relentless contemporary events, *longue durée* historical epochs have been effectively camouflaged under mostly journalistic analysis, supported by sporadic events, stripped of their much deeper roots and more ephemeral consequences. We need to see through that smoke screen. To gainsay the rising crescendo of such common and widespread supposition, as I propose here, is to navigate through a critical gateway leading toward a much more enduring insight into the changing historical circumstances of our age, applicable as much to "Islam" as to "the West" that has thus identified it by identifying itself. Black people become darker by this juxtaposition, and white people ever more sharply insular. "The center," as Dussel puts it, "has imposed itself on the periphery for more than five centuries. But for how much longer? Will the geopolitical preponderance of the center come to an end? Can we glimpse a process of liberation growing from the peoples of the periphery?" The question is no longer rhetorical—and the liberation will have to be two-sided, geared toward an epistemological liberation that is emancipatory on both sides of the binary of "Islam and the West," or "the West and the Rest."

Representing a wider range of similar sentiments, Gilles Kepel's *Jihad: The Trail of Political Islam* traces the rise of Islamist political movements in the late twentieth century, beginning with the success of the Islamic Revolution in Iran in the 1970s, continuing with the mobilization of Islamist movements in Afghanistan against the Soviets in the 1980s, and concluding with his assessment of the most recent, and more violent, manifestations of the phenomenon at the threshold of the twenty-first century. Such selective time spans are historically flawed, too short, analytically too limited, and as such theoretically misguided and misleading—cherry-picking events, cutting them loose from their meaningful context. We need to place the current Islamist movements (particularly in their most violent forms of ISIS and al-Qaeda) in a larger frame of reference, in the global context of their categorical opposition posited against "the West," and with a concluding argument that the historical uses and abuses of that binary opposition between "Islam and the West" have had a politically productive history but have now categorically exhausted their analytical credence and even usefulness—and that we are historically at the threshold of a new phase in Islamic social history, with the allegorical imperative "the

West" having imploded unto itself, thus no longer able to posit its reading of "Islam" as its legitimate interlocutor. In the current dominant discourse, both "Islam" and "the West" are talking to dead interlocutors. The objective today is to liberate these exhausted master tropes and let them rest in peace, so the changing realities of the world that include but have surpassed these two depleted master tropes can begin to reveal themselves.

One crucial move necessary for confronting such blatantly flawed historiography is thinking through a corrective lens to Edward Said's *Orientalism* (1978). We must take a few steps before and then a few steps beyond Edward Said and try to historicize his classical argument, which for him began as a Foucauldian question of the relation between knowledge and power, was then transformed into a literary problem of representation, which he then took to a political hot spot and applied to the modes of knowledge production at the service of European colonialism. The absolute metaphor of "the West" that was so central even to Said's critique of Orientalism has now imploded and no longer exists, while "Islam," a principal focal point of Orientalist knowledge production, has a fortiori lost its historic interlocutor it had found in the course of Muslim encounter with the European colonial modernity. The world is at the cusp of a new global reconfiguration of its emerging metaphors. The current resurgence of the contradictions posited between "Islam and the West" is a ruse political posture hiding some far more potent geopolitics of power.

We need an analytical and historic, and not a mythic and symbolic, reading of the fetishized events of 9/11—that is the only way to dismantle the fictive power of the trope of Europe and all its shadows. A direct reaction to the tragic events of September 11, 2001, Samuel Huntington, Bernard Lewis, and Gilles Kepel's extended arguments represent a rising concern about the nature and function of a militant Islam that not just during the last quarter of a century but in fact over the last 200 years has marked the passage of Islamic societies into a critical encounter with European colonial modernity—a fact that all hasty analysis categorically disregard. We need to frame any assessment of the rise of militant Islamism in the context of Islamic societies in their historic encounters with European imperialism. My reading of similar issues that these leading observers have raised is more dialectical and located between "Islam and the West" rather than endemic to "Islam" as such, more global to an imaginative geography that entails "Islam and the West" than local to Islamic societies held and observed in fetishized abstraction. We need to examine what has happened in Islamic societies in the context of the principal binary opposition presumed as categorically valid between "Islam and the West." The construction and juxtaposition of two principal nemesis—"Islam and the West"—have been chiefly responsible for cross-essentializing the presumption of these two polar opposites as cosmic enemies. How this binary came about and what havoc it has wreaked in the world—that is the task at hand. The thinking that these scholars represent is trapped within this binary—although we need to go over and above and beyond it. The issue is ultimately a pathologically Eurocentric epistemology, trapped in its own Euro-universalism, spinning around itself, chasing after its own tail. We must stop this charade. It is no longer funny, amusing, or even irritating.

The U.S. military campaign against Iraq and in Afghanistan before that, as well as the unending "war on terror," are not wars targeted against Muslims as Muslims. The inclusion of North Korea—with practically no Islamic character to its principally Buddhist, Confucian, Christian, and Marxist cultures—in President Bush's infamous "Axis of Evil" doctrine is a clear indication that these campaigns and military operations point to an entirely different direction—an imperial military project that includes many Muslim states. Many Muslim countries are effectively supporting the United States in its "war on terror." Pakistan, Saudi Arabia, and the whole spectrum of the Arab Persian Gulf states are its military bases of operation. Jordan provides active and Turkey strategic support to the U.S. military campaigns in the region. Not even all Muslims oppose the U.S. invasion of Iraq, as the active collaboration of Muslim Kurdish population of Iraq with the invading army clearly testifies. But none of these facts figure in the overriding picture of hostility and incompatibility presumed and made operational between "Islam and the West." The power of this Manichean metaphor has long since overextended its relevance to reality—and precisely for that reason it is long overdue categorically to dismantle and overcome it—and it will not be ended until and unless the centrality of the metaphor of Europe at the heart of its Eurocentric imagination is dismantled. The naked lives of Muslims and the naked truth of a post-European imagination are at stake.

Death and Resurrection of Europe

There is a profoundly Christological conception of Europe now rising among some leading European thinkers, Christlike perceptions of its repeated deaths and resurrections. Europe is self-imploding, to be sure, narratively and normatively, falling and rising into and from pieces from one end to another—crucified, as it were, buried, and resurrected. From Greece to Spain, from the Macedonian claim on Greek heritage to Catalan xenophobic nationalism, the European identity crisis moves from economic to political to moral anxieties of origin and destination. "UK Brexit proposal," according to Bruno Le Maire, French minister of economy and finance, "would spell 'end of Europe.'"[10] According to *Financial Times*, "French minister warns EU cannot support blueprint that would weaken the bloc. France's finance minister has insisted that Theresa May's blueprint for the UK's future relationship with the EU is unacceptable because it undermines a central tenet of the bloc and would spell 'the end of Europe.'" Such doomsday predilections are definitive to the existential fears of Europe, worrying for its very meaning—from its past to its present and a fortiori its future. The Brexit, in other words, has thrown not just a political or economic but in fact a moral and imaginative monkey wrench at the whole idea of Europe beyond its limited implications for the United Kingdom itself.

The existential fear has inevitably assumed deeply Christian iconography—precisely at a time when the fear of the Muslim immigrants has haunted Europe. According to the Bulgarian political scientist Ivan Krastev, three (no less, no more) ideas of Europe are failing, while a new one is emerging.[11] "Is Europe failing?" he asks rhetorically, to which he responds:

> There is plenty of evidence to suggest so, from the constant bickering over NATO contributions, to the proliferation of half-baked deals to regulate migration, to the growing signs of authoritarianism in Eastern Europe. Yes, Europe has repeatedly failed over the past 70 years, and those failures have been the building blocks of Europe's success.

Europe, in other words, is immortal in its mortalities—Christlike crucified on the cross and yet resurrected: it dies and resurrects ever so stronger, and closer to divinity that it has always been. Ivan

Krastev sees the current condition casting doubts on three kinds of Europe: the *first* is the "postwar Europe, which is the original foundation of the European project. This is the Europe that remembers the horrors and destruction of World War II, the Europe that once lived in constant fear of, and determination to prevent, the next war—a nuclear one—which would be the last war." The *second Europe* is: "Europe as a post-1968 project—the Europe of human rights and particularly the Europe of minority rights. The powerful impact of 1968 on the European mind is defined by the widely drawn conclusion, amid that year's unrest and revolutions, that the state is something that defends citizens but also threatens them." Finally, the *third Europe* is the one that is anxiety-ridden by virtue of the "2015 immigration crisis, ... a turning point in the way European publics viewed globalization. It marked both the end of post-1968 Europe and the failure of a certain idea of post-1989 Europe, as we are witnessing a once unifying consensus falling apart." So: 1944, 1968, and 2015—the three moments when Europe died onto something and was reborn and resurrected. All of these dates have perfectly legitimate political reasons to assert themselves and yet collectively they transcend into a mythic Christian moment.

The European crisis of its (Christian) identity was precipitated by this "immigration crisis," by the mere appearance of Syrian (Muslim) refugees at the door of the Europeans' doubting self-assurances. Krastev concludes:

> The refugee crisis was Europe's 9/11. In the way 9/11 pushed Americans to change the lens through which they see the world America has made, the migration crisis forced Europeans to question some of the critical assumptions of their previous attitudes toward globalization. The migration crisis also led to questioning of the reality of a unified post-1989 Europe, not simply because Europe's west and east took very different positions when it comes to what they owe other people in the context of the refugee crisis, but because it revealed the existence of two very different Europes when it comes to ethnic and cultural diversity, and questions of migration.

"The refugee crisis was Europe's 9/11." Just look at that sentence and marvel! Refugees running away from war zones in the making of which the colonial history and the military arm of Europe, NATO, are implicated is tantamount to a gang of criminal thugs ramming airplanes full of passengers into buildings. Europe had no colonial history, and the United States commands no dysfunctional global empire. Just: "The refugee crisis was Europe's 9/11." These analysts are vested in selective amnesia and sanctioned ignorance. In the mythic Christology of European deaths and resurrection, history no longer matters. Such xenophobic thinking fades in light of the underlying metaphysics of the death and resurrection of multiple Europes. One Europe, two Europes, or in fact the absolutist Christological three Europes—the Father, the Son, and the Holy Ghost: does any one of them owe anything to "other people"? When Britain, France, Belgium, or Germany was robbing the world blind, what were these eastern European countries doing in the Austro-Hungarian Empire? Whatever eastern European countries owed others, they paid back fairly and squarely as best evident in the slaughter of the European Muslims in Kosovo, when Milosevic was doing to Muslims what these neo-Nazi fascists in eastern Europe wish they could do with Syrian refugees, if they only could. The genocide at Srebrenica and Žepa, committed by Bosnian Serb forces against Muslims in 1995, and the wider ethnic cleansing campaign by the Army of Republika Srpska (1992–1995), when thousands of Bosnian Muslims were slaughtered or forced into exile from their homeland under the command of the war criminal Ratko Mladić, where the historic premonitions of the fear of the "refugees crisis" in more civilized bourgeois terms.

Upon his political rendition of the European Trinity, Krastev concludes on a hopeful note—a Christian desire for resurrection and salvation.

> Seventy years ago, Europe managed miraculously to turn the destruction of World War II into the foundation of its peace project. It succeeded at turning the antiestablishment anger of 1968 into political progress. It succeeded in less than two decades at uniting a Europe divided by 50 years of Cold War. If Europe has managed to turn so many failures into success, one can certainly hope that it will achieve the same miracle again today.

Eastern European observers like Krastev speak for a segment of Europe that wants a piece of their Europe and will not have any

Syrian refugee come and take it away from them; they will provide western Europe with its cheap labors, political scientists, and neo-Marxist philosophers even (Slavoj Žižek). Arabs and Africans need not apply. The shadow of Europe cast upon itself resurrects its Christian memories of itself—where Muslims become the extension of its Jewish others. "Can we glimpse a process of liberation growing from the peoples of the periphery," Dussel pointedly asked. The answer is decidedly yes, but heralded by those people of the periphery who have symbolically or physically moved to the presumed center to decenter it.

Five
The Postcolonial Paradox

Over there is like here, neither better nor worse. But I am from here, just as the date palm standing in the courtyard of our house has grown in our house and not in anyone else's. The fact that they came to our land, I know not why, does that mean that we should poison our present and our future? Sooner or later they will leave our country, just as many people throughout history left many countries. The railways, ships, hospitals, factories, and schools will be ours and we'll speak their language without either a sense of guilt or a sense of gratitude. Once again, we shall be as we were—ordinary people—and if we are lies we shall be lies of our own making.[1]

Tayeb Salih, *Season of Migration to the North*

How would Europe look like from the vantage point of one of its former colonies, Sudan, via a seminal novel that although has by now become something of a classic, if not a cliché, it still resonates a central verve that more than half a century after its initially shocking publication, it can still preoccupy and engage any young reader from any side of the Mediterranean. For years I have taught Tayeb Salih's *Season of Migration to the North* (1966) to my students at Columbia and elsewhere, and witnessed the shock it generates for its first-time readers. I also met the late Tayeb Salih (1929–2009) in person in the early 1990s, when I was a young assistant professor at Columbia University and my senior colleagues who knew him had invited him for a lecture on our campus.

Europe is too much in the light of itself. It must cultivate the good habit of looking at itself from a different perspective, particularly from the vantage point of those among its erstwhile colonial victims and victors who are now looking at it with different lenses. As one such colony, Sudan was initially part of the Ottoman Empire until the British Christian missionaries began to infiltrate the region, convert Muslims to their faith, teach them how to turn the other cheek, as they paved the way for the British colonial officers to come to Sudan and deliver those slaps in the face. By 1881, the Sudanese had revolted against the Ottoman rule, and by 1899, Sudan became a British colony, and remained that way until 1955, and the following year in 1956, the Sudanese finally had become independent. Just about two years later, in 1958, General Ibrahim Abboud led a military coup against the civilian government, and by 1962 a civil war began in Sudan. In 1969, Gaafar Nimeiry launched a military coup, or what he called "May Revolution," and he remained in power until 1985. This is the precolonial, colonial, and postcolonial history of Sudan in a nutshell—the collapse of the Ottoman Empire, the rise of Arab and Muslim nations in revolt, and their entrapment inside the European imperial onslaught on their worlds. The period of postcolonial independence was replete with degenerative military coups and corrupt autocratic dictatorships. It was during the tenure of Nimeiry that Tayeb Salih wrote and published his seminal novel.

At the heart of *Season of Migration to the North* is Mustafa Sa'eed, a deeply and troublingly colonized character, confused, self-loathing, murderous, and pathological. Self-loathing and equally troubled by his sickly attraction to British women, Mustafa Sa'eed caters to women's Orientalist fantasies, in which he casts himself as an African conqueror of British female bodies, driving them either to suicide or else killing one of them. Mustafa Sa'eed finally returns to his homeland a broken and defeated man, fallen between two stools of Africa and Europe, neither here nor there, with no healthy claim on either. In his reflections on this novel, Edward Said compares it with Joseph Conrad's *Heart of Darkness*, though narrated in reverse, with Mustafa Sa'eed as the "mirror image of Kurtz … [who] unleashes ritual violence on himself, on European women, on the narrator's understanding." Said observes:

> The interventions and crossings from north to south, and from south to north, enlarge and complicate the back-and-forth colonial trajectory mapped by Conrad; what results is not simply a reclamation of the fictive territory, but an articulation of some of the discrepancies and their imagined consequences muffled by Conrad's majestic prose…. The post-imperial writers of the Third World therefore bear their past within them as scars of humiliating wounds, as instigation for different practices, as potentially revised visions of the past

tending toward a postcolonial future, as urgently reinterpre-
table and redeployable experiences, in which the formerly
silent native speaks and acts on territory reclaimed as part of
a general movement of resistance, from the colonist.[2]

What Said here aptly calls "the back-and-forth colonial trajectory" is of course neither limited to Conrad's seminal novel nor
indeed to Salih's reversing it. The world at the receiving end of European colonialism did not sit idly by waiting for Conrad or any
other European novelist to write their version of what had happened in the heart of their homelands to reverse it and feel
vindicated. We must remember also that the crucial "reclamation of
the fictive territory" Said notes here is neither exclusively English
nor in fact European, nor, perforce, confined to the literary form. In
prose and poetry, film and fiction, drama and art, critical thinking
and creative gestures, and in languages and forms, Europeans did
or did not understand that the colonials were more than just colonials at the receiving end of European incursions, and as such have
expressed and articulated their sustained course of reactions and
rebellions long before and long after Conrad or any other European
novelist. The most dubious phrasing in this passage, however, is
when Said proposes "the post-imperial writers of the Third World
therefore bear their past within them as scars of humiliating wounds."
This is certainly not the case, though of course true about Mustafa
Sa'eed and his pathological character. One cannot and must not
extrapolate from this deeply troubled character or even the brilliant
novel in which he is staged, or even ten other novels like it, that the
post-imperial writers "bear their past within them as scars of humiliating wounds." Reclaiming that past could and has been as much
reinvigorating and enabling as recuperative and pathbreaking. The
world may indeed have been wounded in the course of European
imperialism, and it was, but "humiliation" was most certainly not
the only or even the paramount response to those vile acts.

Faceless Masks?

But if not "humiliation," then what and where was the paramount
anticolonial sentiment, or even more fundamentally, what was the
metaphysics of our morals, to use the language of a seminal European philosopher? How did we get ourselves together? How did

we gather? If Mustafa Sa'eed is murderously pathological, and he is, then who and how and what was normative postcolonial metaphysics of our morals? Are we all faceless masks? Were we all faceless masks before Frantz Fanon wrote his brilliant *Black Skin, White Masks* (1952) or Said in his *Orientalism* (1978)? Sometimes postcolonial theory has a very short memory.

The condition of postcoloniality the world inherited in the aftermath of European imperial conquests was from the very beginning a productive paradox, a creative crisis, in and of itself a postcolonial condition of contradictions, at once enabling and disabling, opening and closing, resistances to it. In my *Theology of Discontent* (1993), I have already demonstrated in some detail how the production of Islamic ideology in resistance to the U.S. and European domination of Muslim lands was itself a deeply Eurocentric project. The condition of coloniality enabled a new mode of knowledge production in confrontation with the very idea of Europe, but at the same time it effectively disrupted and foreclosed the preceding conditions (in multiple forms and varied contexts) of knowing and acting. The European and then American empires had glossed over the previous imperial conditions of knowledge and power—so that the postcolonial subject formation had become perforce fragmentary, allegorical, memorial, always already contingent on the stable metaphor of "Europe." The condition of postcoloniality was conducive to that fragmentary mode of subjection, and therefore the postcolonial subject became a shadowy and allegorical figure. The postcolonial person had become integral in the formation of that fragmentary subjection of himself/herself, the product of an interface between European colonialism and the postcolonial subject it had foregrounded and foreshadowed. That postcolonial paradox, I contend, has now been resolved and absolved, and the post-European person is freed both from within and from without Europe, which can now only be used under a worldly erasure, or Europe as ~~Europe~~.

Before we can begin to understand that post-European person, we must have a clear conception of the path the postcolonial subject has traveled upon and through this Europe and its global shadows. When we look at the biographical genealogy of a postcolonial person today, we need to wonder if there is any face behind the masks we see—or are these mere faceless masks, feeding on the "humiliation" of which Said just wrote? What would a mapping of the metaphysics of our morals look like, if we were to use Kant's language, in the condition we like to call postcolonial? Suppose the sustained criticism of Europe is necessary but not sufficient. Let me take you to a crucial encounter between two seminal European thinkers and we will then part ways with them and go back to our own condition of postcoloniality. I have always been mesmerized by a simple reflection of Gramsci in his *Prison Notebooks* about Kant. "'Kant's maxim' act in such a way that your conduct can become a norm for all men in similar conditions," Gramsci suggests, "is less simple and obvious than it appears at first sight."[3] As the editors of the *Prison Notebook* point out, Gramsci has inadvertently added the phrase "similar conditions" to Kant's phrase, and it is precisely this apocryphal phrase that Kant never uttered on which Gramsci dwells in his comment. "Kant's maxim," Gramsci interjects, "presupposes a single culture, a single religion, a 'world-wide' conformism." That "single culture" is the Europe of Kant's philosophical imagination, and of Gramsci's philosophical habitat. Gramsci defines that European condition in his own terms:

> The objection which would not seem right is this: that "similar conditions" do not exist because among the conditions one must include the agent, his individuality, etc. What one can say is that Kant's maxim is connected with his time, with the cosmopolitan enlightenment and the critical conception of the author. In brief, it is linked to the philosophy of the intellectuals as a cosmopolitan stratum.[4]

The truism that both Kant and Gramsci are limited in their conception of "cosmopolitanism" is of course self-evident but not sufficient. The question will remain: What precisely are the contours of other kinds of cosmopolitanisms, of which both Gramsci and Kant were unaware, and what other worlds could exist to enable such cosmopolitanisms, and in those worlds, what is the groundwork for the metaphysics of our morals, if we were to liberate a European philosopher language and put it to good use elsewhere? Our questions, however, cannot by definition be asked in purely abstract forms and must by necessity be concrete where we wonder how we consolidated the groundwork for such metaphysics—as we picked up our pens (the way a Native American used a Winchester gun to shoot back at those who built it) and began to write in terms defiant of the European will to power?

If the postcolonial person was not a faceless mask, a person without a personhood, and merely a wounded soul carrying the burden of his or her own humiliation, we will need to begin to map the metaphysics of our morals. What has held our worlds together, in terms definitive to our historical experiences and geographical whereabouts? The only way I can begin to answer that question is to map out the manner in which my own generation was born and raised during the Pahlavi period (1926–1979) and then traveled abroad in search of wider horizons, eventually detailing the soft certitude of that metaphysics. This Iran is the Iran of Jalal Al-e Ahmad, Simin Daneshvar, Ahmad Shamlou, Forough Farrokhzad, and Gholamhossein Saedi, as the towering icons of much more. These names mean very little outside Iran—lost as they are in the provincialism of "Iranian studies." But they were the opening horizons of our world onto the wider universe, the wide and inviting windows through which we saw the world. This was the Iran of the Cold War, the Iran of Soviet scholarship on our history, of Russian and American literatures. "The West" existed only as a curious icon, and we had become conscious of this "West" as the classical site of imperial conquest. What we called America was a terra incognita, made known to us via the military coup of 1953, at once inviting and repellent. The idea of the Arab world became palpable after the Arab-Israeli War of 1967, overriding the nasty stereotype of the Arabs manufactured by the racist narratives of the Pahlavi period. Latin America became a reality soon after the Cuban Revolution and when that small island opened our eyes to a vast continent. Che Guevara had traveled on his motorbike from Argentina to Mexico, and so did we with him when we read his *Motorcycle Diaries*. Our conception of Stalinist Soviet Union soon morphed into that of eastern Europe, which soon after the Prague Spring (1968) appeared as occupied territories to us, the backyard of Europe, backward and repressive dominated by retrograde Soviet Union and Soviet Stalinism. The Prague Spring gave rise to Eurocommunism, and later we came to know of the Frankfurt School—soon after I arrived in Tehran in 1970 for my college education.

As for Africa, the same way that the Cuban Revolution had opened Latin America to us, the Algerian Revolution had opened Africa. Fanon had theorized, as Césaire has sung it and Patrice

Lumumba practiced its politics. Japan for us was a success story, in the fate of globalized capitalist modernity in its own terms, a kind of modernity that did not compromise its sense of self-dignity, and also an example of a nation that emerged triumphantly from the ashes of its nuclear holocaust. Yasujirō Ozu, Kenji Mizoguchi, and Akira Kurosawa vastly complicated that picture for us. China came alive in Pearl S. Buck's *the Good Earth* (1931), as did India with Gandhi and Nehru and Satyajit Ray, and Egypt with Abdel Rahman Al-Sharqawi and Youssef Chahine. African Americans entered our horizons through the civil rights movement, and then with JFK, MLK, Muhammad Ali, and Malcolm X. Through Western movies we came to know the antebellum South and Native Americans—before we reversed the camera gaze and saw ourselves in African American slavery and Native American defiance. Through the anti-Vietnam war movement, we pivoted from the idealism of U.S. youth to the revolutionary resistances of Southeast Asia. "The cosmopolitan enlightenment and the critical conception of the author" Gramsci had detected in Kant we lived in terms alien to both. "The philosophy of the intellectuals as a cosmopolitan stratum," Gramsci did not know, had far more than one European rendition of it.

What was holding us together through the thick and thin of this emerging historical consciousness and mapping out the groundwork of our morals was our critical thinking and self-assurances, in our prose and poetry, in our rich films and expansive fiction, where we imaginatively traveled around the globe, tested our convictions and reached for and through new horizons by standing on solid and enabling ground every time we said "I." It is that robust and self-confident "I" that concerns me here. We began rooted in a firm domestic ground, anchored our existence on who and what we were and then we branched out. How did we get there? What biography, morality, politics, poetry, philosophy, film, fiction, theater formed and framed our moral whereabouts? No, by no mean did we bear our past within us "as scars of humiliating wounds." Quite to the contrary: We were reclaiming our pasts in a radical contemporaneity that had the widest, healthiest, and most confident trusts in our futures. You could not have Ahmad Shamlou recite his poetry in your ears, or Abbas Kiarostami screen his liberating vision in your mind's eyes and feel "humiliated."

The Rise and Demise of Religious Intellectuals

My concern here is with the moral imagination of the world into which my generation was politicized—its dynamics and vicissitudes—and how soon after the consolidation of the Islamic Republic it was categorically destroyed. It is that vulnerability of the moral subject that is at stake here. The Iranian Revolution of 1977–1979 was the culmination of a cosmopolitan worldliness that had emerged from the early nineteenth century to the time of the revolution. How that embracing pluralism degenerated into this fanatical Islamism is precisely the path where militant ideologies take over and devour the revolutionary culture that had embraced and enabled them? Via this quick excursion into the modern Iranian social and intellectual history, I wish to underline the structural vulnerability of this moral subject under the invisible European gaze.

The Iranian Revolution of 1977–1979 staged the cosmopolitan worldliness of a postcolonial culture in decidedly pluralistic terms.[5] One particular branch of this multifaceted revolutionary culture that I extensively documented after the violent consolidation of the Islamic Republic, the Islamic trajectory of it, later degenerated into an oddity that called itself "Roshanfekr-e Dini (Religious Intellectual)." Whereas the Islamist component of that revolutionary culture was conversant on equally footing with its multiple alternatives, the postrevolutionary Islamism represented by these state-affiliated intellectuals was boldly intolerant and militantly abusive. If we are to liberate our postcolonial predicaments from the dire consequences of the Eurocentric imagination, such colossal calamities as these "religious intellectuals" are precisely where we detect the European gaze continuing to distort and disfigure the moral imagination that has historically enabled the postcolonial person to say "No!" Through these "religious intellectuals," and particularly at the moment when they think they are being "Islamic," Europe continues to cast a distorted image across the Arab and Muslim world. In the guise and misguided presumption of "religious reform" or even "religious reconstruction," these Muslim intellectuals, as they thus brand themselves, were far more concerned with being Muslim in a militantly nativist form than with critical thinking, and to the degree that they had any critical bone in their thinking, it was at the service first of the ruling Islamic Republic and then when the ruling regime jettisoned them out of the ruling elite, of a crude abstraction called "Islam itself." As "religious intellectuals," these cadres of militant Islamists at the service of their Islamic Republic were engaged in a belated, outdated, and recalcitrant dialogue with a dead interlocutor they called "the West," or its local and regional proxies, and as they did so they plunged the normative and moral atmosphere of the time further into a colonized state of mind. No critique of Europe as a ruling global metaphor is complete without a simultaneous critique of its extended shadows cast deeply upon the nativist dispositions of these colonized minds.

From a multifaceted and pluralistic cosmopolitanism that led to the 1977–1979 revolution, which included Islamist ideologies but was not limited by them, the embracing intellectual disposition of Iran systematically degenerated into a fanatical obsession with a critically unexamined and entirely ahistorical "Islam," ideologically infested with the interests of the ruling Islamist State, and while the country was ruled by a militant clerical Shi'ism. These "religious intellectuals" were squarely at the service of the ruling regime before they exhausted their usefulness and were summarily dispensed with, jailed, or else forced into exile. Best represented by the ideas of Jalal Al-e Ahmad and Ali Shariati, which were formed in defiance against the Pahlavis and in solidarity and conversation with non-Islamist ideas in and out of their homeland, the kind of Islamic critical thinking evident at the Pahlavi period had been informed in dialogical dialogue (both hidden and manifest) with other critical thoughts on socialist or anticolonial domains. With the leading "religious intellectual" Abdulkarim Soroush, whose ideas were made public at a moment of Islamist triumphalism in the early revolutionary period, all the alternative emancipatory languages were declared defeated, discredited, and their exponents jailed, executed, or purged from universities. This Islamist triumphalism, with Abdulkarim Soroush as its chief postrevolutionary ideologue, systematically destroyed all its pluralistic predecessors, declared them obsolete, and unilaterally declared Iranian society to be a "Jame'eh-ye Dini (Religious Society)." Under the disguise of fighting with the United States during the Iran hostage crisis of 1979–1981, and later the Iran-Iraq War of 1980–1988, the ruling Islamic Republic systematically destroyed the pluralistic culture from which it had emerged, and these "religious intellectuals" were there to serve it in this nasty business. The revolutionary condition soon degenerated the post-colonial paradox into a single-minted, violently one-dimensional flat-footedness definitive to the very cast of these "religious intellectual" discourses.

Although accused of having had a major role in the university purges of the 1980s, the leading "religious intellectual" Abdulkarim Soroush turned against other religious thinkers like Reza Davari Ardakani, accusing him of being corrupt and illiterate and a product of the "Nezam-e Sofleh-parvar (The Ignoble-prone Regime)." The language of exchange among these religious intellectuals became increasingly violent and accusatory, especially after they left their homeland and began living in exile. Soroush has repeatedly explained, but never convincingly to his ardent critics, that he did not close the universities but opened them "to Islamize" them. Like a number of other "religious intellectuals," Soroush was forced to leave his homeland carrying the stigma of having initially helped the Islamic Republic to consolidate its ideological monopoly of violent politics and totalitarian ideology. Soon a cantankerous contestation emerged among these intellectuals and Soroush was even accused of having claimed to be a new prophet, an accusation he vehemently rejected. One was charged with being ignorant, the other a prophet, a third illiterate, the "religious intellectuals" had become each other's worse enemies. The ruling Islamist regime in Iran stood by and watched them self-destruct.

The most significant aspect of these religious intellectuals is the manner in which they emerged in a critical vacuum created by university purges, mass execution of their revolutionary rivals in prison, brutal censorship of alternative voices, the violent silencing and exiling of oppositional thinkers, and a fanatical fixation with their "Islamic" thinking as truth. Today, Iranians at large hear the phrase "religious intellectuals" and think morally compromised, politically opportunist, and intellectually dubious careerists who took advantage of their proximity to power to take over the postrevolutionary public sphere and map out their ideological agenda without any serious thinker among them ever daring to question the very premise of their Islamist thinking. They soon performed their services consolidating the dubious ideological foregrounding of the ruling state, and they were summarily purged and forced into exile, where they are now turning against each other, causing a belligerent tempest in their teacups.

The prerevolutionary thinkers like Jalal Al-e Ahmad and Ali Shariati were important because they gave voice to a repressed, denigrated, and ridiculed dimension of their contemporary critical thinking.[6] At a time that Third World socialism and anticolonial nationalism (both religiously amusical) were the two dominant ideological languages of the time, Al-e Ahmad and Shariati, chief among others, offered an enabling way of thinking more at home in Iranian and Shi'i history. In the course of the postrevolutionary mayhem, however, Islamism was now triumphant and in full power. Aided and abated by these very "religious intellectuals," the ruling regime purged the universities of their ideological opponents, imprisoned and silenced their dissidents, and for about a decade solidly articulated whatever it is that they thought needed saying, categorically calming the totality of Iranian political culture—with all their intellectual opponents silenced by the state. Even with that treacherous collaboration with a viciously repressive regime, these "religious intellectuals" did not produce much more than just forcing their intellectual opponents into silence. With all their pomp and ceremony, they never reached the daring critical imagination of a Nasr Hamid Abu Zayd in Egypt or the literary panache of Mohammed Arkoun in Algeria. But nevertheless, so far as it gave full-throttle intellectual depth to the Islamist aspect of modern intellectual history, and although rooted in a dark and diabolical collaboration with the ruling state on the model of Heidegger's collaboration with the Nazis, what they did in articulating their positions was necessary, so that for posterity, the world would know the poverty of their "philosophy."

The most cultic of these "religious intellectuals" is Abdulkarim Soroush, who as a trained pharmacist put together a panacea of seductive prose and what his critics consider to be of little substance, but still attracted a following in circumstances that the Islamic republic he served had presided over the most destructive history of social sciences and humanities.[7] Used and abused, these "religious intellectuals" were then all kicked out of their home and habitat and found themselves in foreign circumstances where they scarcely spoke or understood the literary, academic, and scholarly languages of their host countries, and thus led a mostly isolated and exilic (if not altogether parasitical) life. And yet they continued to fake an authority they now lacked. Subsequent reflections by historians of this movement divide them into three categories: reform of religious thought, reconstruction of religious thinking, and then something they call supra-religious spiritualism. It is a closed-circuited project of naval-gazing—scarcely important outside their limited circles now mostly living in exile, writing in Persian, discussed in vociferous blogosphere. Accusations of prophecy and new revelation might indeed be an exaggeration as it is leveled against Abdulkarim Soroush by his former disciple Akbar Ganji. But the demise of religious intellectuals has a much simpler sociological explanation: For about a decade when the ruling regime had served, slaughtered, and pacified their intellectual opposition, they freely and without challenge did as they pleased. This fact had two paradoxical results: Their voice become increasingly monological as they systematically destroyed the polyvocality of the Iranian intellectual scene and robbed it of its innate heteroglossia and yet they did produce a significant body of critical thinking against their own clerical counterparts. But in the process, they had exacerbated the colonial gaze of European modernity on their Islamist discourse without the benefit of the postcolonial criticism (Al-e Ahmad and Shariati in their own domains). They had superseded under Islamist censorship they had willingly served.

All, of course, was not lost in the Iranian moral imagination with these morally compromised "religious intellectuals." Soon after the revolution, the Iranian artistic scene, cinema in particular, picked up where the aesthetic imagination of the previous generations had left off and went one way as these "religious intellectuals" stagnated even more in their exile. All that had happened in film, fiction, prose, poetry, and critical thinking before the revolution now sublated into this magnificent cinematic adventure staged on the global scene, responsive to the pulse of the nation that had occasioned it. "Religious intellectuals," on the other hand, were clueless that there is more abiding truth, more embracing grace, more elegance, aesthetic sublimity, and metaphysical purpose in a single picture of Kiarostami than in their entire verbose regurgitations of Rumi and Hafez put together. There is an anger, a defiance, a cursed fury about the generation these "religious intellectuals" have left behind back in Iran, about which they are entirely clueless. That energy had found vocal, visual, and aesthetic expression in Iranian film and underground music. Today, we look at them and wonder exactly what it was that these "religious intellectuals" were doing in addition to offering their political allies in the ruling regime a

simulacrum of ideological legitimacy? Their entire intellectual project was to shoehorn a vast cosmopolitan culture, regional and
global, into the tight and gaudy space of their limited ritual imagination of what it means to be a Muslim. If they challenged the
legalistic imagination of Islamic law (Fiqh), they thought they had
engaged in a revolutionary project. To this day, they remain entangled within a tightly limited critical and creative imagination,
illinformed about vital ideas that are agitating the world at large,
and at the twilight time of their demise they gather in windowless,
graceless, rooms rented on some university campus regurgitating
the poetry of Rumi to tired and aging audiences who have nothing
better to do than listen to a miasmatic musing of their guru. The
scene is quite gloomy, particularly when they share it on Facebook.
But California is the land of such gurus and new age mystics in the
crowded space of which these "religious intellectuals" are one
among myriad of other voices. At the end of their short, deeply
flawed, and in fact blood-soaked history, these "religious intellectuals" seem to be blissfully unaware of their own whereabouts.
Dually marginal, remotely distanced from their homeland, and entirely parasitical in their host societies where they live, they lead a
defeated and demoralized life.

The Gathering of All the Renegade Texts

The purpose of this quick excursion into the rise and demise of
"religious intellectuals" in Iran was to see how the comparative plurality of responses to colonialism is as much invigorating as any
exclusionary and absolutist claim to such responses is, in fact,
categorically catastrophic. Not until the breakout of the Green
Movement in Iran (2009–2010) did the complete intellectual bank-
ruptcy of "religious intellectuals" become widely known and publicly
evident. As I have argued in some detail, that crucial social uprising
had nothing to do with these "religious intellectuals" or the re-
formist politics that had hoped to speak for a belated Islamism.[8] As
I have demonstrated, the Green Movement was the commencement of a civil rights movement predicated on the societal modernity
of a postcolonial condition entirely domestic to the cosmopolitan
worldliness of countries like Iran or its neighbors. In a similar vein,
the Green Movement in turn was the precursor of the Arab Spring

(2010–2012), in which a particularly poignant disposition of the post-Islamist moment became publicly evident and politically staged.[9] The university purges that had happened in Iran to enable those "religious intellectuals" also demonstrates how Islamism or any other kind of nativism is the pathological side of postcolonial paradox best resolved by comparative postcoloniality that is the antidote against such self-defeating triumphalism. That proposition in turn leads us to the realization that decolonizing universities and modes of knowledge production, that is to say exactly the opposite of what these "religious intellectuals" sought to do in Iran, is a crucial testimony of what a liberating curriculum might be able to achieve. Now I wish to share some details of one such decolonization of the curriculum at Columbia University, where I teach, by way of showing how bringing a plurality of colonial and postcolonial experiences together is one such crucially liberating ecology of curricular liberation.

First I must set the scene. Over the summer months of 2009, my department finally moved from Kent to Knox Hall on the Columbia campus, high upon a hilly street off the edge of Harlem, on the northern wing of the Union Theological Seminary on 122nd Street, between Broadway and Claremont, where we would now call the new home of our department, MEALAC but soon to be altered to MESAAS. MEALAC stood for Middle East and Asian Languages and Cultures, and by the summer season of our migration to the north, the acronym had consolidated a solid degree of notoriety for itself beyond what the letters signified. MESAAS stood for Middle East, South Asian, and African Studies—an awkward acronym, potentially uneasy, divisive, and contentious concoction that made no one particularly happy or sad, but we all concurred to accept and ignore at one and the same time. The aging denomination of the senior faculty did not sustain much synergy for any contentious fight, either to resist vacating our old home at Kent Hall or to change our name, one way or another, and our junior colleagues opted, prudently, to limp along.

The move to Knox Hall was the culmination of a tumultuous episode in the history of our department when we had become under severe attack by the Zionist contingency from outside the academy, unhappy with our curricular and/or political positions on the United States and Israel, particularly with the legacy of Edward Said in our university in general and our department in particular.

This attack had nothing to do with fact and truth. For decades, the eminent Israeli scholar, my colleague Dan Miron taught courses on Hebrew and Israeli literature as well as on Zionism, while my other colleague Joseph Massad taught a course on Palestine. The political consternation targeting us was only the tip of the iceberg. Much more serious was the epistemic change in our modes of knowledge production within multifaceted disciplines that were now decidedly in a post-Orientalist moment of creative crisis—and of which our political detractors were blissfully ignorant. The whole discipline of anthropology, including our own department, was in deep crisis, as was English and comparative literature, when non-European languages and literatures were pushing for theoretical recognition.

Because of the linguistic turn in Heideggerian philosophy, now through Jacques Derrida and Gayatri Spivak, dominant in departments of languages and literatures, departments such as ours had become among the most exciting places on our and many other similar campuses—chaotic but creative and impatient. We were not European, and that magnificent fact was crucial in reimagining our disciplinary and scholarly project beyond the wildest dreams of old-fashioned Orientalists. The political crisis we faced only exacerbated and underlined the far more fundamental normative crisis we faced in the history of departments such as ours. What were we doing exactly? What were our intellectual and disciplinary missions? These questions at this point were not just epistemic; they were existential. I remember when Timothy Mitchell became our chair (2011–2017); he initiated a series of conversations with me, as a former chair of our department, and other senior department members about what even to call our department. This crisis in the university represented the crisis of the discipline and the moment that in my own work I had called "post-Orientalist" and even "post-Area Studies."[10] We were now in a moment when we needed to trace back the link between history and theory, between geography and power, and between hermeneutics and aesthetics, all of which had been blurred and confused in our sort of departments.

We were categorically suspicious of Eurocentric disciplines, but not in a dogmatic or uniformal way. My senior colleague George Saliba was radically altering the periodization of sciences by dwelling on the repressed facts of sciences produced in Arabic. His work was in many ways emblematic of what was happening in our department. At the same time, we in the academy were all conscious of the fact that we no longer represented anything, for we had become an abstraction to ourselves, entirely on the margin of the radical corporatization of the American university, using us as window dressing and sequestering us as politically irrelevant, socially marginal, intellectually entirely on our own. Our upper administration, systematically harassed by our political enemies, was protecting us on the abstract notion of "academic freedom," but they had no moral or intellectual investment in what we were doing. That made our Zionist detractors furious as they mobilized one slanderous letter or website or book after another, maligning us to our senior administration, asking them to silence and/or fire us. The most exciting scenes at this point, I thought, were visual and performing arts, precisely because of their undecidability. Teaching cinema had become a glorious way out of this political banality for me and many of my colleagues. When I organized a Palestinian film festival, it drove the Israeli lobby up the wall. By now, classical Orientalism, classical colonialism, one corresponding to another, had yielded to a newer form of knowledge-power production. Edward Said had theorized these conditions and made them accessible in a vernacular outside the proverbial provincialism of the English departments. We were running with Edward Said into directions he had not anticipated. My *Persophilia: Persian Culture on the Global Scene* (Harvard, 2015) was a key moment in that direction.

My own thinking in these departmental and disciplinary contexts was perforce guided toward the manner of knowledge production within postcolonial societies that were now the subject of our critical thinking—from Asia and Africa that our department covered to Latin America where I now began visiting and giving lectures and conversing with colleagues from Mexico to Argentina. In my *Arab Spring: The End of Postcolonialism* (2012), which had emerged from this context, I offered and argued the end of postcolonialism, not just as a historical episode or political predicament but far more pointedly as a mode of knowledge production conditioned on the moment of coloniality. The condition of postcolonialism, as indeed the condition of coloniality preceding it, was from the very beginning a productive paradox, at once enabling and disabling, opening and closing. It enabled a new topography of knowing and being, but it also effectively disrupted the precolonial conditions (in multiple forms and varied contexts) of subjection, for the European and then American empires had glossed over and camouflaged the previous imperial conditions of knowledge and power—so that the subject formation for the postcolonial person had become perforce fragmentary and/or allegorical. The condition of post/coloniality was conducive to that fragmentary mode of subjection, whereby the postcolonial person had become a shadow, an allegorical figure. Postcolonial people had become integral in the formation of that fragmentary, allegorical, and above all shadowy subjection of themselves. The objective at hand was to release the postcolonial person from that historical predicament. This is where I had detected the new organicity of the postcolonial critical thinker entering a new mode of being and knowing.

This condition of postcoloniality was the reason why the rhetorical question posed by my distinguished Columbia colleague Gayatri Spivak, "Can the Subaltern Speak?" (a text that has been as influential, and rightly so, as Edward Said's *Orientalism*), is so definitive to it, for it is both its inaugural question and its definitive turning point—and that is also precisely why David Scott suggests the very condition of coloniality began as a romance and is now to be read as "tragedy."[11] For such reasons, the critique of postcolonial reason becomes perforce radically contemporary, confused with postmodernism (Poco, Pomo, as Gayatri Spivak always jokingly called them), remains decidedly on the theoretical surface, lacks historical depth, and thus necessarily the subaltern becomes historically mute, as indeed the critique of Orientalism becomes limited to that of power and representation, rather than resurrecting any historical consciousness. The critique of "the West" thus becomes fetishized and ahistorical and ends up corroborating further what it wishes to dismantle. The condition of postcoloniality, in short, prolongs the myth of "the West" (as both Orientalism and "Can the Subaltern Speak?" paradoxically do) and in effect destroys the radical defiance where subjectivity is no longer allegorical and fragmentary, formed as a shadow-subject, where all postcolonial people become like Mustafa Sa'eed, a shameful repository of "scars of humiliating wounds." Ending the myth of "the West" and coming to terms with the globalized empire will make us aware of the aggressive fragmentation of the globalized postcolonial subject where the possibility of a unified subject is no longer effectively contested by the myth of "the West."

The mostly quiet but quite radical curricular changes that were happening in my department, in close collaboration with the initially Center but subsequently Institute for Comparative Literature and Society in 1998—of which I was a founding member—had by now resulted in the publication of my *Can Non-European Think?* (2015). The publication of that book had in turn initiated a series of conversations around the world (in Asia, Africa, Latin America, and Europe) beyond my expectations. Soon after its publication in May 2015, I received an invitation from Professor Sebastian Cobarrubias of the University of North Carolina in Charlotte, inviting me to join him and his colleagues to further elaborate the themes of my book. This invitation was fairly typical of many others, occasioned by various translations of the book, including into Arabic and Spanish. Professor Cobarrubias is a geographer at the Department of Global, International and Area Studies at University of North Carolina in Charlotte. He had invited me to speak at their interdepartmental colloquia that had just started at UNC-Charlotte between the Global, International and Area Studies Department and their Anthropology Department. He and his colleagues had found the issues I had raised in my *Can Non-Europeans Think?* as an important step in challenging particular canons (scholarly, popular, and otherwise), and that fields such as anthropology and global studies, as he put it, "are sites where those canons need to be challenged and or preempted." In his invitation, Professor Cobarrubias had specified that he and his colleagues were looking for discussions that can challenge their thinking on "inter-/anti-/post-disciplinary research and also in exploring the incorporation of decolonial/postcolonial thought into undergraduate curricula at a public institution of this nature." He further specified that he had participated in the Duke-UNC Chapel Hill working group on De-Coloniality/Geopolitics of Knowledge with Walter Mignolo and Arturo Escobar and was currently a member of the "Colonialism Interno" working group focusing on "migration, decoloniality, [and] Europeans in today's Spain." All of these remarks were of course music to my ears—and clear indications that what we were thinking and doing at Columbia went far beyond our iron gates.

On my way to Charlotte, I was thinking how in my own work the condition of postcoloniality was neither temporal nor spatial. It was analytic, historic, and decisively disruptive. The condition of coloniality that had happened before it was not something that happened there and then—but always here and now. The condition of postcoloniality is therefore an act of permanent revolutionary disposition—or what in my book on Arab revolutions I had called "delayed" or "deferred" defiance. Coloniality was and remains an epistemic condition of knowledge production, a condition that had predated the preparatory stages of colonialism and thereafter succeeded it in its various gestations of anticolonial, neocolonial, or particularly postcolonial conditions. It is therefore a particular take on knowledge and power: where *coloniality* is a clear and naked condition of *governmentality,* whereby the colonial subject becomes the carrier and the cause of his and her own de/subjection. To overcome that stage required the radical dismantling of the metaphor of "the West," with the same epistemic violence that we were so deeply de-subjected that Mustafa Sa'eed's pathological violence had become putatively definitive to us, so that Edward Said's detection of "wounded humiliation" had become definitive to our character.

Upon arriving in Charlotte and delivering my talk I shared with my hosts the proposition that the colonials had become knowing subjects precisely at the moment when they had become de-subjected, when a gun was put to their head and they were told they were free from the bondage of dark ages of their "traditions." What is this de-subjection? I wondered aloud. Colonial people are subjected into coloniality, a subjection that is contingent on their de-subjection, that conditions even or particularly any and all of their attempts at de-subjection for re-subjection, makes it almost impossible. This philosophical impossibility of becoming a postcolonial person casts a long and damning shadow at what it means to be a colonial person, and how in the world it is possible to be freed from the conditions of that coloniality, that colonial extension of governmentality. All disciplinary formations within the academic cultures of North American and western European universities—and by extension the manner in which they are cloning themselves around the world—are definitive to the colonizing cultures and quintessentially instrumental to this condition of coloniality as governmentality. From anthropology and sociology to political science and history, from literary historiography to studies of art and architecture—the entire spectrum of social sciences and the humanities is constitutional to what Gramsci saw as the role of education in foregrounding ideological hegemony of the ruling master tropes of "the West"—if I were to bring Gramsci into postcolonial domain and think with his mind.

The way out of this cul-de-sac condition of coloniality, I was thinking to myself on my flight back to New York, is outside the compromised parameters of disciplinary and departmental domains and through the emancipatory power of unruly and homeless texts that the condition of coloniality has produced, and we read them in various contexts and yet they dodge their restraining order and refuse to succumb to any penitentiary punishment. These texts have emerged from the trenches of fighting colonialism, and they will not be disciplined into any regime of knowledge. Subversive texts like those written by Bartolomé de las Casas, Karl Marx, Theodor Adorno, Walter Benjamin, José Martí, Frantz Fanon, Malcolm X, Aimé Césaire, W. E. B. DuBois, Jamaica Kincaid, Ashis Nandy, C. L. R. James, Jalal Al-e Ahmad, Ali Shariati, James Baldwin, Albert Memmi, Richard Wright, Patrice Lumumba, Emile Habiby, Roberto Fernández Retamar, and so on, refuse incarceration into any discipline, department, or regime du savoir. They seduce their ways into departments, disciplines, and syllabi and do mischief before they are detected and expelled. I have gathered them all at my postcolonial theory courses and read them with my students along with certain kindred souls in film and fiction, hoping to create a condition of critical synergy that agitates all claims to disciplinary power and authority. These are unruly texts from battlefields of history. The whole field of postcolonial studies, we might say, is a veritable attempt to domesticate, neuter, and spay these texts into digestible morsels for North American and western European campuses—and then beyond into the domains of pedagogical imperialism where they generate and sustain both in cloning themselves and in generating nativist responses to their hegemony. Try as they may, the professoriate ranks fail to domesticate these renegade, defiant texts.

On periodic occasions, chairs of my department who have come after me—Sheldon Pollock, Timothy Mitchell, and Mamadou Diouf—have gathered us around departmental "retreats," where we share these thoughts with colleagues doing work in Africa or in the larger Arab and Muslim world. I and other chairs before me had done similar gatherings, basically trying to figure out how we were evolving as a department, and what our intellectual project might be. My position on all such gatherings has been articulating the reasons it is imperative to recognize these epistemic transmutations, and then through their fragmented and ruinous history retrieve the historical potency of texts that had defined us and archive their allegorical contemporaneity. Otherwise, I think, American universities are the graveyard of an aggressive transmutation of these critical texts into digestible sound bites as those campuses are being cloned around the globe as commodified brands. These are unruly texts that fit and belong to no particular discipline or field of academic discipline or department. They habitually defy and misbehave wherever you place and expect them to behave and yield or serve one discipline or another. These texts disallow themselves to be appropriated and put into work for any disciplines or academic disposition that expects them to forget their militant origin and defiant dispositions. These texts were not written by academics, scholars, and professors or else by graduate students who wish to become those figures of disciplinary authority. These texts, ipso facto, being what they are, habitually disturb and unsettle any form of totalizing narrative that seeks to abuse them to produce a grand metanarrative that informs the neutralizing forces of knowledge production.

These texts, I believe, are the fragments, the remains, the relics, and the ruins of the empires they have disturbed and sough to dismantle, and as such they have reached us as the allegorical allusions to and for our future revolts. They might be put into and sought to be incarcerated inside syllabi and libraries and studied by tenure-track professors and students to get professional recognitions and advanced degrees. But they run away back to the allegorical memories of our future defiance. They are never totally decipherable. They need to be read in streets, back alleys, open squares, and mountaintops. They were written with blood and tears. They are the continuation of a list of books titled "*list-e kotob-e zalleh* (the list of books that will misguide you)," handed to me by a passerby in a bus station in Tehran the day I arrived from the provincial town of Ahvaz to go to college. I went through the motion of attending college and getting my degree, but that list was my core curriculum for the following four years—and then beyond into my professional career toward more advanced degrees and into the ranks of the professorates in Ivy League universities. I never lost touch with that piece of paper and its list of books from a bus station in Tehran.[12] Much of my syllabi over the last four decades includes extensions of that piece of paper.

These unruly texts seduce various departments and disciplines into adopting them into their curricular programs where they enter as a Trojan horse, do their mischief, before running away back to revive the original battlefields from which they emerged in the first place. Consider *A Short Account of the Destruction of the Indies* (1542) by the Spanish Dominican friar Bartolomé de las Casas: It is a mischievous text par excellence. A priest originally wrote it to his king, warning him of the abuses to which his soldiers were subjecting Native Americans. Today, it reads as one of the earliest primogenitures of the discipline of anthropology exposing their imperial pedigree of informing the colonial conquest of the New World. The text has also been dubiously read as one of the earliest documents of Christian liberation theology, anticipating Gustavo Gutierrez by centuries. But the text also informs against itself—for it is one of the earliest sources documenting when Christianity begins to recast itself at the service of capitalist modernity and its colonizing logic. Bartolomé de las Casas reports so graphically of the body torture and punishment of the natives that his work offers Foucauldian evidence of some of the earliest transmutations of torture into doctrinal governmentality.

Today, *A Short Account of the Destruction of the Indies* reveals all of those traces and still some more. Living as we do through a new and amorphous empire, these texts come alive in those battlefields of history that we need to learn and rethink. They are the signatures of battles lost and won, and they map out the multiple souls of the postcolonial person who could not possibly belong to this globalized empire but must perforce inhabit it. That inability is inhibited and thus you become truer to yourself the closer you get to the truth of these texts and the more distant you grow from the fiction of being any hyphenated American. Histories vary, geographies change, circumstances alter: constant has remained the capitalist logic of systematic exploitation, the silencing of the natives, the narrative enabling of the victors. All that remains is our ability at reverse reading: reading the text against the grain of its history, brushing it counterclockwise, as it were, tickling its hidden fancies out into the open.

In our contemporary history in which we read these renegade texts, European imperialism operated through colonialism, colonialism generated anticolonial nationalism, which in turn resulted in fragmented nations: fragmented nations were perforce trapped inside domestic postcolonial tyrannies exacerbated by the amorphous empire that had no center or peripheries. These runaway texts are the fragmented remnants of those bygone empires, carrying within them the pains and sufferings, hopes and aspirations, of nations, of people brutalized by those empires and their colonial holdings into our conditions of coloniality. Fragmented nations were alienated from their common sufferings by being divided into postcolonial states and their false consciousness of ethnic or linguistic or sectarian nationalism. Read in that light and comparatively, they reveal the transnational public spheres from which they emerged. Read this way, these texts overcome their false entrapments into postcolonial nation-state projects as "national literature," and reveal their common traces as fragments of the empires they have destabilized and dismantled.

From these fragmented relics, a composite picture arises like a complete reflection of a face into a broken mirror. In and of themselves, these texts are fragments. Together they are the composite collage of a worldly vision that enables alternative worldings. Read separately, they will dissolve into nativism. Read together, they reveal a whole new world. Imagine if Mahmoud Darwish was read only by Palestinians or Arabs, Vladimir Mayakovski only by Russians, Faiz Ahmad Faiz only by Pakistanis, Ahmad Shamlou only but Iranians, Nazim Hikmet only by Turks, and Pablo Neruda only by Chileans. What a horror! Now imagine them read together and a whole picture emerges much more embracing than merely the summation of them all. We are the products of those multiple and concurrent worldings, the subject of their world imaginings. They imagined us together. We must remember them together.

Liberation Geography

In *Season of Migration to the North*, Mustafa Sa'eed is not a person but a trope, the figurative representation of a degenerate colonized prototype. The postcolonial person might indeed appear as full of contradictions, but that person is not a repository of "scars of humiliations." Who and what then is a postcolonial person? To say that the postcolonial person is someone somewhere beyond the reach of Kant or Gramsci is necessary but not sufficient. That person is no doubt vulnerable to the absolutism of postcolonial fear and fanaticism that shows itself in strange creatures that call themselves "religious intellectuals," self-alienating themselves from the totality and infinity of their postcolonial historicity—and yet resurrected in massive social mobilizations like the Green Movement and the Arab Spring, after which "the religious intellectuals" are rendered once again irrelevant and thus recede back from society to the basements of reading their belated mysticism to their small band of tired old disciples. Those social uprisings and how we are to read them are contingent on a renegade band of rebellious texts if the universities do not become Islamized by a cadre of fanatics or else trapped in a commodified liberal pacifism from which they must be liberated by any means necessary. The condition of the postcolonial paradox will always remain a creative crisis, for as colonialism was global, so it can only be liberated globally and comparatively, when the fate of postcolonial nations is brought horizontally together to be freed from the vertical dominations of truth and power between the white supremacies and colored people they have ruled. The result will inevitably lead to a global pluralism, a collective and comparative awareness of critical theory against the grain of coloniality. Thus read, the "list of books that will misguide you" will rescue both Fanon and Adorno against both Eurocentricity and the fanatical nativism that actually extends, exacerbates, and corroborates it.

The move from the trap of "the religious intellectuals" (as the most potent manifestation of a colonized mind going with a hatchet at their ancestral faith to reshape Islam on the model of Eurocentric modernity) to the emancipatory moment of the Green Movement in Iran and the Arab Spring across the Arab world marked a passage from the degenerative implosion of the condition of the postcoloniality into a vastly more enabling liberation, with paradoxical potency, a momentous occasion when historical agency could see beyond the trap of "Islam and the West." From the rise of the Arab Spring to the global intifada occasioned by the Eurozone crisis and marked by Brexit on one side and Occupy Wall Street on the other were acts of epistemic liberation that brought back the power of runaway texts, creating a whole new geography of liberation for the world at large. From the publication of Amy Allen's *The End of Progress: Decolonizing the Normative Foundations of Critical Theory* (2016), we might consider the crucial occasion when the emancipatory power of postcolonial theory and the enduring significance of critical theory finally came together—both rescuing each other from stagnant feudalism.[13] What had in effect occasioned the rise of the Frankfurt School, which Allen set here to set free, were the horrors of the Jewish Holocaust forcing European (German, in particular) thinkers to question their unexamined trust in reason and progress, and yet their ignorance or negligence of the larger colonial world had seriously limited the range of their own project. Here is where lies the significance of Amy Allen's book.

What Amy Allen does in this book is precisely where the enduring terrors of coloniality and the most critical body of pathbreaking thinking in postwar Europe come together and pave the way beyond Eurocentric conception of reason and progress. The force of postcolonial thinking thus overcomes the blind spots of European modernity and postmodernity and faces the colonial consequences of European instrumental reason. Decolonization of the Frankfurt School, as her project declares itself, means expanding upon the critical core of European thinking beyond its fictive frontiers and imaginative self-centrality. By exposing the blind spots of critical theory toward colonialism and imperialism, she questions the very idea of modernity and forces critical theory to face its terrorizing consequences upon the globe, long before it brought it home during the Jewish Holocaust. In her reading, critical theory is caught red-handed and exposed how astonishingly provincial it has been. The guiding principle for Allen begins where Edward Said left with his damning observation that the critical theory is not only silent on colonialism and imperialism but is in fact integral to the "blithe universalism" of European thinkers.[14] More specifically, Allen says she wants to do for critical theory what Robert Young's *White Mythologies* did for Marxist literary theories, namely exposing the theoretical blind spots of a Europocentric body of thinking that normatively corroborates what it politically declares it wants to dismantle.[15]

In between critical theory and the active theorization of the condition of coloniality even before and beyond Edward Said, the tertiary space of a liberation geography is mapped out where European and non-European thinking, Christian and non-Christian, dissolve into both their alterities. Here, one might see how the post-Christian philosopher's notion of a "nonreligious Christianity" seeks to reverse the course of history and decolonize Christianity form its long and illustrious services to European colonialism ever since Bartolomé de las Casas in the sixteenth century. Theorizing this notion of "nonreligious Christianity," the eminent Italian philosopher Gianni Vattimo has extended his seminal notion of *il pensiero debole* ("weak thought") to a kind of postmodern Christianity that is nonviolent and nonfoundational, a kind of "nonreligious Christianity" as he calls it that might wholeheartedly return to the bosom of humanity.[16] I have followed the thinking of Gianni Vattimo even before I met him at our Casa Italiana on Columbia campus in 1995, when the director of the academy Maristella Lorch had invited him for a series of lectures on our campus—and then on a couple of other similar occasions at both Columbia and New York University when we were both part of panels on civilizational dialogues. I had already read and knew his idea of *il pensiero debole*, and in fact had included his books in my courses on postcoloniality. His two seminal works, *The End of Modernity* (*La fine della modernità*, 1985) and *The Transparent Society* (*La società trasparente*, 1989), were instrumental in my thinking, a link between his notion of "weak thought" and the kind of liberation theodicy, alterity instead of identity, at the core of my own critical rethinking of Islam beyond its catastrophic consequences after the Islamic revolution in Iran.

Vattimo's Christianity as a "weak Christianity" is exactly the opposite of what those "religious intellectuals" were doing with their triumphalist "Islam itself," an epistemically violent Islam they belligerently cast against their "secular" enemies. In my *Islamic Liberation Theology* (2008), I had moved in a similar direction when I thought through a bringing-together of Islam closer to Latin American Christian liberation theology, which in his own particular philosophical language is what I believe Gianni Vattimo is doing with his "weak Christianity." Vattimo's initial impetus toward his confession that he "believes that he believes" is, of course, a Kierkegaardian moment of existential confession that brings Christianity back to its inaugural moment, negotiated between two professors of philosophy in the course of a conversation on a public phone, as he describes it early in his book.[17] I had come to my Islamic liberation theology not through Vattimo but decidedly through Emmanuel Levinas's theodicy, mapped inscrutably, as it is, on the face of the Other. I had turned Levinas's face of the

Other, which to me sounded too European (I have always wished Levinas were more Jewish than European in his philosophy—it would have made him closer and dearer to me), into a liberating moment of alterity for post-Islamist theology. Somewhere in between Asef Bayat's post-Islamism, Levinas's face of the Other, and Vattimo's weak Christianity, I could now see, the liberation theology of all these three religions come together to bear witness to the liberating alterity at the heart of the postcolonial person.

Six
Europe: The Indefinite Jest

Precisely because *Europe* is the name for universality, that is, for an openness and exposure to the other, the very injunctions that constitute universality also require that this name, as a proper and singular name, and as a name of a singularity, be abandoned.[1]

Rodolphe Gasché, *Europe, or the Infinite Task* (2009)

Perhaps it is not accidental that beginning with Edmund Husserl (1859–1938), European philosophers, phenomenologists in particular, have paid close attention to what it means to be European. In Husserl's seminal text, *The Crisis of European Sciences and Transcendental Phenomenology* (1936), there is already evidence of the rising anxiety of a towering German philosopher thinking about a moment of categorical crisis rising from social and political to critical consciousnesses. As a victim of Nazi racism, Husserl's philosophical reflections on what it means to be German (in racial or spiritual terms) had obvious implications for what it means to be European. Emerging from moments of existential crisis in Europe itself, the question inevitably reached back to its transhistorical domains to the Greek origins Europeans had imagined for themselves. Today, too, whether we are in the presence of the most radical or the most conservative European thinkers and scholars (from Slavoj Žižek to Niall Ferguson), we are in fact witness to a fundamental fear of foreigners and what it means when the fragile identity of being "European" is threatened by the proximity of an unknown and unknowable "alterity" as they call it. Whereas at the time of Husserl, with the internal European rise of fascism that had prompted what it means to be European, for the more recent and contemporary philosophers, decidedly the arrival of Arabs, Muslims, and Africans has triggered the selfsame fearful questions. For we who are neither beholden to nor fearful of Europe, our task today is to make these foreigners familiar to the European philosopher by making their own familiarities with themselves foreign to them.

The allegorical disposition of the thing called Europe, the fictitious link to a manufactured conception of "the ancient Greek," the categorical claim of this Europe on that Greece—these are the issues European philosophers all take for granted, as they engage in further mystification of the factual link they have actively imagined between their Europe and that Greece. This fiction needs to be dismantled.

The trajectory of such critical reflections, however, is not geared toward doubling down on the strangeness of strangers by making ourselves even more strangers to ourselves too—a kind of double estrangement and alienation (or what W. E. B. DuBois called "double consciousness"), in which we will be lost to ourselves and thus civic life itself will be made impossible. But through the common space of familiarity, the foreigner in us and the familiar in them could find new spaces of coming together, not in a gesture of philosophical feigning of *hospitality* but in urgent existential needs for *solidarity*. We are not the enemies of Europeans, though Europeans have made strangers of us. For them Europe is an essence; for us it is an accident. They insist on mystifying it; we must persist in historicizing it. They may or may never be cured of the universality of their Europe, which at times they seem to wish to shove down the throat of the world at large, first by imperial and colonial conquests, and now by sheer power of their philosophical imagination. We respect that philosophical imagination, but we must insist on cutting it to its proportionate sizes. On the ruins of their belligerent persistence in and through their *Europe,* we find the relics of a world beyond their reach that once was, and a world that we need to imagine not against but beyond their *Europe.*

Europe: The Infinite Chore

We must think beyond Europe but through Europe—so when all is said and done on the precious ruins of Europe, we overcome its atrocities. This is not just a collegial courtesy to European philosophers. It is a matter predicated on the entangled self-mystification of Europe, of Europeans, and their Europeanism. In his formidable study, *Europe, or the Infinite Task: A Study of a Philosophical Concept* (2009), Rodolphe Gasché successfully turned Europe to the status of a philosophical proposition. Opting decidedly to examine the word *Europe* as a philosophical cognate away from its political implications, Gasché has mapped Europe into the philosophical cornerstone in the works of four eminent European philosophers: Edmund Husserl,

Martin Heidegger, Jan Patočka, and Jacques Derrida. His project is admirable in the way he seeks to sublate the concept of Europe over and above the globalized market economy of indefatigable flattening of ideas into noises. His limitation, however, is rooted in his European inability to see other worlds equally if not even better equipped to engage in rationality, universality, or openness. These worlds are not in juxtaposition or opposition to Europe—Asian, African, Latin American, Islamic, Buddhist, and so on. These worlds transcend Europe, master its abilities and disabilities and reach for a more leveled space for critical thinking. Such worlds are not named. They are invisible under the radars of our habitual Europeanization of the universe.

"Europe is intimately tied to the very idea and promise of reason and rationality," Gasché attributes this thought approvingly to Husserl.[2] More than his actual thought, and his seminal (unfinished) text, *Die Krisis der europäischen Wissenschaften und die transzendentale Phänomenologie: Eine Einleitung in die phänomenologische Philosophie* (*The Crisis of European Sciences and Transcendental Phenomenology: An Introduction to Phenomenological Philosophy*, 1936), Husserl becomes the principal figure through which Gasché assigns to Europe no less a task than defining the quintessence of our humanity at large—not just the European humanity (to which he and other Europeans are of course entitled) but all our humanities, no matter how far or close to the idea of Europe (not its geographical location) we might be. If we were to discover a new planet in some other universe on which human life would be possible, that planet too would be "European." Through Husserl Euro-universalism, as Gasché reads him, becomes Universal—while the world at large, the subject of this Universalism, has no say in the matter. "Although the European spirit is born in Greece," Gasché repeats after Husserl, "it manifests itself properly only with another primal establishment, which occurs in the Renaissance, and which is at once a re-establishment [*Nachstiftung*] and a modification of the Greek primal establishment."[3] Here, as elsewhere, is where a cliché chronology that consolidates Europe in its self-referential teleology back to an innocent Greece anachronistically becomes the central time line of the complete identification of Europe with philosophical humanism writ Universal. This is the moment when universality assumes a spatial form and calls itself Europe, a period that Gasché considers "Universality in the making," when "the very idea of philosophy as a rational science ... emerges in Greece and ... according to Husserl coincides with the idea of Europe."[4] The world at large, the world outside this Europe and its colonially appropriated idea of "Greece," has had no agency or say in the matter—not even the real Greece, either the ancient Greece or the present Greece. What matters is the European invention of a Greece to its liking. The Greece of the European imagination was and remains the passive object of European self-universalization, with Husserl at one end and Gasché at the other end of this European anxiety seeking to overcome it by philosophically reasserting the European designation as the locus classicus of the love of truth manifest.

Being European

Gasché's exquisite book is an extraordinary evidence for us to see how a learned contemporary European philosopher reaches back to his philosophical ancestry to reassert Europe in one of its direst moments of categorical crisis. When Gasché turns from Husserl to Heidegger, a crucial epistemic linkage in his underlying teleology, he starts with a discussion of how the word *Europe* has been used interchangeably with "Occident" or "the West." He takes issue with this conflation of these words.[5] When focusing on Heidegger's "Letter on Humanism," Gasché tells us how for Heidegger "the West" was not to be thought as a region different from the Orient, but "rather worldhistorically out of nearness to the origin."[6] "Europe" is what is near to Being, the Orient is what is far. The Orient is not Being. The Orient is non-Being. The Orient is not. "The Occident would seem to refer to the present time and is, compared with the Orient, a late phenomenon within the history of being." More specifically: "destiny guides the spirit on its way from the Orient to the Occident."[7] The Orient is in short what was and is not anymore. This is utterly brilliant, for it reveals how as we move from Husserl to Heidegger, in Gasché's reading of the two seminal European philosophers, *the present* and *Europe* become synonymous with the worldhistoricality of truth as destined to move away from Orient (which means the world at large) toward Europe. The self-realization of Europe as being is contingent on being away from Orient (meaning the whole world). The world fades into nonhistorically, into non-Being, as Europe emerges as the ultimate destination of being, of humanity. We the world, the Orientals, are strangers to this European worlding of the world, backward not by virtue of any moral, imaginative, or existential shortcoming, but by virtue of our very being the past-present absentees in European Being. We have no choice in the matter. We cannot strive to be better human beings even by getting closer to Europe. We were all stillborn. The accident of our birth makes us nonexistent in European Being.

There is an infinity to this Heideggerian totality. Heidegger is particular that Europe was not just "the proper time-space of destiny," but also "something waiting to happen, something still to come."[8] Predicated on its manufactured Greek origin, there is an indefinite futurity to this Europe, a metaphysical destiny, rooted in Europe but cast into the unknown future—thus not just Being but in fact Time becomes European. We, the world outside Europe, are checkmated outside existence, outside Being—willingly. There is no escaping it. Heidegger thought both the United States and Russia as the two enemies of Europe.[9] This according to Gasché is the decisive turn in Heidegger's thinking from 1935 forward, when he shifts from "fundamental ontology" to "the History of Being."[10] In this turn, Germany lies at the heart of Heidegger's Europe, directly rooted in his Greece, "and in resistance to what from both sides [the United States and Russia] endangers their ability to reconnect with the question of Being."[11] Russia and the United States, on both sides of Heidegger's Europe, are purgatorial. They are the polluted backyards of Europe, protecting and inoculating Europe against threats from the beyond of those bumper zones.

It is all but inevitable, in fact predictable, that "the thought of Being that irrupts in ancient Greece is a prodigiously strange thought; for Heidegger the birth of this thinking coincides with the advent of Europe and the West."[12] This is not logical, historical, or even geographical. This is pure philosophical fantasy. Before Europe, there was no thinking, nor will there be any thinking after Europe, and this Europe has an exclusive, colonial claim on Greece. This is not a matter of speculative metaphysics. It is the very definition of Being, for "in the same way as Husserl, Heidegger traces Europe or the West back to Greece, not, however, to the emergence in Greece of rational science but to the breakthrough in Greece of the question of Being, and hence to the emergence of philosophy an attentiveness and exposure to Being."[13] This may or may not be a fact about Greek philosophy. But the fictive, allegorical, claim of Europe on this possibility is pure fantasy. As Gasché rightly reminds us, this is not a mere matter of the ontology of a philosophical choice. It is much more than that: "The thought of Being, as that thought which genuine commencement of Europe is, is equiprimordial with a conception of what or who is human."[14] Being human means being European, being European means being human. If you are not European, you are not human. The only thing you can be if non-European is nonhuman. Gasché clarifies emphatically: "According to Heidegger, Parmenides saying that thinking and Being are the same contains the 'determination of Being-human that is definite [*massgebend*] for the West, and just as decisively it contains an essential characterization of Being.'"[15] You may hope that we mortal Orientals may escape this fate sometime in some remote point of history, but alas: "The beginning of Europe and the West ... is a beginning in the genuine sense because, in principle, it is free of all traces of the religious.... This beginning ... is characterized as primordial history, as *Ur-geschichte*."[16] We mortal non-Europeans are outside history, ahistorical, the Heideggerian philosophy makes us impossible beings.

For Heidegger, Gasché tells us, Greece is the originary world of tragedy. Heidegger's world is not the natural world or the life-world of Husserl.[17] Instead, he is in search of "that poetry that is 'the originary language of a people,'" and he finds it in Sophocles's *Antigone*. "This Greek sense of Being-human, which arises in early Greece and sets the stage for Europe and the West is itself uncanny, precisely in that it shows that to be is to be homeless."[18] Europe and Europeans are uncanny, homeless away from their Greece (which is not to be confused with the real Greece). The moral of the argument follows handsomely:

In the same way as Husserl, Heidegger considers Greece to be the sole origin of Europe and the West. However, saving the West from the imminent threat that it faces by way of an originary recreation of its history not only requires the people of the middle—the German people—to reflect on what is their own by reaching to the one singular other—Greece—that concerns it most immediately, but, as Heidegger suggests in "Wege zur Aussprache" 1937, this task is also a task incumbent on all other European peoples.[19]

Between Husserl and Heidegger, Greece becomes a manufactured philosophical prototype, a trope, from which Europeans in general, Germans in particular, are to re-create their originary homecoming. Heidegger might insist to claim this originary point for Germans in particular, but other Europeans need not worry. They should all do the same for themselves. The world at large, the non-Europeans—well they are just that, they are non-Europeans, nonhumans. They need not apply. They have no place either in Husserl's or Heidegger's Europe or in Gasché's articulation of an infinite task for it. What is crucial here is the existential denial of even homelessness for non-Europeans, categorically condemned from birth to death to be just that—non-Europeans: black to their whiteness, inferior to their superiority, backward to their forwardness, raw material for their philosophical machinations, spectators to their gesticulations of "Europe as an infinite task."

Caring for the (European) Soul

Gasché continues his philosophical mapping of "Europe" as a concept from Husserl and Heidegger to the Czech phenomenologist Jan Patočka (1907–1977), who like his German counterparts thought Europe "is not primarily a geographical or purely political concept."[20] Particularly important, Gasché tells us, is the fact these philosophers have all turned to Europe as a concept and a reality prompted by their contemporary crisis. For Patočka, it was imperative to retrieve the "spiritual origin" of this concept of Europe as Gasché is mapping it in this book. These European philosophers were preoccupied with the overwhelming notion how "deepening the foundations of European rationality is capable of putting humanity onto a new road, and of overcoming the crisis of the principle of Europe."[21] If Europe were in crisis, in short, the whole world would be lost forever. The crisis of who and what and wherefore they are is not just a European predicament but a global predicament. If Europe is in crisis, the entire fate of our humanity is in crisis. This is the centerpiece of all these philosophers' preoccupations from Husserl to Heidegger to Patočka, as Gasché maps out their respective philosophical love letters to their beloved absolutist abstraction, "Europe."

By closely examining such major works of Patočka as *Heretical Essays* and *Plato and Europe*, Gasché informs us that in the writings of this Czech philosopher from eastern Europe, "a truly new, and original, conception of what is European emerges."[22] There are of course variations on the theme: For while Husserl thought "the origin and telos of Europe is a genuinely rational science," and while Heidegger thought "Europe or the West is grounded in the oblivion of the thought of Being," Patočka believed "Europe as Europe arose ... from ... the motive of the care of the soul."[23] More specifically, Patočka believes "Europe, especially western Europe, but even that other one [namely, eastern Europe, Gasché interjects], arose out of the care of the soul." More emphatically, "this is the embryo out of which arose what Europe to be ... The care of the soul [as] the central theme around which ... the life plan of Europe crystallized." Patočka and Gasché trace this "care of the soul" all the way back to Plato, particularly to *The First Alcibiades*.[24] This indeed is a marvelous philosophical romance to read, so many deeply moving love letters by such eminent philosophers written to a distant abstraction, each in a different diction. But alas, in none of these varied gestations of the European philosophical romance, does any human being outside Europe have a snowball chance in hell to see his or her mortal being reflected.

Gasché consistently reminds us "the emphasis on the spiritual heritage of Europe is motivated by the diagnosis of Europe's decline, as well as of that of the world at large."[25] Here the emphasis that Gasché and his European philosophers put on "the world" is quite crucial—for in their estimation, not just Europe but the world is in crisis, and Europe and its eminent philosophers are here to help, to think for us all, reminding us that Europe means "the care for the soul," our European soul, of course. If you were ever so unfortunate to have been born in Timbuktu or Kalamazoo, you better search for and detect your European soul and start caring for it. If you do not find it, you can of course dye your hair blonde, wear a pair of blue contact lenses, whiten your skin, and unflatten your nose the best you can and convert to Europeanism and start saying "Hail Mary" a few times until a lost European soul began dawning on you. What is astonishing here is how no human being who is not European is presumed to have a soul beyond the grasp of the European colonial claim on Greek philosophy and what has happened to it in the hands of these European philosophers—all of it, no doubt, beautiful and compelling in and of itself. But it has absolutely nothing to do, nothing to say, about the world beyond their European noses, itself a figment of philosophical imagination.

There is a genealogy to the European sense of responsibly or what Gasché call "Europe-Responsibly." In a remarkable anthropomorphic move, Gasché writes, "if Europe did not remain simply Greek, but also allowed the Hebrew element to become an essential ingredient of European civilization … it is 'perhaps … because there are certain immanent components in the Greek thinking itself that required something like that.'"[26] Gasché and Patočka are quite generous and even ecumenical in this liberality of having other cultures (Jewish in this case) feed Europe where and when it is needed. Even more generously, Roman, Byzantine, and Islam too have chipped in "for the formation of Europe." But none of that is to distract from the fact that "the history of Europe, the only history that, according to Patočka, merits to be called so—is 'foremost a history of the soul.'"[27] This only history that matters begins with "the emergence of humans who master the original dilemma of human possibilities by discovering the authentic, unique I."[28] Such observations indeed abound in Gasché's exquisitely learned book—from which emerges a uniquely qualified European philosophical voice in no uncertain terms declaring there is no humanity, no history, no agency, no caring for the soul, indeed no soul, outside or beyond the European reach.

Gasché repeatedly emphasizes that Husserl and the other philosophers he examines closely turned to the notion of Europe and what it means when Europe was in crisis. The same is or might be suggested to be true of his own time to turn to Europe and what it means. The publication of his reading of Europe (as an Infinite task) in 2009 is in the full aftermath of the collapse of the Berlin Wall, the dismantling of the Soviet Union, and then the liberation of eastern Europe from Soviet bondage, the formation of the European Union, and the rise of "the refugee crisis," and ultimately the Brexit and other right-wing xenophobic manners of neofascism in this very "Europe" he is studying with such learned philosophical care. That is, of course, perfectly understandable. Under such dire circumstances, Europeans need to reconfigure who and what and where and wherefore they are. And yet (paradoxically) the more they do so the more they get themselves entangled in a philosophically miasmatic (if not delusional) fixation with Europe being rooted in a fictive Greece of their own making. Take their Greece away from them (their fictive Greece, for they have no use for the

real Greece), and they would be like that proverbial cat with its
whiskers clipped.

When a Jewish Algerian Remembers
the European Past

Gasché finally turns to Derrida, an Algerian-French Jewish philosopher, to resolve a major tension Gasché correctly detects in his
philosophical articulation of Europe—the dual and mutually exclusive claims of Greece and Christianity on it. Gasché begins by
turning the most iconoclastic Jewish philosopher of our time into a
conservative thinker who believes philosophers must "take responsibility for that heritage of discourses in what Europe is."[29] Gasché
insists on "the fact that for Derrida the prime responsibility of the
European is one toward the tradition of the discourses and counter-
discourses concerning his own identification."[30] What is remarkable
here is how radically the essentialized notion of "Europe," even
with the most revolutionary thinkers, turns them into conservative
guardians of the gate, of the "tradition." From within this tradition, Derrida identifies the "essential Christianity" at the heart of
Patočka's notion of the care of the soul.[31] Gasché of course insists
that Patočka's Christianity is a heretical Christianity. Thus begins a
full discussion of the difference between the Platonic and the
Christian conception of responsibility. This evident difference is
poised, if left alone, to rip apart the very notion of a unified Europe.
Is Europe Greek or is Europe Christian?—the discussion of the
issue of responsibility is entirely contingent on answering this
thorny and potentially destructive question.

The issue is quite serious for "as we have seen," Gasché tells us, "there
is no place for secrecy in the Platonic paradigm of responsibility.
The Platonic model is a democratic model based on responsibility
as universally accessible knowledge and on a demand of transpar-
ency."[32] Derrida resolves this paradox by refusing to privilege one
over the other. He proposes the very "aporia of responsibilities" to be
definitive to "the relation between the Platonic and the Christian
paradigms throughout the history of morality and politics."[33] Gasché
and Derrida's ingenious resolution of the paradox is to suggest: "The
conflicting exigencies ... of the concepts of responsibility require
the invention of a new way to revive or replay the figure, concept, or

idea of Europe. European responsibility is, first of all, this openness to *both* traditions of responsibility that characterize its history—namely Platonism and Christianity."[34] I say this is quite ingenious because under the current aporia of laying a colonial claim on both Athens and Jerusalem, on both Greek philosophy and Christianity, these distinguished European philosophers turn the lemon of their conceptual cul-de-sac into the lemonade of openness and generosity of their spirit. What belies this philosophical colonialism, however, is the fact that it is of all things a Jewish philosopher who comes up with this gimmick to bring Plato and Christianity together and the fact that this "openness" is suddenly closed and frightened out of its liberal wits at the sight of a single Syrian or Afghan (Muslim) or Somalia (African) refugee child—for they are neither Greek nor Christian in the manner "Europe" has manufactured these to tropes.

Along with Derrida, Gasché insists the question of Europe is universal, global, and therefore of utmost urgency not just for Europeans but in fact for the world at large. "The question of Europe is not merely one question among others. It is, rather, as Jacques Derrida remarks 'a question that will always be of current interest.'" If this is so, it is because this question is not only of current interest to Europeans but also because it is a question that by essence projects itself beyond boundaries, particularly, those of a geographical, political, and cultural entity called "Europe."[35] But why—we non-Europeans might be permitted to wonder? Who said so? Why should an astoundingly provincial provenance and its crisis of identity, however mightily expressed in thundering philosophical terms, be of any serious concern to anyone else in the world. What allows European philosophers first to indulge in self-universalization and then get caught up in their own philosophical fantasies? There is no shred of credibility to think the European question is of any global significance beyond this habitual European self-universalization. As intruders into their august gatherings, we read them politely and wonder. But their questions are theirs. Not mine. Not ours.

There are moments when the truth of the larger world beyond the limited claims of Europe begins to shine some reason on this gathering. "As a pure idea, however," Gasché admits, "the idea of philosophy as an infinite task can, in principle, have no geographical or historical roots, and 'in this respect, Europe should be able [as Derrida notes] to be replaced by Asia or by Africa.'" But Gasché immediately reverses himself: "And yet, in spite of the refusal—particular to phenomenological idealism—to grant the European *eidos* the status of an empirically datable and localized event, Europe, in Husserl's works, is said to be 'philosophy's spiritual place of birth, its mysterious and immaterial residence,' the place where philosophy inhabits, in his words, 'the heart of certain men.' Europe, consequently, is endowed with an eidos that is also specifically European."[36] This is fine, of course. Europeans can have their philosophy and enjoy it—as a philosophy specific to them, and perfectly glorious at that. Their problem is a bizarre gestation of European philosophical imperialism. They want to shove it down the throat of people around the globe, claim universality for it, and yet insist on calling it European! These are very fair-minded and reasonable people. They are the best of the best philosophers. But there is a philosophical blindness to their insights. They cannot see other peoples might be busy wondering about the world too. If they did so, then they must be Europeans.

It is a revelation to read Gasché's extraordinary book cover to cover and see his brilliant and caring mind so utterly bewildered. Here we see how the father of deconstruction, Derrida, checks his deconstruction radicalism at the gate of Europe, for as Gasché tells us "the intimate link that Derrida conceives between Europe and (phenomenological) philosophy sets the stage for his ongoing interest in the question, leading him to present himself, over time, as a philosopher of Europe." Imagine that. The philosopher who does not allow one brick to stand on another in the making of a single sentence, still insist on being European, his Algerian Jewish origin notwithstanding. More specifically, we learn: "As a thinker of Europe, Derrida has broached the question of Europe on numerous occasions, but this does not mean that he is simply a European thinker." Let us recall what he says at the end of *The Other Heading:* "I am European.... But I am not, nor do I feel, European in every part, that is, European through and through.... I feel European among other things."[37] Derrida, in sort, wants to have his European cake and eat its deconstruction too. Who is of anything "in every part"? Am I Iranian in every part? Is someone an Arab in every part, an Asian, a Latin American in every part, or "through and through"? Would that phrase not imply that some are European, in every part and through and through, a prototype of the European? That is pure Aryanism. That is pure fascism—even to assume such a thing exists, against which Derrida is sometime less of a European.

What a frightful construction to assume by the very father of deconstruction.

Gasché is invariably honest about the irredeemably racist fore-grounding of the European project. "As Husserl's exclusion of Eskimos, Indians, and gypsies from European humanity demonstrates, the danger of understanding European identity from a purported spiritual unity is that such a conception of European identity risks foreclosing any openness to the other, to everything non-European."[38] He is, of course, right. The idea of Europe could not possibly be so open-minded as to accept such undesirable elements. Europe is Greece, a fictive Greece, Greece is Europe, a fictive Europe, and Europe is philosophy, a decidedly ethno-philosophy that feigns universality—that is the trajectory Gasché articulates through his philosophers of choice, though entirely unbeknownst to himself. "As Derrida reminds us," Gasché tells us, "what we can rigorously call 'philosophy' exists nowhere other than in Greece. While there are certainly very powerful bodies of thought elsewhere, which are other than philosophy, philosophy as a specific project of the thinking of being was born in Greece."[39] If we were to follow the mythic fiction of European philosophical self-understanding, this is precisely what follows. Things begin to fall apart when we remember the real Greece, and the allegory of Europe that will be dismantled if that real Greece were to be placed where it was, within a geographical topography long before the myth of Europe was invented categorically and conceptually to colonize and claim it.

At issue here is not just the proposition that non-Europeans cannot do philosophy without polluting the very word *philosophy*. Far more importantly is the exclusive claim that the anxiety-ridden word *Europe* wants to lay on Greece. Take this Greece from Europe and it will collapse. In the process, though, Gasché has to be careful not to ethnicize Europe: "As Derrida remarks, this appeal to the tradition"—that is, Husserl's and Heidegger's conception of "the entirety of philosophy ... on the basis of its Greek source"—amounts neither "to an Occidentalism, nor to a historicism."[40] Well, I do not know how to break it to the distinguished European philosopher: it actually does. But neither Derrida nor Gasché would be willing to yield that with Occidentalism and Historicism combined the whole universal presumption of Europe will in fact fall flat on its nose. More specifically, Gasché tells us, "indeed, if for both Husserl and

Heidegger the advent of philosophy is of the order of an irruption (*Aufbruch* or *Einbruch*), or the result of a call or claim of Being that occurs in Greece, then the Greek or European *eidos* cannot be reduced to the factuality of this occurrence. Derrida, for his part, does not contest this phenomenological recourse to the origins of the philosophical tradition in the Greek event."[41] If for both Husserl and Heidegger, each in their own way, Greek philosophy is so coterminous with the very idea, the very possibility, of Europe, and a fortiori European philosophy, the origin of that myth is in fact predicated on a geographical and historical delusion. Here the question is not the fact that the Greek sources reached the philosophical ancestors of Husserl, Heidegger, Derrida, and in fact Gasché himself first through their Arabic translations and commentaries, but the fact that these later philosophers so violently and ungratefully disregard that medium and lay a colonial claim directly on Greek sources. But why? By what authority? Who said a German, a French, or any other modern or contemporary European philosopher has more claim on Plato than any other philosopher in Asia, Africa, or Latin America? This very simple fact never bothers Gasché or his philosophical Europeanists.

The subordinate clauses of Gasché's phrasings are as important, if not more, than his basic arguments. When he says, "Before I broach Derrida's novel interpretation of the source of the philosophical, and hence of Europe, let me pause here long enough to …" This casual equating of the Greek with the philosophical, and the philosophical with Europe, is a most crucial nervous tic agitating the subconscious of the text, where the non-Greek, non-European are excluded with the adage of the nonphilosophical. The triangulating frame of "Greek, philosophical, and Europe" into a closed-circuited triumvirate decidedly disallows any interference and disruptions by alien elements. All these three corners of the triangle—Europe, Greek, and philosophical—are an entirely ahistorical, figment of an agitated puritanical imagination.

In the age of multiculturalism, as it were, more recent European philosophers more openly in the public eyes do not mind admitting non-European influences:

As opposed to Husserl and Heidegger, and more emphatically than Patočka, Derrida highlights the multiplicity of the sources and identities that intersect in the European heritage.

He writes, for example, that "if the heritage of thought (of truth and Being) in which we are inscribed is not solely, neither fundamentally nor originary Greek, it is no doubt because of other intercrossing and heterogeneous affiliations, of other languages, and other identities which are not simply additions [to this heritage], or secondary accidents (Jewish, Arabic, Christian, Roman, Germanic, and so forth). This is certainly so because European history has not only unfolded a Greek deal [une donne grecque]."[42]

Both Husserl and Heidegger were writing in the insular Germanic province of their philosophical prose. They never had an Arab, Muslim, or Chinese person reading over their shoulders as they wrote. But Derrida, as an Algerian Jew, did. What he says here, though, is not to be confused for generosity of his cosmopolitan spirit. When it came to Europe, he was indeed more Catholic than the pope. For Derrida too, philosophy could only speak Greek. Forget about Arabic; philosophy could not even speak Hebrew.

Be that as it may, it is important to take note of the fact that it took a Francophone Algerian Jewish philosopher to think about Europe and its philosophy even in the dubious terms of "influences on it": "In his reflections on European identity Derrida has consistently demanded that these other moments be taken into account. In *Rogues*, for instance, he contends that it is indispensable to examine 'what gets passed on, transferred, translated from Europe by pre- and post-Koranic Arabic, as well as by Rome.'"[43] The sentence and the sentiment behind it is of course entirely confused and ill informed. The phrase "pre-Koranic Arabic" decidedly confuses the Islamic (in both Arabic and Persian) spectrum of Greek philosophical tradition that includes the Koran in its epistemic universes but is not reduced to it. The trouble for these European philosophers is of course entirely rooted in the false assumption that Greek philosophy is exclusively theirs. It is not.

The power and significance of Gasché's book, so committed to Europe as Greek, Greek as philosophy, and therefore Greek and philosophy as exclusively European, is that he will never allow his readers to entertain the illusion that Europe can be robbed of its exclusive claim to both Greece and to philosophy: "At this juncture," he poignantly warns us, "a note of caution may be warranted. What is at stake in this interrogation of the uniqueness and originality of the Greek source of philosophy (and Europe) is not a desire to replace the Greek by the non-Greek. As Derrida has forcefully shown in 'Violence and Metaphysics,' any interpellation of the Greek by the non-Greek is possible only in the language of the Greeks. Only in this language is it possible to state that the question of the non-Greek is a question that is silenced and forgotten in the language of the Greek."[44] This is powerful and significant, I say, because it allows us to see that in Gasché's text as the summation and summary of the philosophers he examines, there is no room for philosophy outside the Greek he and his comrades have invented and carved out exclusively for Europe. You pull that Greek from under their feet, they will fall flat on their noses. Islamic and Jewish philosophies (particularly in the pluralities of their articulations) are the Achilles' heels of this delusional European invention of the Greek. They must consistently belittle, ethnicize, exoticize, and alienate such other non-European takes on the real and historical Greek to enable themselves as exclusively Greek.

But that is not all. It is not sufficient to deprive others of philosophy, agency, morality, and authorial voice. The authorial voice of the other must be suffocated by making it subservient, no matter what it says to Europe. "Derrida writes," Gasché quotes him, "that nothing can so profoundly solicit the Greek logos—philosophy—as this irruption of the totally-other; and nothing can to such an extent reawaken the logos to its origin as to its mortality, its other."[45] We are the mortality of the Greek logos, its very negation, by virtue of our very being, our very existence. We breathe and we negate philosophy. They invent an ahistorical Greek, claim it to authenticate a delusional Europe, lay a categorical claim on that Greek logos, and all of that to deprive the humanity at large from reason and dignity. We were here to serve, to tickle the fancy of the European philosopher, as their "totally other," as the totally other of Greek. We are here to be scarified on the altar of the "totally the same." Gasché entertains the possibility of this "infinitely other" to be "Jewish." But again, only as subservient to the Greek of their European imagination, not the real Greek, of course, of there and then, or of now and here.

Gasché derives that European insatiable cannibalism of eating all its others to nourish itself home: "I intend to argue not only that Greece is the origin of Europe because of this 'indestructible and unforeseeable resource of the Greek logos' but also that the priority that Greece enjoys in determining Europe's *arche* and *telos* derives precisely from its intrinsic nonidentity."[46] The first task is more urgent than the last, or as important: first to lay a flawed European claim on Greece, and then to sustain the cannibalistic delusion that the more Europe as Greece devours its others, the more it becomes Greek, inimitable, and singular. This is all for Gasché to push forward the proposition of "a Europe that can understand itself as having its origin outside itself":

> Europe's origin is nonidentical to itself; it would thus be a mistake to conceive of it as primarily Greek, with additional Jewish, Christian, and Islamic elements. Rather, Europe's origin is open to multiple origins from the beginning. However, this conception of Europe is made possible, specifically, by the West's philosophical heritage—its Greek heritage—in that from the beginning that which was Greek allowed alterity to circulate within the logos ... constituted by an openness and a hospitality that is extended not only to the non-European but also to unpredictable, unforeseeable otherness.[47]

Again, this is for Europe to have its exclusivity unto itself and eat its others too. The European others are there to serve Europe and consolidate its wobbly claims on Greece. This will guarantee Europe's universality without losing its particularity. So, anyone can do philosophy so far as it is done in specifically European terms, so it can insist "on continuing to call such a conception of unconditional openness and hospitality to the other by the name of Europe."[48] Gasché can thus always be trusted to provide and assure Europeans of their inviolable singularity: "... a cautionary remark is warranted. Such a figure [Europe as a figure of conversion and passage into other(s)], does not entail reversibility of self and other, what is one's own and the foreign, the familiar and the alien."[49] More specifically, reassuringly: "Reversibility is without risk, since the other, or the foreign to and into which the self-reverts, is only the opposite of oneself (thus the self can always reassert itself in the other, or reappropriate it) ... without the threat posed by its promise Europe would not be a promise to begin with. Without its inherent danger it would also lack all universal appeal."[50] These hilarious gymnastics of going back and forth to others and reverting back to oneself are precisely the farcical position the European philosopher finds himself when trying to be fanatically committed to its fictive Greek origins and yet sport a bit of liberal ecumenicalism.

Holding On to or Letting Go of Europe

"For many," Gasché readily admits, "universality is a European invention. It is a philosophical and, for some, an ideological construct that intends to justify and embellish its historical pretensions with respect to the non-European world. Universality is generally considered to amount to Europe's historical and cultural imposition on the rest of the world and to imply an overriding and denying of all singularities."[51] That is a flawed argument. The European universality is not imperially imposed on other people's singularities, but on their alternative universalities, which Gasché here completely ignores, disregards, or perhaps a bit too cleverly sidesteps. But even that admission is only a subterfuge to insist and persist on the universality of Europe in a manner that accounts for, absorbs, accommodates, and in fact underlines other people's particularities—robbing them of their possible universalities in the meantime. "For those who seek to understand universality as a simple translation of the merely factual power of Europe and European arrogance," that will be we non-Europeans of course, "the connection that I have made in this book—between the thought of universality and Europe—will only serve as further confirmation of what, in essence, is a misunderstanding of universality—namely, that universality is dismissive of particularity and singularity. Universality, however, or for that matter, reason, is not a threat to particularity per se. On the contrary, particularity only makes sense with respect to universality."[52] This is indeed an excellent, quite shrewd, categorical move. They, the Europeans, get to keep their universality; we, the world, stick to our particularities, positively denied of any chance of alternative universalities, and we will all live happily ever after sticking to our particularities under the generous, magnanimous, and hospitable universality of Europe.

What is remarkable is the fact that Gasché is fully aware that "resistance to associating this conception [of universality] with 'Europe' is to be expected since that name, today, smacks of parochialism."[53] He further admits: "If 'Europe' is taken to refer to a geographical entity, or to the however-ill-determined economic, cultural, and political identity of present-day Europe, one would be hard-pressed to discover any traces in it of the radical openness to the other advocated by the new conception of universality and world." His solution to this predicament? "But if universality and Europe are intrinsically linked, then this can only be the case if 'Europe' is not understood as a geographical entity but, in Husserl's words, as a spiritual figure, in short, as a philosophical concept." But why? By what authority? Why should Europe, and only Europe, be understood in those universal terms? Why not Africa, Asia, Latin America, the North Pole, Kalamazoo, Timbuktu, why not the Chinese, the Indian, the Islamic universality? Whence this exclusionary arrogance that only one word, and only this particular word must be associated with universality? Have there been any other claims on such universalities? Could there be any other name with similar claims on universalities? Whence this imperial arrogance over universality preserved for Europe?

At a crucial point, Gasché plays "the philosophical card": "if it seems problematic to relate a newly enlightened conception of universality to something called 'Europe,' it may also be because of a lack of clarity regarding the relation of the philosophical concept of Europe to Europe as a particular part of the world—something that is more generally reflected in the relation between universality and singularity."[54] But there are no historical, theoretical, or even "philosophical" reasons to buy into that proposition. Muslims had a philosophical claim on the Greek long before this Europe was invented or any one of the philosophers Gasché examines had come around. But he still insists:

> Husserl's, Heidegger's, Patočka's, and Derrida's reflections are all attempts to reawaken the demand for universality and for a world (that would be one world shared by all) in the name of Europe. Undoubtedly, some other great world-cultures have raised themselves to the thought of universality. It is therefore not a question here of arguing that thought—which is thought only on condition of seeking universal validity—only emerged with the Greeks. Yet only in Greece did thought develop in a way that had no likeness anywhere else. Though this is certainly not sufficient to argue for the supremacy of Greek thought, more important is the fact that it is only in Greece that thought became defined as such.[55]

The question here is not even to doubt if indeed Greek thought was the only thought with a claim to universality, and that the Egyptians, the Chinese, the Jewish, or the Zoroastrian thoughts did not have any similar claims to universality, and in fact cosmogonic universality. Let us even assume that indeed Greek was the only such claim to universality. What has it got to do with "Europe"? Islamic philosophy for one had a claim on that Greek universality centuries before the word and the idea and the claim (all colonial) of "Europe" was invented to lay this bizarre, ahistorical, entirely ideological claim on the Greek.

Gasché's last-pitch battle in this losing war continues to the very last pages of his learned book. He speaks of "nostalgia for a lost Europe," of the "temptation to claim that only European rationality has the privilege of uprooting itself and of having alone the disposal of alterity, of other cultures and traditions," and of "Europe" "of universal openness and responsibility to the other."[56] But all of it to conclude:

> The name of Europe must be maintained to designate the thought of universality, hospitality, and responsibility that arose in Europe and, drawing on the resources of this tradition, has found its most radical development in the thinkers I have discussed. However, in order for there to be the other and the event, for responsibility, hospitality, and history to take place, the name *Europe* must also be abandoned. Jean-Luc Nancy has proposed "to rename Europe 'Euruopa,' the one that sees far into the distance, to no longer name her." As the one who looks far ahead, Europe can leave its name and all of its presumed identity behind. Yet, to simply drop Europe's name would also mean to cease being faithful to its memory. In fact, it is not simply a question of either being faithful to the memories of Europe or of preferring the openness of the open to its opposite. Rather, the question is how to meet both contradictory exigencies of preserving and abandoning Europe's name at the same time. Only by simultaneously facing these inexorably aporetic injunctions can there "possibly" be such a thing as *the* world.[57]

At this point one feels truly sorry to see grown-up philosophers so desperately cling to a word like a security blanket without which they have no clue what to do with themselves. It is at one and the same time sad and pathetic, unseemly and juvenile. Why Europe, whence this urge for universality, by what right this dubious claim to hospitality, responsibility, all housed and supposed in the thing that calls itself by the name "Europe"? The world is neither the other nor the event. The world is at variant with itself, housing fragments and multiplicities of itself, all its Europes and its others, selfed and othered repeatedly, all the while at home where it is, in need of no condescending "hospitality." Yes indeed, "the name Europe must also be abandoned"—and no not with any cognate like "Europa." The world is full of memories, many memories, in no need of any single word to trigger such memories. The world is not the opposite of Europe. The world can and has left Europe behind. The world in its multiplicities is not any possibility. It is an actuality, a reality, a truth, if we were not blinded by "Europe."

On the Poetics and Politics of the Otherwise

Now: suppose Europe is no longer there—Europeans have dissolved into the bosom of what is left of the worlds they ravaged and abused, into other worlds they have arrogantly denied, violently suppressed, philosophically obscured. What then? What other worlds exist to welcome them and embrace them and forgive them with no rancor and no fear? We travel from one end of the world to another—from Asia to Africa to Latin America, from India to Pakistan to Iran to Turkey to Palestine to Martinique to Cuba to Chile to Japan to China. Are there visions of the world that Europe has either denied or repressed or else museumized, ethnicized, anthropologized, or else has scarce seen, sensed, abused? In each of these worlds, from one end of our planet to the next, there is a poet, an artist, a filmmaker, a painter, a photographer, a dramatist, building on the fragments of the worlds rising and falling, capturing the soul of their people caught in between these worlds, in a poem, film, painting, photograph, paragraph. We will, however, first need to rescue these works of art from the pigeonhole of "Third World literature" or "Third World art" the First World theorists have put as a trap on their ways, then we need to teach Europeans humility and have them learn deserving to sit at their feet and patiently and politely and quietly behold the worlds they have emotively mapped. There and then they will see a tapestry of poets of pictures and proses awaiting at the gates of the world after Europe—where they have lived the world beyond Europe, unbeknownst to Europe.

Those worlds are not hostile or even alien to Europe—if they were to step out of their Platonic cave and look back at their own shadows cast upon the wall of these worlds familiar to us but strangely foreign to them. There and then they will see and hear Pablo Neruda reciting in a Spanish slightly different from their European Spanish, sitting next to Nâzım Hikmet singing in a Turkish not dreamt in their Constantinople, next to Vladimir Mayakovski in an unfamiliar Russian, side by side with Faiz Ahmad Faiz in a melodious Urdu of which they did not hear in their British Raj, right in the vicinity of Mahmoud Darwish in an epical Arabic their Israeli settler colony had occasioned but could never understand, all of them the familiar neighbors of Ahmad Shamlou watching them in his rebellious Persian whose diction was cried out loud soon after their CIA had toppled a democracy alien to their Greek origins. The sight is joyous to us, vertiginous to the European at first, but if they were to persist, they can hear their Irish W. B. Yeats and their German Rainer Maria Rilke and their French Stephané Mallarmé in them. They will fail to translate the foreignness of these poets back to their familiar prosody, and yet their strange poetry will make what was familiar to them foreign to their ears and what is foreign in them now suddenly becomes familiar.

They turn around and they see in a corner gathered Satyajit Ray, Akira Kurosawa, Yasujirō Ozu, Chen Kaige, Abbas Kiarostami, Ousmane Sembène, watching each other's visions of the invisible. If they were to sit down and watch (with) them, they will see the reflections of their Bergman, Fellini, Truffaut, Hitchcock, and John Ford, and yet something strange will remain in the sunrise and sunset of their horizons that is the beginning of a renewed worldly wisdom. The world philosophizes in a poetry and a vision that is made of the fragments of all other worlds colliding, collapsing, resurrecting in the fragility of a moment when we dream of worlds not seen in the wildest dreams of their Europe. In these worlds they will see us neither angry nor beholden, neither Europhobic nor Europhiliac—happy where we are, fearful of a future we all face. The worlds of our poets and our artists, the worlds in which we live, the worlds that enable us, after all European philosophers did to deny us agency and universality, to say "I," is not made of any Oriental fantasies of European vintage. We have made vast and beautiful worlds, empowering and forgiving worlds, out of the relics and fragments of the world of the ruins Europe has left behind.

The path toward these worlds, living and breathing beyond the European garrison state of their minds, however, must be mapped out from within the European world they know to bring the European thinkers along with us to the feast of the world beyond their limited imagination. To be fair to Gasché, he is not the only European philosopher trapped in the delusion of European universality. "Even if one admits," this is none other than the towering Marxist thinker Antonio Gramsci in his seminal *Prison Notebooks*, "that other cultures have had an importance and a significance in the process of 'hierarchical' unification of world civilization (and this should certainly be admitted without question), they have had a universal value only in so far as they have become constituent elements of European culture, which is the only historically and concretely universal culture—in so far, that is, as they have contributed to the process of European thought and been assimilated by it."[58] This is incurable Hegelianism manifest—the world has been there to move the Geist along to deliver it to Europe and happily resign and recede. Here is where we see the European malady of self-universalization is not limited to liberal and extends well into radical thinkers.

Upon this premise, Gramsci then proposes that "even European culture has undergone a process of unification and ... has culminated in Hegel and the critique of Hegelianism." Beyond that Hegelian moment, Gramsci believes in his time "a new way of conceiving the world and man is born and that this conception is no longer reserved to the great intellectuals, to professional philosophers, but tends rather to become ... popular." This may very well be the case, and the age of the grand philosophical narrative of Europe is over. But even in this Marxian populism, Gramsci remains committed to the European universalism. For in understanding the constituent elements of this "new way of conceiving the world," Gramsci remains as provincially European as everyone else. The advantage of Gramsci's perception of "a new way of conceiving the world," however, is that it at least opens the European provincialism to the wider world, of which he has a limited, pathologically Eurocentric, conception. But beyond his limitations, there is another Marxist thinker with a much more liberated imagination.

Through her, we can hope to carry the rest of European critical thinkers along with us to the world beyond their blindfolded visions.

Rethinking the World in Postcolonial Terms

The significance of Rosa Luxemburg as a leading Marxist thinker of her time is usually overshadowed by Marx himself. But there are reasons from the vantage point of a postcolonial critical thinking to reassess her significance.

The world at large celebrated the 200th anniversary of the birth of Karl Marx (May 5, 1818–March 14, 1883), the revolutionary political economist who immortalized a single act of theoretical genius in his three-volume magnum opus *Das Kapital* (1867–1883). People around the globe had legitimate reasons to remember how the German political economist had redefined our enduring understanding of the material foundations of our economic class, social life, political positions, and ideological proclivities.[59] The Marxist vocabulary of theorizing the economic foregrounding of social and political (and even religious) forces have now become integral to our social sciences and the humanities —used and abused by friends and foes alike. It is fair to say, generations after his pioneering work, Marx's ideas of historical materialism, of class struggles, and particularly his critique of capitalism have still become the common parlance of our reading of the world.

In a world ravaged by the wanton cruelty of predatory capitalism, the enduring wisdom of Marx's theory of capital and its political consequences continues to guide the course of our struggles for global justice. Marx, however, was incurably Eurocentric in the very cast of his critical thinking. Although he was fully aware of the expansionist proclivities of capitalist economy, Marx never fully developed a theory of how colonialism was the modus operandi of this capitalist tendency. Although in the 1850s, Marx wrote copiously in his essays for *New York Daily Tribune* on various aspects of European colonialism, his Eurocentric blind spot led him to his notorious notion of "Oriental despotism" and the scandalous argument that colonialism was actually good for India for it "modernized" the subcontinent. He had a global vision of the rise and demise of capitalism, and yet he saw the world from a decidedly European critical thinker's perspective, with the world at large at the receiving end of his (however liberating) ideas. The world had to be modernized first, come to terms with European capitalist modernity before it could reach equal footing with the liberating force of communism.

Such theoretical blinders and political blunders barred the extension of Marx's own insights into a more global theory of capital and its political consequences. When it came to his perception of the non-European world, Marx was as much an Orientalist as the rest of his European contemporaries—though he of course wished to see the world liberated globally from the terrors of an abusive capitalist system. But when he said "workers of the world unite," he basically had European workers in mind. The rest of the world had to be liberated from their feudal ways and "modernized" before reaching the revolutionary consciousness of his European audience. The necessary and crucial task of extending Marx's groundbreaking ideas to the world at large remained for the next generation of Marxist critical thinkers, the German Jewish revolutionary thinker and activist Rosa Luxemburg (1871–1919) in particular. In the figure of Rosa Luxemburg the debilitating blind spots of European thinkers find a way out of their Platonic cave.

There is a manner in which we can read what today we call postcolonial theory that in fact begins long before such seminal thinkers as Aimé Césaire, Frantz Fanon, Malcolm X, or Edward Said, and is rooted in such radical Marxist thinkers as Rosa Luxemburg, who early in the twentieth century was busy thinking far more globally about the significance of Marx's thought—even more poignantly than did Marx himself. As a Jew, a woman, and a socialist revolutionary, Rosa Luxemburg was in a unique position to think about the meaning of Marx's ideas from the vantage point of disenfranchised segments of the world in or out of Europe. As a Jew, she was the internal other of Europe, as a woman its gendered alterity, and as a socialist revolutionary its nightmare. In figures like Rosa Luxemburg, people around the globe have a solid inroad into recalling Europe into the bosom of the world at large.

In her groundbreaking book, *The Accumulation of Capital* (1913), Rosa Luxemburg demonstrated how capitalism expands the domain of its predatory operation globally to exploit resources, abuse cheap labor, expand its insatiable need for new market, and accumulate ever-increasing surplus value. European imperialism, she suggested, was the military machinery to enable and facilitate this globalization of capital. Without Rosa Luxemburg's correction of Marx's theory of capital, his blindfolded Eurocentrism would have had two fatal deficiencies. He could not account for the European longevity of the capitalist system and he would have been irrelevant to the colonial extension and consequences of capitalism. Luxemburg's argument that the endemic crisis of the capitalist system propels it to imperialism and colonialism effectively brought the realm of the colonial into the critical apparatus of Marxist thinking. In her critical reading of "the three world empire" (UK, Russia, and USA), she underlines "the vital part played by an unlimited supply of means of subsistence, of raw and auxiliary materials and of labor power which is just as necessary for a capitalist industry computed in terms of a world market as the demand for finished products." She points out how just "the history of the English cotton industry, a reflection in miniature of the history of capitalism in general ... [has spread] over five continents throughout the nineteenth century."[60] Her vision of how the global economy worked had already brought Europe into the bosom of the world at large.

To be sure, in his *Imperialism: The Highest Stage of Capitalism* (1917), published about half a decade later, Vladimir Lenin too connected the economic vicissitude of capitalism and the military logic of imperialism together, arguing military expansionism was the mechanism through which European countries delayed the endemic economic crisis in their own countries. Other major Marxist theorists like Karl Kautsky and Nikolai Bukharin had also paid close attention to the link between capitalism and imperialism. These figures were pioneering theorists dismantling the racist assumption that colonialism was instrumental in the process of so-called "modernization." It was because of them that "modernization" was exposed for what it has been: a euphemism for colonization. What is crucial in this trajectory of critical thinking is the active de-Europeanization of Marxism, effectively liberating it from Marx's own provincialism.

In an excellent recent book, *Marx at the Margins* (2010), Kevin Anderson has sought to rescue Marx from his European provincialism and offer us, with some degree of success, a different version of Marx. The only problem with such revisionist accounts and other Marxist theorists seeking to expand Marx's insights is that even in their closer attention to global consequences of capitalism, they have remained Eurocentric in the sense that even in their "world system" theories à la Immanuel Wallerstein, they still believe in a "core periphery" dichotomy between capital and its colonial consequences.

There is no "core" or "periphery" to the global operation of capital and the military forces that seek to sustain it. The ruling elites in the United States, European Union, Asia, Africa, and Latin America are as much the beneficiaries of the system they violently uphold as those who are disenfranchised by it are dispersed in these very places. The central argument I have sustained in this book is precisely rooted in this dissolution of the metaphor of "Europe" into the larger global conditions and consequences of late capitalism, where in fact no essentialist allegory of this sort holds any meaning anymore.

Eurocentric racism is a mere ideological veneer to the hard-core economic logic of colonialism and imperialism. Predatory capital is color-blind and gender-neutral. It abuses white and colored labor identically, and it makes no difference to its maddening logic if you are a Donald Trump or a Saudi prince, an Egyptian general, an Indian entrepreneur, a Russian oligarch, or a Chinese businessman. Those who are abused and maligned by the selfsame system are as much among the poor of the United States and Europe as they are in Asia, Africa, and Latin America. Color and gender codification of power (and allegories like "Europe" or "the West" that sustain them) are mere false consciousnesses to the economic logic of power and domination. The migrant laborers, more than 300 million of them, roaming around the globe in search of a half-decent wage, are neither in the center nor in the periphery of any system. They are the most obvious victims of the predatory capitalism made invisible by a false geography of "center and margin," or "core and periphery," or "European and non-European." By giving detailed accounts of the British economic atrocities in India, and French colonialism in Algeria, Rosa Luxemburg anticipated the more detailed accounts of postcolonial theories by decades—and she did so from the heart of a Europe she thus pushed out into the world. By bringing the presumed margins of the self-centering Europe to global consciousness, she enabled the postcolonial theorist a veritable voice at the worldwide gathering of critical thinking—and she did so not despite but through her birth and upbringing as a European. To that Europe, she was a Jew and a woman, the two most compelling others of Europe that thereby de-othered the world, as she de-Europeanized Europe.

Seven
Mapping beyond the Postcolonial Artworld

The world has to be ready for certain things, the artworld no less than the real one. It is the role of artistic theories, these days as always, to make the artworld, and art, possible. It would, I should think, never have occurred to the painters of Lascaux that they were producing art on those walls. Not unless there were Neolithic aestheticians.[1]

Arthur Danto, "The Artworld" (1964)

All I am trying to do is to calmly remove the human from the dungeons of oppression and murder and deliver it to a place where it is possible for its body to be spread wide across the face of the earth, in order for it to be broken and thereby released from the legacy which makes it an oppressed creature.[2]

Día al-Azzawi (1975)

On November 26–27, 2018, as my writing of this book was coming to an end, I was invited to deliver a keynote at an art forum in Doha, Qatar. My hosts were Mathaf: Arab Museum of Modern Art in collaboration with Doha Institute for Graduate Studies (DI). Conceived by Abdellah Karroum, the director of Mathaf, and Ismail Nashif, the chair of the Department of Anthropology at DI, the conference was designed to explore what they had termed: "Expanding Geographies of Resistance on Modern and Contemporary Art," a theme conceived in parallel to the Fall 2018 Mathaf exhibitions "that deal with social and cultural histories, with a particular focus on the post-independence era in North Africa and the Middle East."[3]

The invitation was an opportune and very much welcomed occasion to think through the decidedly non-Europe scene where the artistic stage offers a critical space to wonder how the forced aesthetic dissolution of the work of art into the political, the particular predicament of the non-European artists at large, is predicated on the appeal of *the public* that was now in such a state of disarray. The need for staging, and the urge to place oneself in the eye of the beholder, were crucial to see in what particular term *an aesthetic intuition of transcendence* is possible for an artist outside but not alien or hostile to the European purview. Without this intuition, self-reliant and domestic to an artist's home and habitat, no liberation from the towering metaphor of Europe and all its cultural trappings (while engaging with them) will ever occur. The more the non-European artist, I contend, appeals to the public it must imagine, the more the abstract forces of his or her own art begin to assert themselves and demand attention. "Third World artists," thus branded, especially when they begin to package themselves as being "in exile," are deeply vulnerable. The "exilic" protestation is quite a perilous position—it sells but more than what the artists think is selling. The artists, thus made "exilic" go to the public, mitigated through museums, galleries, and biennales, to perform and stage, and there and then come back to the solitude of their own soul and studio to discover the vacuity of the public and perforce the ephemerality of the work of art they have performed. The exercise is deeply traumatic and destabilizing—however lucrative it may be in the market. Here the sublime and terrifying recognition downs: "The crowd is untruth," as Kierkegaard would say.[4] Exploring the fear and fascination associated with the crowd, we can see the critical and creative in conversation to overcome Europe (or even worse, "the West") as it has historically barricaded itself against the world.

"To see something as art," the prominent philosopher of art Arthur Danto proposed in his classic essay on "Artworld" (1964), "requires something the eye cannot decry—an atmosphere of artistic theory, a knowledge of the history of art: an artworld."[5] The world the postcolonial art world faces today more than half a century after the writing of that seminal essay extends precisely from that "atmosphere of artistic theory" all the way to that register Danto called "the history of art," and even more crucially what holds these two poles of theory and history together (who gets to theorize which history) to define the "world" in that "artworld." Danto began his seminal essay with a reference to Hamlet and Socrates who "though in praise and deprecation respectively, spoke of art as a mirror held up to nature." The comparison leads Danto to some exquisite observations about how "Socrates saw mirrors as but reflecting what we can already see … [while] Hamlet, more acutely, recognized a remarkable feature of reflecting surfaces, namely that they show us what we could not otherwise perceive—our own face and form." Our issue has always been whether any other face than those splendid countenances of Socrates and Hamlet are in fact visible or could ever be visible in that mirror. How and when and why did a European mirror held between the factual Greece and the fictive Denmark becomes "the mirror"—there's the rub!

Between Museums and Universities

Our two distinguished hosts in that Doha gathering, Abdellah Karroum and Ismail Nashif, had joined forces and asked us to reflect on what they termed "the Expanding Geographies of Resistance on Modern and Contemporary Art, a theme conceived in parallel to the Museum's Fall exhibitions program that is dedicated to several generations of artistic practice that deal with social and cultural histories, with a particular focus on the post-independence era in North Africa and the Middle East."

Prior to this meeting I had known Ismael Nashef and was familiar with his scholarship since the establishment of the Doha Institute. I was also quite familiar with and felt quite at home at Mathaf, which I had known even before Abdellah Karroum assumed its leadership. I consider both these fine institutions, Mathaf and DI, as pillars of the two complementary forces of *reason* and *aesthetics* (or truth and beauty) that our two hosts wished for us to examine. My thoughts on the theme and occasion of the event were therefore in solidarity yet with a healthy dose of critical reflection if their objectives went far enough in achieving what they had set to achieve. "Conceiving of the Museum and Academy as sites for debate," they had told us, "we bring together key voices in contemporary museum and research practice, from different geographies and generations, to share case studies and negotiate new horizons that crisscross institutional limits." I shared that concern about the institutional limits of both the academy and the museums and yet had a far more radical conception of how those geographies would expand.

The crucial wordings of our hosts, I thought, had left open the use of the phrase "sites of debate" for us to read as both debates within an art museum or within an academic institution, as well as debates between these two different and potentially contradictory loci—one of the *reasonable* and the other of the *beautiful*, one of *thinking* and the other of *feeling*, one of the *hermeneutic* and other of the *aesthetic*, one of *depth* and the other of *surface*. Were we gathered at that conference to engage in debates on either or both these sites, or were we there to engage in debates in between these two sites? The fact that this two-day conference had been divided between the two sites of DI and Mathaf at least signaled to the wishes of our two hosts to invite us to think through the institutional and discursive interface, if not contestation, between the two locations.

Our hosts had informed us: "The two-day forum/conference focuses on bridging scholarly and curatorial perspectives to collectively rethink contemporary research practices on modern and contemporary eras, when the large majority of countries were struggling with conflicts and change." To me the declaring of this "bridging scholarly and curatorial perspectives" spoke of the trajectory of an ambitious project that is fully aware of the chasm that has over decades if not centuries—and in fact historically and epistemically—emerged between these two sites of European modernity, which the world at large has received through its colonial gestations. Consider the recent news that surfaced while we were in Doha in November 2018, that a report commissioned by the French President Emmanuel Macron had called for thousands of African artworks in French and other European museums, all stolen during the colonial period, to be returned to their original owners—namely African countries. If we were to move to France, both the university and the museum were the privileged sites of European colonial modernity—of active contestation between the scholarly and the curatorial—common in their epistemic and aesthetic conquest of Africa. But is the world at large—in Asia, Africa, Latin America, and in this case the Arab world too—beholden to that contestation? It seems to me that our distinguished hosts had implicitly challenged that bifurcation.

Here I thought it was perhaps necessary to recall how historically the origin of modern museums and music halls is very recent, basically in the eighteenth century, when the rise of bourgeois public sphere replaced the church and the palace that were the site of art and music—whereas the origin of modern universities (whether in medieval Europe or in the Islamic madrasa system) is much older and began as the site of the education of the priesthood and the princely, but eventually expanded to public universities we know today. It is therefore crucial to keep in mind that as spatial designation of the bourgeois public sphere and perforce public reason, the university and the museum are in and of themselves floating institutions contracting and expanding based on the historical vicissitude of the public sphere of which they are integral—ranging from revolutionary to reactionary. It might even be suggested that the rise of biennales has challenged the institutionalized museums by attending to the site specificity of the work, and perforce art world, of art and the ephemerality of its whereabouts.

Expanding Geographies

As our two hosts put it—one a Palestinian anthropologist from Israel and the other a Moroccan curator educated in France: "One of the major questions in this framework, is how the museum—particularly new museums in rapidly developing contexts—can lead and facilitate the expansion of knowledge to make visible and chart previously silenced areas of art and knowledge production? How can it contribute to revise dominant narratives and reopen the floor to encompass and reflect the multiplicity of voices and practices in the Arab world and beyond?"

Here, it seemed to me the project of expanding the knowledge of making "visible ... previously silenced areas of art and knowledge production" deliberately uses the mixed metaphor of seeing and hearing, of visibility and silencing, to point to the curatorial and epistemic foregrounding of what and how and why we get to see and hear and thereafter theorize as a site of feeling and knowing, of curatorial and scholarly choices we make within a frame of knowledge and power ordinarily beyond the political limits of our aesthetic or hermeneutic choices. The mixed metaphor also marks the limits of what we scholars and visitors to museums can or could or should or might even aspire to see and know. Should we not be content with Naji al-Ali's Handala (the iconic cartoon representing the task of witnessing the Palestinian sufferings), turning his back to us in dismay to face the bitter fact of the phenomenon, or more pointedly will we not be paralyzed with shame if we were to look at Día al-Azzawi turning the face of Handala around to stare at us? He, Azzawi, the Iraqi artist, the kindred soul of the martyred Palestinian artist, Naji al-Ali, may have earned the privilege of seeing the face of Handala, but have we the shameful witness

Día al-Azzawi's Handala, after Naji al-Ali's iconic image. Courtesy of Día al-Azzawi.

to Palestinian suffering also earned that privilege? The question here is as much moral as epistemic—of facing the limits of what an artist can see and a scholar cannot or should not.

Let me quickly add here: the caution I propose in marking the distance between the curatorial and the scholarly is equally crucial in the distance between the event and the artist. There is a sanctity and an inviolability to certain events that an artist must be cautious not to trespass. I have already written about occasions when in the rush to be socially responsible, an artist violates the sanctity of the event and trespasses its inviolability, as in the case of the Syrian child Alan Kurdi, done by Ai Weiwei, or the terror of Abu Ghraib done by Botero.[6] In both these cases my position has been to come to terms with the distance the work of art must keep from the sanctity of the event. Of course, art as the simulacrum of the sacred and art as bordering with the sacrilegious have a close affinity. No one is or should ever be in a position to tell an artist what to do or what not to do—and the same hold true for a cultural critic on what to think and what not to think of the obscenity of an art market that rushes to frame and sell just about anything.

During this conference, our hosts had informed us:

> Using the platforms offered by Mathaf and DI we aim to expand and deepen the interrelations of art and research by addressing the connections between collections, production, display, and historical narratives. The focus throughout both days is on bridging scholarly and curatorial perspectives to collectively rethink contemporary research practice. This is achieved by approaching art and research through the following axes: Art and Society; The Artist as Citizen and storyteller; Art Histories in Contexts of Social Change; and Art and politics in post-independence and pre-revolution era.

These I thought were indeed admirable, timely, if not a bit of a tall order for a small gathering there in Doha, but nevertheless serious steps in the right direction of decolonizing the narrative of what our hosts call "post-Independence" and "pre-Revolution era." Such post- and presuppositions speak of a teleological thrust that is politically predetermined, which is of course necessary but insufficient if they are not to lead us to a cul-de-sac of a historicist determinism that may in fact end up robbing art of its open-ended mystery and cut and paste it to a deeply colonial chronology. There is also a more paradigmatic consideration to be kept in mind—whether arts (*Geisteswissenschaften* or *Kunstwissenschaft*) and social sciences (*Sozialwissenschaften*)—to use them in their more precise Germanic traditions—are not indeed those proverbial apples and oranges.

Of course, we need not do what the Germans or Indians or Argentines have done. There is a local historicity to every transnational front to Eurocentric imagination. In noticing that regional particularity, we pluralize and enable the worldliness of the movement. But in doing what we had hoped to do there in Doha, we needed to pay closer attention to the geographical metaphors our hosts had suggested to us. The very title that our hosts had assigned to our gathering: "Expanding Geographies of Resistance on Modern and Contemporary Art" needed crucial attention. We should take that "expanding" and that "resistance" in more than just their existing geographical and political senses or registers. We can, and indeed we must, begin with the *planetary* and the *political* terms the two concepts suggest but then swing into that "beyond" and see where it can land or suspend us. Here I underlined a slight discrepancy between the English and the Arabic text of the program, where the English word *beyond* does not appear, but merely the juxtaposition between the Arab world and the world at large "al-'Alam al-'Arabi wa al-'Alam 'Amma." That binary at the expense of that "beyond" would in fact be even more crucial to keep in the Arabic text as well as in the English text.

Be that as it may, the "Expanding Geographies" will inevitably lead us beyond the limited colonial cartographic imagination of "the West and the Rest," "the West and the East," and by extension the Arab, the Iranian, the Muslim, or any other such designation, as in the First or the Third World. In fact, the very designation of "national art" within colonial divides and postcolonial frontiers will also have to be critically examined and discarded. In my previous work on Palestinian and Iranian art, I have already argued in some theoretical details how the formation of any notion of "national art" is predicated on the historical condition of a "national trauma," and the very nature of such traumas are by definition transnational and transregional, conditioned by a state of coloniality that might be post-Independence, as our hosts put it, for Egypt, or Qatar, or Jordan, but it certainly is not for Palestine.[7] The Palestinian pause in our condition of coloniality then perforce pushes the boundaries of national traumas into larger, even allegorical, dimensions.

I have extended this argument to a larger examination of the comparative assessment of world cinema in which I have argued such major movements as Russian formalism, Italian neorealism, French New Wave, New German Cinema, and then the rise of Chinese, Iranian, Palestinian, or Cuban cinema are all formations of national cinemas on specific national traumas—and perforce each and every one of them point beyond their rooted national particularities. Palestinian cinema is predicated on the trauma of Nakba because of the European Zionist colonial project, as Cuban cinema emerged during the Cuban Revolution, and so on. I have also suggested a similar pattern with major poets of the twentieth century ranging from Vladimir Mayakovsky from Russia to Pablo Neruda from Chile, to Mahmoud Darwish from Palestine, to Nâzım Hikmet from Turkey, to Faiz Ahmad Faiz from Pakistan, to Ahmad Shamlou from Iran. When you put the geography of these poetic affinities together, an entirely different geography emerges, liberating us from our postcolonial frontier fictions—and the ethnicized affinities they project. Such vision of liberating transnational public spheres exponentially opens up the horizons of the very idea of "expanded geographies."

The same is true of literary and scholarly works in both our own and previous historical epochs—where conflating geographies defy the European cartography we have inherited. In our own time, consider the fiction of Juan Goytisolo and Emile Habiby, the scholarship of Américo Castro and Fernand Braudel, the revolutionary prose of José Martí and Ali Shariati, the critical thinking of Gayatri Spivak and Enrique Dussel—all of which you can trace back all the way to Ibn Khaldun's historiography and Al-Biruni's comparative anthropology. All these figures cast not just a transregional but in fact supranational literary and historiographical prose that feeds on an entirely different geographical imagination than the one we imagine from our colonial and postcolonial histories. One might even consider the cross-occupation exchanges between Anton Shammas when opting to write his *Arabesques* in Hebrew and A. B. Yehoshua's barefacedly racist objection to it—in which episode we read a Palestinian reappreciation of Hebrew as a Palestinian language in the face of the Zionist occupation of Palestinian land. Such exchanges systematically dismantle the assumptions of colonial occupations in powerful linguistic and literary reversals—and thereby defy the postcolonial geographies in decidedly emancipatory directions.

A Transregional Consciousness

Such comparative and transregional consciousness does not just transcend our existing nativist geographies or colonial categories. They actually generate new topographies of literary, poetic, and aesthetic sensibilities, all in the context of what in my book on Arab revolutions I have called a "liberation geography." Here we see similar if not identical national traumas leading to transnational liberation geographies that no curatorial or scholarly encounter can any longer ignore. This recognition also has serious consequences for such ethnicized nation-building project as Arab, Iranian, Turkish, or a fortiori French, German, or English, and so on. An entirely different geography of the globe emerges here. In my *Persophilia* (2015), I have demonstrated in much more specific details, particularly in art and literature and philosophy, how the formation of the bourgeois public sphere was (contrary to the grain of Habermas's theory) from the very beginning not exclusively European but decidedly transnational. It was upon that transnational public sphere that arts and literature, poetry and politics were formed. The world of art, from the very beginning, was a regional and global marketplace of ideas, never limited to any given language or culture, nation or polity. The very idea of the "the West" and any binary that was cast against it was ipso facto colonially conditioned, an ideology of false and falsifying consciousness, against the very grain of factual history. That factual geography needs to be retrieved, not reinvented.

Let me give you a specific example here. If we look at Picasso's *Guernica* (1937), we may detect aspects of its visual imagination in Charles de Steuben's *Bataille de Poitiers, en octobre 732* (1837). This masterpiece eventually finds its way into Día al-Azzawi's *Sabra and*

Shatila Massacre (1982–1983). On February 15, 2003, just a week before the U.S. invasion of Iraq, I had a young friend raise *Guernica* when I delivered a speech against war as Colin Powell had ordered a replica of *Guernica* covered at the UN when he presented his lies to justify that war. When I visited Mathaf in November 2018, Abdellah Karroum showed a work of Día al-Azzawi that he says was inspired when he saw Iraqi airplanes flying over his roof in Baghdad to go bomb my hometown in southern Iran. I raised that *Guernica* in a speech against Iraq war in New York, when U.S. fighter jets went on their way to bomb Día al-Azzawi's hometown. This circulatory geography creates its own emotive universe. It constitutes a trans-aesthetics of renewed significance. There is a geography to the artwork itself, where we no longer are trapped inside the limiting discourse of the anxiety of "influence." The art world creates a force field of its own. The point is to decenter any European assumption of centrality. There are multiple force fields, moving into and out of each other in aesthetic direction. There is no center; there is no periphery to these movements.

Let me move to another continent to make a similar point. Diego Rivera and other Mexican muralists, notably David Alfaro Siqueiros and José Clemente Orozco, deeply affected artists during the New Deal in the United States. Jackson Pollock considered Orozco's *Prometheus* at Pomona College "the greatest painting of the twentieth century." Pollock's *Naked Man with Knife* is a tribute to it. One can repeat the same transregional affinities between African art and Picasso, or between Persian art and aspects of Gauguin, Matisse, and Kandinsky's work. What is crucial here are the aesthetic and formal encounters among artists themselves, crafting a world of their own, entirely independent of colonial, imperial, and a fortiori national geographies. Such potent geographies liberate artists in multiple emancipatory ways.

One can point to similar stretches in cinema among the works of Yasujirō Ozu in Japan, Mani Kaul in India, and Abbas Kiarostami in Iran—all masters of a-descriptive visual registers thriving on immediate indecipherability. The task here is not to decipher their indecipherability or search for the chicken and egg of their "influence" on each other. That is an entirely useless exercise. The point is to map out the formal, aesthetic, and emotive universes that collate in the shifting horizons of emerging works of their art. In the same vein, if we were to look at the work of the Iranian artist Azadeh

Dia al-Azzawi, Sabra and Shatila Massacre 1982–1983. Courtesy of Dia al-Azzawi.

Akhlaghi, we see how her fixation with historical traumas are turning into obsessive-compulsive passion for the detailed reenactments of events she has never seen. These reenactments turn actual historical locations into transcendental spaces where they are, and where they were, but now in an entirely ahistorical way. In the same way, consider the term Zainab Bahrani uses to describe Día al-Azzawi's work as "modern antiquity," in which the historical moment, the temporality of the work of art, contracts into an archetypal instantiation beyond any periodic passage of time.[8]

The collective work of at least eight Iranian artists from two generations in New York—Manoucher Yektai, Sohrab Sepehri, Amir Naderi, Nicky Nodjoumi, Nahid Haghighat, Shirin Neshat, Ardeshir Mohassess, Kamrooz Aram, and Ramin Bahrani—projects a whole different conception of home and homeland with a fusion of memory and materiality best evident in the work of all of them but particularly those of Nodjoumi and Mohassess. These artists make it difficult to decide if they are Iranian or American, or

Nicky Nodjoumi's The Oaths of Infidels (2017). (The Third Line). Courtesy of Nicky Nodjoumi.

Iranians living in New York, or Americans remembering Iran in their artworks, or perhaps a creative and indecipherable fusion of both. The physical geography here yields to an emotive aesthetics at once in and out of homeland.

Equally important is the work of Iraqi artist Monkith Saaid (1959–2008), who left his homeland and went to Syria, and then spent years studying sculpture in the Netherlands, before returning to Damascus and then Baghdad after the fall of Saddam Hussein. His short sojourn in New York and his marriage to his Iranian wife Rebecca Joubin (who wrote and published his biography), the mother of his youngest daughter Jenna, all map a geography far beyond the reach of the Iran-Iraq war or Arab-Persian binaries.[9] What is crucial here is neither the Iraqi origin nor the European sojourn of Saaid's life, but the mapping of his aesthetic trajectory that consistently defied all geographical limitations and assumptions.

These conflating geographies map out the traumatic nuclei of works of art that are at once rooted and yet defy the provincialism of any nativist definition of homeland. Día al-Azzawi would not have become the Día al-Azzawi we know today if he had not moved to London, nor did he stop being an Iraqi artist once he did. On the enabling trajectory of that paradox running from Baghdad to London to Doha, the aesthetic particularities of an artist are formed in and out of a homeland—or of a homeland of the artist's own making. Such intersectional geographies require a radical re-thinking of both curatorial and scholarly presuppositions about works of art—or how we see and how we write art. On the borderline between the museum and the academy dwells a critical bifurcation between aesthetics and hermeneutics, between what art is and what aesthetic theory can hope to grasp—thus putting a paradoxical twist to Danto's notion of "Artworld." In the aftermath of the Holocaust and the terror of instrumental reason, Adorno sought to safeguard the experience of the aesthetic from reason, as did Derrida after him, before Christoph Menke in his seminal study, *Die Souveränität der Kunst: Ästhetische Erfahrung nach Adorno und Derrida* (*The Sovereignty of Art: Aesthetic Negativity in Adorno and Derrida*, 1988) sought to explain the sovereignty of art to subvert reason without submitting to Adorno's negative dialectics or Derrida's deconstruction. Adorno and Derrida had posited art and aesthetic experience as a medium for the dissolution of nonaesthetic reason, and in fact as a critique of reason. Art is both autonomous and sovereign, and ipso facto it subverts the rule of reason. Art, Menke purposes, entails no knowledge and its negativity toward reason cannot be articulated as an insight into the nature of reason: Art is sovereign not despite but because of its autonomy. That conception of art implicates a vastly different geography for it beyond the Eurocentric imagination of Menke himself.

Now the question is: When we wish to bring the academy and the museum closer together, do we wish to close that gap or would that gesture not indeed deepen that fact? Abusing the work of art and putting a political price on it, for or against "Independence," or any other such lofty ideal, endangers its enduring mystery. If anything, if academics come close with their verbosity, it is to study humility. In the Arab and Muslim world, we have produced some precious few works of art with enduring mysteries that transcend the predicament of our pathological politics. Our politics is one of defeat and misery—just one quick look from Syria through Palestine to Yemen is sufficient. In the midst of this Nakba writ large, we need to sustain an aesthetic of hope of salvation. It might be wise not to drag them down to the politics of our despairs. No doubt our art is rooted in social and political realities we have lived. But we have also transcended and sublated them in our works of art. We need to reach up and dwell on those moments of self-transcendence and be very careful not to bring them down with a disposable political price tag.

In between the space of the museum and the space of the academy, art crafts a tertiary space, where we might consider gathering. In his seminal work, *The Relevance of the Beautiful (1986)*, H. G. Gadamer puts together the three forces of "play, symbol, and festival," expanding on that premise in his specific hermeneutical setting, taking issue with the idea of aesthetic experience as individuating (*Erlebnisse*). Here he emphasizes that within the experience (*Erfahrung*) of the work of art, one is always socializing in terms initiated and occasioned by the work of art itself. The act of the aesthetic for Gadamer is always already social—and we might add trans-social, given the layered traumas at the roots of the world of art, or as Danto would say "Artworld." For Gadamer, the experience of the work of art is equally trans-subjective, where time and space are suspended and an agency of an entirely different potency crafted. On the occasion of art as festival, the work of art constitutes the person as the collective, the artist as the prophetic voice and vision of an aterritorial liberation. "In the festive the communal spirit that supports us all and transcends each of us individually represents the real power of the festive and indeed the real power of the art work."[10]

On that festive gathering where art occasions an agency beyond political compromise, the aesthetic act remains a truth and a reality sui generis. Here we might suggest three ways of understanding palpably aesthetic occasions like Andrei Tarkovsky's *Mirror*, Sergei Parajanov's *The Color of Pomegranates*, Arby Ovanessian's *Lebbaeus Whose Surname Was Thaddaeus* (1967), Bahman Jalal's desert photography, Juan Miró's final lines, or Koorosh Shishegaran's abstract paintings. The absolute otherness of the aesthetic event occasioned here can be (1) pulled inward into purely aesthetic terms with no connection to the world, (2) pushed outward into pointedly political terms, and (3) sustained as a mode of poetic implosion of the act of art. My position is emphatically on the third option, when art as a poetic implosion resonates through the world and makes it meaningful and trustworthy. If, as Fanon said, "Europe is literally the creation of the Third World," the critical dismantling of Europe is almost entirely contingent on this creative imagining of a geography that re-creates and transcends Europe and the Third World into a transcendental geography of liberation that only art can imagine.

Nowhereville

Let me conclude my argument with a quick reference to Abbas Kiarostami's inimitable patience with detecting the superlative aesthetic intuition of transcendence in his visual veracities. Here I want to mark an affinity between Kiarostami's masterstrokes and a deeply entrenched concept in Shahab al-Din Suhrawardi's (1154–1191) epistemological cosmogony that he called *Na-Koja-abad*, a term we usually associate with the Arabic philosophical concept *al-Alam al-Muthul*, corresponding with the Platonic phrase of "the world of ideas," or the "world of forms." The Greek words, εἶδος (*eidos*) and ἰδέα (*idea*) come from root *weyd- or *weid- "seeing." This eventually through its Latin and German renditions comes to us as "theory of ideas." In its original Persian, however, the term that Suhrawardi uses is best translated as "Nowhereville." In Nowhereville we have a sense of inimitable spatiality, while in the

Platonic "theory of form" there is a strong element of speculative visuality. In both cases, Greek or Persian, our humanity is cast in a condition of forgetfulness, in which we can see works of art as visual allusions to those forms we have forgotten upon entering our earthly existence. This is art at its supreme moments of aesthetic remembrance of things past, and therefore of inexplicability—the occasion of a poetic implosion that derives from repetition and stays at the door of total silence and blankness of the page as Rumi said: "Be a blank page of unwritten piece of paper."

My proposal here is the factual evidence of Kiarostami's cine-aesthetics visually alludes to what Suhrawardi called "Nowhereville" (Na-koja-abad), somewhere that is nowhere but that is perfect in its whereabouts. We are sure that it exists, for it is a locus of civility, civilitas, and urbanity, or Abad/Ville, but we cannot locate or even point to it. As such, as both speculative metaphysics in Suhrawardi and ocularcentric visuality in Kiarostami, they both allude to things that we sense but cannot see. I am not suggesting any causal relationship between Suhrawardi's Illuminationist philosophy (Falsafah Ishraq) and Kiarostami's ocularcentric cinema. But I am suggesting that in what French scholar Henri Corbin called the "visual recitals" of Suhrawardi, we may detect a philosophical foregrounding of Kiarostami's cinema.[11]

Let me now cut from medieval Persian philosophy through Abbas Kiarostami's artwork to an Iranian exilic poet like Esmail Khoi currently living in the United Kingdom, where he considers himself living in what he calls "Bi-dar-koja"—a self-made coinage best translated perhaps as "Wanderwhere." From *Na-koja-abad* to *Bi-dar-koja* is from Suhrawardi's idyllic Nowhereville to Khoi's exilic Wanderwhere, from a philosopher at home in his philosophical abode to a poet at a loss for words in his exilic homelessness. With a hint, knowing or unknowing, to Suhrawardi, Abbas Kiarostami in his visual poetry found himself at home both in and out of his homeland, while trapped inside his exilic Persian poetry while living in UK. Khoi lost himself in exile from and exiled in both his homeland and his mother tongue. In his visual poetry, Kiarostami was liberated from his nativist provincialism, while in his exiling diction Khoi lost touch with the material territory of his poetic birth certificate. Khoi is thus exiled into self-diasporic peripheries of self- and cyberspace. Here we need to think through a floating conception of geography, in which multiple factual and imaginative geographies conflate into an interpolated and aterritorial planetarity. This planarity is first and foremost polynomial and thus rooted in changing forces of worldliness. It thus braces from cyberspace to outer space with full awareness of the fragility of the Earth on which we live.

On the face of this fragility, when European modernity has yielded and dissolved itself into its own belated postmodernity, looking for multiple or alternative modernities I am afraid is a bit too little too late. The condition of colonial modernity, which is precisely the manner in which the world at large has received European modernity, is where we can determine the location of our artworld. We are in fact back to the archival moment of our tiniest constitutive locations like Doha, a little peninsula open and close to nowhere and everywhere, where the accumulation of a critical mass of artwork from across the Arab and non-Arab world will in fact dissolve the binary of the Arab and the non-Arab world into an aterritorial planetarity yet to be named. Let us learn from our past and say that planetarity is no longer geocentric.

Eight
Is Peace Possible?

The puppet called "historical materialism" is always supposed to win. It can do this with no further ado against any opponent, so long as it employs the services of theology, which as everyone knows is small and ugly and must be kept out of sight.[1]

Walter Benjamin, *On the Concept of History* (1940)

Nist vash bashad khiyal andar jahan
To jahani bar khiyali bin ravan

Like naught appears our phantasm in this word
A whole world you can see riding upon a mere phantasm.

Rumi, *Masnavi* (1273)

Let me now ask perhaps the most vital question of our time: Is peace possible? Whether or not beyond the absolute and absolutist metaphors of division, domination, and submission—"the West and the Rest," "Europe and non-Europe"—is any notion of peace at all conceivable for us, and if so, peace in what sense? Peace as in absence of war, or peace as absence of conflict, peace as absence of opposition, or peace as absence of dialectical force field of history? If we are not to bring the idea of peace to the borderline of death—as in "rest in peace" (RIP)—then we need to think peace in the realm of the living, where a different dialectic of reciprocity and pluralism must be imagined between humanity and the environment, between and among the classed, gendered, and racialized binaries, between manufactured cultures and warring civilizations. The only meaningful peace at the inaugural moment of that future history is "the peace of mind," peace not just *on Earth* but peace *with Earth*, a peace that will allow the overcoming of these hostile and warring binaries within and without nations and their overriding myths—where *alterity* can be fathomed to replace *identity* as the site of consciousness: not who we are but who we are talking to—with the full recognition and internalization of the other's humanity. To reach the shores of that consciousness, I intend to navigate with Walter Benjamin on history, with Emmanuel Levinas on "the face of the other," and with Jalāl ad-Dīn ar-Rūmī when he sings: "upon a phantasm rides their war and peace!" If truth is a mobile army of metaphors, and if Europe is literally the creation of the Third World, what other metaphoric mobility can reinvent the world that in the lyrical words of Hafez will "rip the heavens open" and reimagine it anew?

Finding a Common Idiom

On April 16–17, 2015, I was invited to Arizona State University to deliver a keynote in the conference they had put together and called "People's Peace." Our distinguished colleagues thinking this conference through and hosting our conversations over these two days had asked us to reflect on "cultural idioms of peace" that in their judicious phrasing "are evident in many forms." They had further stipulated that "People's peace is a resource that resides in the hopes, dreams, and visions of everyday, ordinary people." The direction of our thinking was guided "to generate further attention to the lived experiences that people draw upon to become agents of peace." We were encouraged to explore how "peace can be best realized when it is put into service by people through their own initiatives." They rightly declared: "This approach to peace requires focused attention on the practical, humanistic values that are lived and find expression in the idioms and practices of different communities." I read all these precious sentiments and I wondered.

Following their lead, I thought to dwell on one such idiom of which I was aware and think it through. I thought this would enable us to explore the question of "peace" as a viable idea and as an absolute metaphor, and wondered if peace is at all possible—and if so, peace in what sense? With the wind of Benjamin's theorization of history as fragments and debris, and the thoughts of Levinas's miraculous demand that the inscrutable face of the other be the primary site of our consciousness under my wings, let me fly toward Rumi and wonder if peace is indeed possible. It is not peace but the territory and time upon which we ask whether peace is possible that is the issue. Where exactly is peace dreamed, where is it drawn, where is it imagined? We cannot be on the East or West of any geography of which we are aware and with which we are alas too familiar.

Rumi's *Masnavi* (1273) has a story about a prince who falls madly in love with a maiden he has just purchased and now owns. In the realm of Rumi's parables, we must, momentarily, suspend our moral judgment about the horrors of slavery and see what he does with such stories. The young maiden, however, soon falls ill, and no physician the prince summons can cure her. In utter desperation, the prince falls asleep, crying in his anguish. In his dream he sees a spiritual master who reveals to him what the issue with the maiden is, and the prince follows the master's instructions and after a rather traumatic twist, unites with his maiden. The story is very famous and has been the subject of much interpretation and speculation. My concern here is not with the story itself but with the passage in which Rumi introduces the figure of the spiritual master, the Pir, in the prince's dream. This passage contains a crucial allusion that I like to borrow.

The mise-en-scene is very important here. The prince falls sleep crying. While sleeping he has a dream. In this dream a Pir, a spiritual master appears to the prince and tells him that tomorrow morning when he wakes up, a stranger will come to him. He instructs the prince to welcome this stranger, for he is the master's envoy. The stranger is a wise physician, and the prince must heed his instructions. *Sehr Motlaq* ("absolute mystery") and *Qodrat Haq* ("power of truth") are all in this stranger's wise counsel as to what to do. The following day the prince wakes up, goes to his balcony, and looks into the horizon waiting for the stranger to come. Lo and behold, he sees a wise person approaching him, appearing like *Aftabi dar miyan Sayeh-'i* ("a sunlight in the midst of shade"). The stranger appeared from afar like a *Helal* ("a sliver of moon"), and he was *Nist bud-o-hast bar shekl-e Khiyal* ("nothingness and being") in the shape of a phantasm. Here then Rumi pauses for a moment of poetic implosion of his narrative:

Nist vash bashad khiyal andar jahan
To jahani bar khiyali bin ravan
Bar khiyali solheshan-o-jangeshan
Vaz khiyali fakhreshan-o-nengeshan
An khiyalati keh dam awliast
Aks mahruyan-e bostan-e Khodast
An khiyali keh shah andar khab did
Dar rokh mehman hami amad padid

Shah beja-ye hajeban fa pish raft
Pish an mehman-e gheyb-e khish raft

A literal translation of the passage would be like this:

Like Naught is phantasm in this world,
A whole world you'll see riding on a phantasm—
Upon a phantasm is their peace and their wars,
And upon a phantasm runs their pride and their shame—
The phantasm that is set like a trap for the Friends of God
Is the image of the Beautiful from the Garden of God—
The phantasm that the Prince saw in his dream
Appeared on the face of this guest
Instead of his servants the Prince rushed forward to welcome him
Approaching that Divine guest coming towards him.

The Pir first appears in the prince's dream and then comes to life while he is awake. The two figures, thus it turns out, are the same: the Pir of the dream and the stranger of the awakened prince. The prince first sees the Pir in his dream and then appears to him as a *khiyal* or a phantasm while fully awake. The narrative ploy fuses reality and dream on the borderline of a phantasm.

I use the term *phantasm* for "khiyal" in the sense that we take the word from Middle English *fantasme*, from Anglo-French *fantosme*, *fantasme*, from Latin *phantasma*, from Greek, *phantazein*, which means to present something like an apparition to the mind. Except in the Arabic/Persian word khiyal, if we take it to the active participle of *takhayyol*, we have a more active agency on part of the person who does the khiyal-ing, as it were. If we dwell on Rumi's little poetic pause, we see war and peace are here proposed as the products of a phantasm, as are in fact pride and shame—namely two binary oppositions, two radical extremes, made possible by being planted next to each other, so much so that the distance between war and peace is just a twist of this phantasm, as indeed the difference between shame and pride. There is a dismissive haphazardness about Rumi's formulation: you see they are warring now, and then they are in peace. Both of them are the working of their phantasm—so that in effect the most radical extremes are nothing but a mere impression of the moment of that khiyal upon which we are riding, the imaginary in which we dwell.

If we follow the logic of the metaphor through, the state of our humanity is caught, "plotted" as Paul Ricoeur would say, in a mental stupor, a false twist of our phantasm, as if all we need to do is snap our fingers and snap out of it just like that. As if all we need to do is just one blink of an eye and—*poof*—the terrifying course of our self-destruction will be turned around, switched off, and we will become evident into a whole different world.

The German Mystics and Their Rumi Souls

Now let's switch register and wonder: Could it be that this switching, this turning of things upside down, as it were, is what Walter Benjamin also meant when he said we need to "awaken the dead, and make whole what has been smashed"?[2] Is this, in yet another fragmentary move, the moment that "the pile of debris," as Benjamin calls it, makes up the whole of our history? Is this what Levinas had in mind when he proposed that the unfathomable face of the Other is, or ought to be, the site of our consciousness? Can we here place Levinas, Benjamin, and Rumi next to each other, in an entirely ahistorical way that might make sense of our history, and through them reach for *an intuition of transcendence* when peace is made possible not in terms domestic to the idiomaticity of the dominant prose of our history—but in terms in fact entirely sublated, uplifted, *aufgehoben*, alienated from the debris we live? "The relationship with the Other, the face-to-face with the Other," says Levinas, "the encounter with a face that at once gives and conceals the Other, is the situation in which an event happens to a subject who does not assume it, who is utterly unable in its regard, but where none the less in a certain way it is in front of the subject. The other 'assumed' is the Other."[3] This is, of course, an impossibility made plausible by replacing the site of consciousness from the Self onto the Other. The history of Europe is the history of "the West and the Rest," of the European Self made possible by the site of all its others gathered into an Other.

But let's talk temporality and spatiality: when and where is it exactly that we can talk peace in terms uplifted from our otherwise entrapped time and space within the current state of affairs? Let me take Rumi's dream as a guide and ask you to consider the fact that I wrote this passage while attending a conference on the Iran nuclear issue and its repercussions for the Arab world in Doha, Qatar, as the Saudis were bombing Yemen. I went to bed at 10-ish in the evening local time and woke up about 1 a.m., and I could not sleep anymore. Rumi's poem was on my mind all day, and knowing I would soon attend the conference in Arizona, I needed to put my thoughts together. So I stopped tossing and turning, just got up, turned on the light, reached for my laptop, and started writing my keynote—these very words I am now reading to you. The Self and all its others gathered in the figurative presence of the Other dissolve in the amorphous moment of the I that gathers them, that summons them, to wonder.

Between Doha and New York, and between New York and Phoenix, both the temporal and the spatial distance cover the topography of the universe between war in nearby Yemen and the peace in the title of "People's Peace"; my question "Is peace possible?" ceased to be an academic exercise in futility but an existential phantasm that kept me awake on the borderlines of a commanding jet lag and a desperate hope. There in Doha, in the solitude of that hotel room, I was awake when I am ordinarily asleep, so in effect, I wrote these words in my sleep, just like the prince's dream. So which is which now? I was standing there in front of my colleagues in Arizona, the evidence of a dream of peace while awake, writing while fast asleep.

Let's call this a temporal implosion, a spatial pregnancy, when and where time and space begin to yield otherwise hidden but not denied promises of their possibilities. We mortals here, in terms very domestic to our lives, have managed to procure the material foregrounding of an intuition of transcendence far away and epistemically liberated from those metaphors that rule over us and decide our fate. On this imploded time and within this pregnant space, we can now safely begin to think liberation. To achieve peace, we need actively to imagine it, will and desire it, and yet cease to try to achieve it but yield to the inner rhythm of this alternative worldliness, impending universe, where the logic and madness of the Earth, its inner breathing with the rest of the universe, announces itself in and out of the surface of the topography of our being in the world, which means not to try too hard to achieve but allow it to achieve us. We are already dwelling in the world beyond "the West and the Rest." We just do not allow ourselves to see it.

From within this world, both within and yet hidden from the world, we sense and live, we come to the conclusion that before achieving peace on Earth, we need to yield to a peace with Earth. But how is that peace possible? Consider the odds: The selfsame and identical greed that is imposing its destructive logic on Earth does the same with the earthly beings. The Earth and the earthlings are used and abused by the same maddening logic that dictates that by 2016, 1 percent of the world population will own more than 50 percent of its wealth, that about a billion human beings go to bed hungry every night, that almost half a billion human beings roam around the globe in search of a backbreaking job to secure a half-descent life for themselves and their family. Whatever madness and reason, whatever logic and lunacy, whatever figure and allegory that has brought us here is not working. The same logic that cast Europeans around the planet to own and abuse it is now at work casting the world against the Earth. That logic and that lunacy will have to be reverse engineered.

Yet again consider the odds: To sustain this abusive relation of power, about half a dozen countries—from the United States and Canada to the UK, France, Germany, Sweden, and Holland, to Russia and China—flood the global market of warmongering with weapons, basically to keep the status quo, for those in power remain in power and those who are victims of power remain victims. People rise in their masses of millions in peace only to be brutalized by those in power, whether by political leaders in the United States, Israel, Syria, Egypt, Iran, or Saudi Arabia, or by the World Bank or IMF in the financial domain. ISIS is the gist, the naked fact, of the absolute and total state, not as the monopoly (as Max Weber suggested) but as the very definition of pure violence. In the face of that naked violence we are powerless, we are *homo sacer*, our *bios* (social life) is reduced to *zoë* (natural life) we become the walking dead, the concentration camp Muselmann, as Giorgio Agamben would say. In the face of such wanton cruelty we see perpetrated by the United States in Iraq, by Israel in Gaza, by Assad in Syria, by Sisi in Egypt, by Saudi Arabia in Yemen, by the ruling regime in Iran against its own people, the whole notion of civilitas is reduced to camps. The world is doing to its inhabitants what Europe used to do to the world.

In the face of these camps, we cannot have peace by pointing, motioning, alluding to peaceful Muslims, Christians, Jews, or Hindus. Their peace is normal. Their wars are abnormal. We must reach for peace, actively imagine it, from within the ruins of these camps, linking the terror of Auschwitz to the indignity of Yarmouk, the horror of Zaatari, the fear and loathing of Abu Ghraib, Guantanamo Bay, Bagram Air Base. From the terror of Auschwitz and other Nazi concentration camps, from which Benjamin spared himself by killing himself, Primo Levi and Emmanuel Levinas survived to posit the face of the other as the inscrutable site of ethical consciousness. That ethical consciousness, not the Zionist abuse of it, is the premise of all our future peace.

From the vantage point of that ethical consciousness, between Rumi's dream and Levinas's mirror, between Primo Levi's poetic prose and Mahmoud Darwish's painful poetry, daring and defiant acts assume their resumed political potency: Noncooperation, civil disobedience, a radical simplification of life, defiant asceticism against the very logic of consumption, dismantling the very dominant logic of capital by systematically expanding the horizons of the inner peace into all corners and discourses of the public sphere while the public space is occupied. These acts should not be remedial, but made agential, predicated on an intuition of transcendence that transforms the crisis of the subject into the force of historical agency. The emaciated body of the Jewish victims of Nazism and the mutilated bodies of Palestinian children under Israeli bombs— from those ruins and debris the critical consciousness of our future will surpass all the received allegories of our time—European or non-European.

This authorial agency, where we begin to write a different future for our posterity, is possible through a switching off and switching on of a vastly different phantasm of peace from the phantasm of war, rethinking what is dignified from what is dishonorable. This can be achieved by first and foremost putting people before power, realities before abstractions, Christians before Christianity, Jews before Judaism, Muslims before Islam, atheists before old and new atheism, agnostics before agnosticism—for reality has escaped the bastille of abstractions, and the abstract vacuity of their commanding metaphysics has obediently yielded to a vastly different intuition of transcendence.

Jews and Gentiles, Muslims and Kafirs Unite!

We are Jews, Christians, Muslims, Hindus, Buddhists, atheists, agnostics to a radically altered worldliness, to a miasmatic fact and phenomenon of a constitutionally different metaphysics—a metaphysics that we live and yet have hitherto failed to theorize, terrorized as we are by the retrograde forces that distort the terms of our theological transcendence into the idioms of our identity politics. The shifting conditions of coloniality are not merely historical. They are also epistemic, emotive, and have therefore altered the parameters of self-othering in the world.

What we have learned from Gustavo Gutierrez and other liberation theologians is not just the fact that the Gospels can be read in a revolutionary and liberating way from the site of the civic, but that the civic needs to be altered to its new pluralistic demography for which a new civil religion (from Jean-Jacques Rousseau to Robert Bellah) might emerge far beyond the manufactured triangulation of the so-called "Abrahamic religions," for as millions of migrant workers are circulatory around and about the capital, then transnational and nondenominational circularity must become the modus operandi of mores and metaphors that become ethically commanding in this civic religion. The battlefield for that peace made possible via this civil religion is not just at the fronts where the U.S. Army bombs Iraq, or Israelis are bombing Gaza, or where Assad kills Syrians, the Saudis slaughter the Yemenis, or ISIS burns the Shi'is, the Yazidis, the Christians, or the Kurds. The battlefield is here and now where the liberal hypocrisy gives room to *Charlie Hebdo* cartoonists, to Bill Maher, to Ayaan Hirsi Ali, to Pamela Geller ad nauseam, planting seeds of horror and hatred in the hearts and minds of vulnerable people, where Clint Eastwood's *American Sniper* (2014) becomes the norm, not the abnormal.

This is where Walter Benjamin's fragments, Levinas's mirror, and Rumi's dream all come together to yield to a messianic materialism of a Jewish, Christian, or Muslim tapestry, where we manage to achieve an intuition of transcendence, where through an *il pensiero debole* ("weak thought"—Gianni Vattimo's idea), the violent metaphysics of foundational thinking yield to the radical hermeneutics of Arthur Danto and his *weak theology*, and thereby the metaphysics of identity yield to the transcendence of alterity, where self becomes an other and stays there for good, where Europeans are liberated into the non-European, and the non-Europeans do not mind the remnants of the European relics in that transaction.

Preventing an achievement of this objective is the fundamental flaw in the binary we habitually make between a *militant* and a *pacifist*. Militants rule, kill, maim, murder, and destroy, and get away with it all, while pacifists bicker, complain, moan and sigh, write op-eds, create alternative websites, update their status on their Facebook pages, send a tweet with a hashtag, or else organize conferences on "People's Peace." The task at hand is to actively imagine and cultivate militant pacifists. Militant pacifists are not passive. They are decidedly active, defiant, assertive. They interrupt, they object, they dismantle the apparatus of power, they follow Hannah Arendt's conception of *public happiness,* seek to secure not just freedom from tyranny but the liberty to participate in politics, in the public domain, organized not just in wards, as Arendt extrapolated from the American revolutionary period but in labor unions, women's rights organizations, student assemblies, and so on—and in all of these while imagining the otherwise. The colonizer and the colonized were different in the abusive relation of power that held them together. We need to reverse engineer that proposition and be democratically united in our cultural differences.

Let me now go back to a question the organizers of that conference had asked us to consider: "What values of peace exist in particular cultural settings? How and why do they persist? How are these values authorized and transmitted from one generation to the next?" My proposal was that the most compelling cultural setting we need to explore is our own daily lives, and the manner in which we dream of peace between nations and among cultures as we persist through the knowledge of the wars that are pulling them asunder. What authorizes these dreams is the *Hayy ibn Yaqdhan* ("Alive, Son of Awake," from Avicenna to Ibn Tufail) living in us, the "living awakenness" that dreams in us while asleep, that writes while dreaming, fights while hopeless, convening a conference on peace while fully conscious of the wars that have terrorized our waking hours.

So suppose this conference is a dream, I told my colleagues in Arizona, taking place as a Rumi metaphor, and thus every single participant that saintly apparition, that walking stranger appearing from multiple horizons, disappearing into different dreams, held together for a moment fully conscious when riding upon that phantasm of peace in the midst of wars, the vision that stops and interrogates us at every border we cross, every airport we land or depart. So, you never know, if you are now here and see me in your wishful dreams, or wishing me so in your own scholarly commitments, academic disciplines, innermost convictions, that compels you to peace.

I wished my colleagues peace in that conference in Arizona, bid them farewell, boarded a plane, and flew back home to my family in New York. On my flight, somewhere between Heaven and Earth, I though to myself: The first and final peace is between Europe and non-Europe. "Europe"—whatever it was, whatever it is: It is and it has been for a long time self-imploding. The world at large, the non-Europe, takes Europe as an icon and an allegory far more seriously than Europe does itself. A symbiotic relationship has emerged between two strangers. Europe as a metaphor is therefore sustained as a towering illusion far more by its critical others than by itself. We need to disengage this fake binary of "the West and the Rest." By contrast, the more Europe's others become self-conscious, the sooner they deny Europe its phantom alternatives. The more Europe's others become self-conscious, the more they discover worlds to which they actually belong. We in the post-European world must actively think of the world without the centrality of this thing that calls itself "Europe." How would a world without Europe look? How would we reimagine ourselves in a post-European world? We are already there, in that post-European world, and yet we have a phantom feeling for that Europe that was once the central metaphor of a colonial consciousness that keeps recasting itself, even in the critique of Europe. The post-European world is at peace with itself.

Conclusion

Wherefore Should We Stand in the Plague of Custom and Permit?

Why "bastard"?
Wherefore "base"?
When my dimensions are as well compact,
My mind as generous, and my shape as true
As honest madam's issue?

Shakespeare, *King Lear*, act 1, scene 2

More than halfway through the writing of this book, as I was putting the final touches on its penultimate draft, in mid-September 2018, I was invited to Berlin to deliver a keynote at a magnificent art collective called Savvy Contemporary. "Dis-Othering as Method: Leh Zo, a Me Ke Nde Za," was the title of the event organized for September 11–15, 2018. The two co-curators of the event, Antonia Alampi and Bonaventure Soh Bejeng Ndikung, had named the overall theme of their gathering "Geographies of Imagination." My journey with this book was coming to an end. Europe and its shadows were now gently merging into each other. The condition of coloniality was overriding any singular claim to any towering empire. The United States was a dysfunctional thuggery. Europe was coming to pieces. China was predatory capitalism ruled by its Communist Party. Russia was flexing its military and cyberwar muscles. Asia, Africa, and Latin America were in turmoil. The world was divided between the rich and abusive 1 percent and the poor and abused 99 percent. There was no East and West or North and South, Europe or non-Europe among them anymore.

The centerpiece of the effective mini-art festival our hosts had organized for us in Berlin was a labyrinth walk-through of some powerful and provocative works of contemporary conceptual art, where invited artists would introduce their work. A musical ensemble called Drummers of Joy held the event together with some magnificent music, while performing artists, novelists, and museum curators, presented and performed their art, after which Nacira Guénif-Souilamas, a French-Algerian professor of sociology and anthropology at University Paris 8, Vincennes-Saint-Denis, and I delivered two keynotes on the theme of the gathering. It was a delightful event, and I was very happy to have been part of it. When we did not have a scheduled event, I was hanging out with Mario Rizzi, an Italian artist friend of mine who lives in Berlin.

For my talk, which I had informed my host would be called "The West and the Rest in Peace," I had prepared a few selected passages from this book but had given them a pointed direction toward the central theme of "dis-othering." I began my talk with a citation from V. Y. Mudimbe in his magnificent book, *The Invention of Africa:* "But it can be admitted that the colonists (those settling a region) as well as the colonialist (those exploiting a territory by dominating a local majority) have all tended to organize and transform non-European areas into fundamentally European constructs."[1] This enduring insight of Mudimbe, I thought, dovetailed perfectly between the themes of this book as I was writing it and the subject of conversation at this gathering in Berlin about which my hosts were deeply, critically, and creatively concerned.

We Troublemakers

We troublemakers, I told my audience when it was my turn to talk, look for trouble. The trouble is hiding inside the innocuous and innocent looking "and": Islam *and* the West, Europe *and* non-Europe, Europeans *and* non-Europeans, and the open space it generates between the colonizer *and* the colonized, the First *and* the Third World. That conjunctive is actually notoriously disjunctive. Whatever comes after that conjunctive is anything but—it does not bring together. It partitions and separates, it is in fact exactly the opposite of bringing together: it creates an appendix, a parasitical expression, a mode of being that is ipso facto subordinate, abnormal, abrasive, odd, in need of some explanation.

The phrase "non-European areas"—the way Mudimbe uses it in his pioneering text, *The Invention of Africa*, is always already colonized. No place on planet Earth is "non-European" in and of itself. Every place is the center of its own universe, of multiple worlds that have been historically built around and about it. Iranians call Isfahan "Nesf-e Jahan," half of the world or more accurately the center of the world. There are similar places in any other parts of Asia, Africa, Latin America, in every single spot on planet Earth, which become "non-European" the minute the Europeans, colonials or colonialists, in either way colonizers, start thinking of it. Very soon those born and raised and nourished morally and imaginatively in that place begin to think of themselves as "non-European," "nonwhite," and then by extension subhuman, an approximation, a rendition, an afterthought, in need of some explanation. A "non-European"—person or place—begins and remains with a negation, with a "non."

Europe is not the first mode of imperial self-universalism that has cast the world at large in negational terms—Arabs called non-Arabs *Ajam*, Greeks called the non-Greeks barbarians, Iranians called non-Iranians *Aniran* (literally "non-Iranian"). The phenomenology of this "non" must be de-Europeanized, conceptually rooted in its historiography, before we move into a postcolonial critique of it. We must not exclusively demonize nor indeed paradoxically privilege Europe, for in both cases we metaphorically de-historicize the condition of coloniality that multiple European imperial imaginings have occasioned. Like a massive mountain, Europe stands before us and does not allow us to see other, even larger mountains behind it. If we are to move beyond "Europe" with a clean slate, we need to seize it at the moment when it has transformed the world into the negative image of itself and called it "non-European," for that is precisely when the world is seen as a European construct. We want gently to deconstruct that construct.

Since the fateful events of 9/11, I have consistently argued those iconic moments marking not the beginning but the end of the two-towering false consciousnesses of our time catapulted between "Islam and the West." The collapse of the twin towers of the World Trade Center in New York and of the twin Buddhas of Bamiyan in Afghanistan mirrored and reflected each other and marked the end of "Islam and the West" as one potent case of "the West and the Rest." From neoconservative to neoliberal pundits, columnists in the United States and Europe continue to write and publish voluminously on the hatred and opposition between "Islam and the West"—as one potent and fertile ground of self-othering machination apace. Theirs is a self-fulfilling prophecy—just like Donald Trump jumping on any incident in which an immigrant is suspected of a crime and yet disregarding mass murders when perpetrated by someone from the demographic outline of what he considers to be his base support.

Today, at a time that seems to mark a resurrection of identity politics—"we Europeans, you Arabs, them Africans," and so on— we are in fact actively dreaming of our and all other alterities. We are dying before our own eyes, before our own deaths. We are being born into our own alterities, into the other than ourselves. There was a colonial condition they used to call "Westernization" of the world. Today, we have entered the phase we might call the "worldification" of "the West." Because selves are aggressively fragmented in the European crisis of their subject, others are lost to themselves too. Because others have come here, selves have nowhere to go. "The West and the Rest" have long since collapsed into each other and lost their binary potency—all the kicking and screaming of racist Europeans and their "identity crisis" will be for naught. The surfacing of the "alt-right" in the United States or the "far right" in Europe are the last long flames of a dying candle, full of vengeance and zest, and not the steady rise of a burning bush. Steve Bannon is a hoax, a self-fulfilling prophet of trafficking between the United States and Europe in search of a pure race just a few decades after his kindred soul Adolf Hitler murdered millions of human beings in a similar endeavor. Consider the terror on the face of Steve Bannon or Stephen Miller, two Trump xenophobic advisers, at the sight of a little Afghan or Mexican boy or girl.

In this context, dis-Othering is a theoretical art and craft of liberation seeking to dismantle the biopower of alienation and perforce the biopolitics of domination. But the underlying metaphysics of that liberation remains a phenomenologically stable identity trope: "Let me be my authentic Arab self, don't bother me with yourself!" But that jargon of authenticity, of return to self, as Adorno diagnosed it is too little, too late. The metaphysical foregrounding we now live is decidedly not identity-driven but emphatically geared toward alterity—toward what we are not and not toward what we think we are. Even Levinas himself failed the test of the face of his Palestinian others. He failed to look at that face. But neither identity nor alterity will do in defining who and what and where and why we are anymore for they are both sedentary—stable and stationary sitting comfortably inside secured walls, whereas the paramount metaphor of our age is beyond those walls—migratory, exilic, and fugitive impermanence like those endless lines of "Syrian refugees" coming out of and going to nowhere. Impermanent mobility rather than stale stability is the towering metaphor of who and what we are and where we think we live. Fictive frontiers, moving signposts, barbed wires, tall apartheid walls, military checkpoints, militarized airports, train and bus stations, stormy seas, leaking refugee boats, drowning parents and dead children's bodies.... Our metaphysics must start there, for it has long moved there. The metaphysics of our being in the world start with the weakest and most vulnerable, not with the strongest sporting a U.S. or EU passport. There is no self or any other on that leaking sinking boat. There is no self or other, and therefore there is no dis-othering on that boat. In dis-othering we are carrying the delusion of a safe destiny from behind secured walls to stormy seas and leaking boats, there to ignore the fact of a perilous journey as the single most defining metaphysical uncertainty of our existence today.

From the Sacred Ashes of Our Dreams

Right there in Berlin while attending this beautiful and uplifting art event and surrounded by young artists, poets, novelists, and critical thinkers coming from around the world, including Europe, it finally occurred to me how the metaphysics of our presence has been globally mapped out where- and whenever we are: the exilic impermanence of stateless peoples, carried inside the bags of homeless migrants who will never reach their destination, for even if they did they will never belong there. We are always "in transit." We have all become Palestinians because Israel is the prototype of all illegitimate states—states built on pure violence and lacking any enduring legitimacy. In my work on Palestinian cinema, I have called its aesthetic condition predicated on traumatic realism. But what does that "traumatic realism" actually mean? You must begin with Nakba as the central drama and trauma of Palestine. Palestine as a collective memory in effect begins at the moment of its abortion. This, as all other traumas, is the present absentee; it is there but it is so traumatic you cannot talk about it, the poetic sounds of explosions (when Mahmoud Darwish recites his poetry and his audience bursts into applause) are the only sounds that speak (to) it, for it is loud enough to conceal the scream. In another metaphor, Nakba is like a master poem a poet does not compose but that all his or her other poems point to. From Darwish's poetry, to Said's critical thinking, to Mona Hatoum's art, to Azmi Bishara's scholarship—all point to it but do not actually name and address it. Nakba is not a name; it is unnamable. We usually translate it as "catastrophe," but Nakba is actually a metaphysical calamity that cannot be named—naming it defines and locates and diffuses it. Nakba is there as the unmoved mover, the primal cause of the Palestinian being in the world. It is a dialectical paradox. It is the invisible (one) in front of any numerical zero in the total population of Palestinians. We have all become Palestinians by virtue of the traumatic origins of all our collective nationhood, all under colonial conditions over which we had no inaugural control.

The supreme sign of Nakba is of course Naji al-Ali, with his back turned toward us, toward the world, and his gaze fixated on the event, on the repercussions of Nakba. As such, Handala is defaced, by facing the event. The character of ES in Elia Suleiman's cinema is Handala turning around from the event to look at us and enabling us to see what he has seen. But what has he seen? ES does not speak. He is not dumb. But he does not speak. He just stares at us, at the world, speechless, because of the enormity of the injustice, the trauma he has witnessed. In Mohammad Bakri's documentary *Jenin, Jenin* (2002), Mohamed Bakri represents Handala by his back being turned to the camera, facing the event too. Describing to him as to what has happened in Jenin is a dumb and deaf witness, who has seen the event but cannot describe it. This is a condition of moral dyslexia—when we cannot describe and the world cannot hear.

This epistemic rupture—when the Palestinian qua Palestinian cannot talk, and were she to talk no one can listen—is where what she is saying is an impossible speech. This is where Elia Suleiman's cinema starts, with visual stuttering, staccatos of fragmented scenes, followed by repetitions, disruptions, of any and all narratives, metanarratives, or topologies of a colonially caused speech impediment. He can only show in fragments, in ruins, always stuttering, whereby his fragments become enduring allegories. Predicated on such fragments, semiotics overcomes analytics, nonlinear over linear, episodic over triumphalist, aesthetics over hermeneutics, fragments over totality, therefore fragments become allegories for itself, and for the world.

I recently read an article on how "Britain Stole $45 Trillion from India—and Lied About It." We learn from the essay, "new research by the renowned economist Utsa Patnaik ... drawing on nearly two centuries of detailed data on tax and trade … [shows] that Britain drained a total of nearly $45 trillion from India during the period 1765 to 1938."[2] That is a lot of money, I thought. But is that a real price tag for a life that has been stripped naked and exposed to the structure of political vulnerability in the biopower of our postcolonial presence—where and when our *bios* are the closest to the *zoë* that scared Giorgio Agamben's theory. It is good to know of the enormity of terror that European colonialism has perpetrated upon the Earth, but can that terror be calculated in dollars and cents or pound and pence? It is remarkable how European philosophers like Agamben become so eloquent when the biopower of their own making begins to do to Europeans what it has done globally to countries it has robbed blind and slaughtered en masse. "The 'happy life' on which political philosophy should be founded," Agamben tells us now, "cannot be either the naked life that sovereignty posits as a presupposition so as to turn it into its own subject or the impenetrable extraneity of science and of modern biopolitics that everybody tries in vain to sacralize. This 'happy life' should be rather, an absolutely profane 'sufficient life' that has reached the perfection of its own power and its own communicability—a life over which sovereignty and right no longer have any hold."[3]

We do as we must—learn a lesson wherever from and whenever it comes, even though in the making of its philosophical abstraction, only Europe and never its victims matters and configures. We too in and about the savagely brutalized world left to ruin by European colonialism wish to think of a "happy life." We also concur that neither the biopolitics of European colonialism nor the kind of science they practiced on us—from political science to anthropology to everything else carrying the bizarre arrogance of "science"—can dictate the terms of that happiness. Happiness—though we must think through the very ruins European colonialism has left for us to own and ponder—without any abusive illusions.

The Center Cannot Hold

The perilous journeys of refugees from somewhere to nowhere are the mirror image of a fragile Earth floating dangerously in the eternity of a space alien strange to us. The condition of coloniality that Fanon and Said had fully understood and theorize, I have argued in this book, with the European "West" on one side and the colonized

"Rest" on the other—has now metastasized and entered a whole new phase where the colonizer and the colonized are no longer divided along any national, regional, or continental divide, that the colonial has always been embedded in the capital, and the capital in the colonial, that imperialism was never anything other than predatory capitalism writ geographically large, and that the current condition of "empire" requires a synergetic reading of class struggles that overrides fictive national and civilizational boundaries. If that were the case, as in this book I have proposed it is, then how do we measure our worldly, global, and epistemological whereabouts—when and where "Europe" is effectively decentered, de-authorized, de-universalized? We must perforce begin from the ground up, from the fractured and allegorized relics of the world we had inherited and no longer see.

A more immediate and critical understanding of the metaphor of "Europe" and its corollary extension into "the West" and its shadows will enable a historic grasp of how their contemporary transmutations have morphed into a site-specific understanding of our world affairs—where we are blinded to our own insights. Without the metaphor of "Europe," the world as we know it will conceptually collapse—and for all the right reasons. The volatile bifurcation between "Europe" as a self-centering metaphor and all its manufactured others (in Asia, Africa, and Latin America) has historically been conducive to the epistemic conditions of knowledge production along hostile and mutually exclusive boundaries, with specific references to Islam and Muslims, as now conceived to be the absolute Other of "the West." Based on this crucial epistemic formation, I have argued here, a mapping of the postcolonial subject the world over will reveal a steady streak of historical, political, and narrative defiance against this Eurocentric conception of the world, not just among Muslims but also, in fact, around the globe, from Asia to Africa to Latin America. We are living on that map. I have sought to make its contours more vividly evident in this book.

I have also sought to point out how an *aesthetic intuition of transcendence* has systematically built up in a decidedly non-Europeanized context to mark and register the manner in which the creative impulse to revolt has become critical in overcoming the very condition of coloniality. This *aesthetic intuition of transcendence* is rooted in generations and histories of protest arts—in film, fiction, drama, and poetry—from Asia to Africa to Latin America. In this book, I have sought to map out the contours of that art in a different geographical imagination. Without that intuition and the creative impulse it sustains, the world will never see itself liberated from the mixed metaphor of "Europe"—its colonialism and its modernity alike. "Europe" will never be defeated or overcome epistemically, even if it were politically—or perhaps particularly when it is politically. "Europe" as the dominant metaphor of global distortion of truth and narrative will only be overcome aesthetically—by poets, filmmakers, novelists, dramatists, and the critical apparatus they occasion. The volatile formation of the metaphor of "Europe," in its epistemic power of alienation, is evident in the modes of political and epistemic resistances it has created. It is only in the varied forms of aesthetic formations that we are witness to a seismic defiance beyond any epistemic control. In the thrust of my arguments, I have neither "provincialized Europe" (as the false premise now puts it), nor sought to strengthen by opposing Europe. I have brought Europe into the larger domain of its own contradictions and thus opened it up to the world at large, the world it has conquered and concealed. By way of showing how against all protesting too much, the metaphor of "Europe" has long since exhausted itself. The massive demographic changes within Europe contextualize the even more potent forces of labor migrations from and into Europe. The rapid globalization of the public sphere on which we live, where the extended links of cyberspace and outer space have all come together, posit a whole different liberation geography, which I have hoped to map out in this book. I have set upon myself the task of theorizing that geography.

I look at the mess of Brexit, the calamity of Trump, and the insidious xenophobia that connects Europe and the United States, and I wonder: The idea of Europe is imploding because it has now hit its most central paradox—it was built by robbing the world and building its own confidence—and now the world is coming back to rob it of its delusions of power. Europe colonized the world territorially and its own disjointed history temporally. It narrated itself backward to Plato and Aristotle and Alexander and Rome as it conquered for itself a planet to rob of its own multiple worlds. Europe was an illusion that soon made itself forget what it was, and now the refugees are bringing back its own repressed memories. Those refugees are the liberating forces of Europe, bringing it back to the bosom of humanity, hard as they resist and despise them.

If we opt for perilous journeys rather than stable destinations as the modus operandi of our thinking, we'll see how the allegories of a new world are emerging from the fragments of the old worlds we still cherish in our minds. These fragments and ruins are our Benjaminian relics—too destructed to be figuratively coherent. We live in ruins and bask in relics. They lack any symbolic consistency any longer familiar to us. Like a Sergei Eisenstein montage, we are in between two cuts. We still don't know what this tertiary space our emerging montages will or would or should signify. All selves and others are collapsing into this new montage, this potent assemblage, where all hitherto legitimate but in effect colonial territorializations are reluctantly de- and thus reterritorialized. In this postcolonial assemblage, the world sees Europe for having impregnated the non-Europe in the course of its violent colonial intercourses. The children of non-Europe, bastards born out of wedlock, are making it through those stormy seas, coming back to haunt their parental officers. Their European siblings have nowhere to go, nowhere to hide, no way to deny their half sisters and brothers—entering as they do with an air of Edmund the bastard about them and reading a letter in their hands—and see how in conclusion I have come back to Edmund the bastard with whom I began:

> Thou, nature, art my goddess.
> To thy law
> My services are bound.
> Wherefore should I
> Stand in the plague of custom and permit
> The curiosity of nations to deprive me
> For that I am some twelve or fourteen moonshines
> Lag of a brother?
> Why "bastard"?
> Wherefore "base"?
> When my dimensions are as well compact,
> My mind as generous, and my shape as true
> As honest madam's issue?
> Why brand they us
> With "base," with "baseness," "bastardy," "base," "base"—
> Who in the lusty stealth of nature take
> More composition and fierce quality

Than doth within a dull, stale, tirèd bed
Go to th' creating a whole tribe of fops
Got 'tween a sleep and wake?
Well then,
Legitimate Edgar, I must have your land.
Our father's love is to the bastard Edmund
As to the legitimate.—
Fine word, "legitimate"!—
Well, my legitimate, if this letter speed
And my invention thrive,
Edmund the base
Shall top th' legitimate.
I grow, I prosper.
Now, gods, stand up for bastard![4]

Notes

One. Europe: A Mobile Army of Metaphors

1. Friedrich Nietzsche, "On Truth and Lie in an Extra-Moral Sense" (1873), in *The Portable Nietzsche*, selected and trans, with Introduction, Prefaces, and Notes by Walter Kaufmann (New York and London: The Viking Press and Penguin Books, 1954): 46–47.

2. For more details on Al-e Ahmad, see the chapter on his thoughts in my *Theology of Discontent: The Ideological Foundation of the Islamic Revolution in Iran* (2nd ed., New Brunswick, NJ: Transactions Publishers, 2005).

3. Friedrich Nietzsche, *Beyond Good and Evil*, trans. Judith Norman (Cambridge: Cambridge University Press, 2002): 5–6.

4. Friedrich Nietzsche, *On Truth and Lies in an Extra-Moral Sense*, in *The Portable Nietzsche*, ed. and trans. Walter Kaufmann (London: Penguin Books, 1954): 46–47.

5. Frantz Fanon, *The Wretched of the Earth* (New York: Grove Press, 1961/1963): 58–59.

6. See "Dalai Lama Thinks Europe Has Let In 'Too Many' Refugees," *NBC News*, June 1, 2016, www.nbcnews.com/storyline/europes-border-crisis/dalai-lama -thinks-europe-has-let-too-many-refugees-n583701.

7. See "Flüchtlinge sollten nur vorübergehend aufgenommen warden," *Frankfurter Allgemeine Zeitung*, May 31, 2016, www.faz.net/aktuell/politik/dalai-lama -tenzin-gyatso-im-interview-zur-fluechtlingskrise-14260431.html.

8. Edward Said, *Orientalism* (New York: Vintage, 1978): 4–5.

9. This is best—most notoriously—evident in the racist take articulated in voluminous details by Niall Ferguson in his *Civilization: The West and the Rest* (London and New York: Penguin, 2012).

10. For the full text of the Chilcot Report, see www.iraqinquiry.org.uk/the-report.

11. Fredrick Nietzsche, *On the Genealogy of Morals*, trans. Walter Kaufman and R. J. Hollingdale (New York: Vintage Books, 167): 19.

Two. Europe, Shadows, Coloniality, Empire

1. Friedrich Nietzsche, "On Truth and Lie in an Extra-Moral Sense" (1873), in *The Portable Nietzsche*, selected and trans., with Introduction, Prefaces, and Notes by Walter Kaufmann (New York and London: The Viking Press and Penguin Books, 1954): 45.

2. A copy of this manifesto is available at fas.org/programs/tap/_docs/2083_-_A _European_Declaration_of_Independence.pdf.

3. *2083: A European Declaration of Independence: De laude novae militae: Pauperes commilitones Christi Templique Salomonici.* Signed: Sincere and patriotic regards, Andrew Berwick, London, England, 2011, Justiciar Knight Commander for Knights Templar Europe and one of several leaders of the National and pan-European Patriotic Resistance Movement—With the assistance from brothers and sisters in England, France, Germany, Sweden, Austria, Italy, Spain, Finland, Belgium, the Netherlands, Denmark, the United States, and so on.

4. Michel Foucault, *The Order of Things: An Archaeology of the Human Sciences* (London and New York: Routledge, 1966/19899): 422.

5. Frantz Fanon, *The Wretch of the Earth* (New York: Grove Press, 1961/1963): 58–59.

6. See Immanuel Kant, *Observations on the Feeling of the Beautiful and Sublime and Other Writings* (Cambridge: Cambridge University Press, 2011): 60–61

7. For an analysis of these and similar pieces of jewelry by the great European philosopher Emmanuel Levinas, see Robert Eaglestone, "Postcolonial Thought and Levinas's Double Vision," in *Radicalizing Levinas,* eds. Peter Atterton and Matthew Calarco (New York: SUNY Press, 2010): 57–68.

8. Ibid.

9. Enrique Dussel, *Philosophy of Liberation* (New York: Orbis Books, 1980): 3.

10. For a study of Agostino Brunias's work, see Mia L. Bagneris, *Colouring the Caribbean: Race and the Art of Agostino Brunias* (Manchester, UK: Manchester University Press, 2018).

Three. Whence and Wherefore "Europe"?

1. Walter Benjamin, "On the Concept of History," in Walter Benjamin, *Selected Writings,* Volume 4: 1938–1940, trans. Edmund Jephcott and others, ed. Howard Eiland and Michael W. Jennings (Cambridge, MA: Belknap Library of the Harvard University Press, 2006): 392.

2. See Niall Ferguson, "The Way We Live Now: 4-4-04; Eurabia," *New York Times,* April 4, 2004, www.nytimes.com/2004/04/04/magazine/the-way-we-live-now-4-4-04-eurabia.html.

3. George Steiner, "The Idea of Europe," which he initially delivered in 2003 at the Netherlands-based Nexus Institute at its annual lecture. For a short version of it, see www.opendemocracy.net/can-europe-make-it/george-steiner-benjamin-ramm/idea-of-europe. For the full version see George Steiner, *The Idea of Europe: An Essay* (New York: Overlook Press, 2015).

4. See Hamid Dabashi, *Persophilia: Persian Culture on the Global Scene* (Cambridge, MA: Harvard University Press, 2015).

5. See Aijaz Ahmad, "Orientalism and After: Ambivalence and Cosmopolitan Location in the Work of Edward Said," *Economic and Political Weekly,* 27, no. 30 (July 25, 1992): PE98-PE116, reprinted in Aijaz Ahmad, *In Theory: Nations: Classes, Literatures* (London: Versos, 1994): 159–220.

6. After the publication of Edward Said's *Orientalism* (1978), we saw the rise of a number of studies on "Occidentalism" or "Europology" or "the West in the mirror of the East," and so on. All of them camouflaging the point I am making

here, that there is no better understanding of "Europe" or "the West" than reading its "Orientalism" in reverse, as a sociopathology of its own anxieties of origin. For a good example of this genre, see Eid Mohamed, *Arab Occidentalism: Images of America in the Middle East* (London: I. B. Tauris, 2015).

7. Bernard S. Cohn in his *Colonialism and Its Forms of Knowledge: The British in India* (Princeton, NJ: Princeton University Press, 1996) looked at the same phenomenon though from the site of British colonialism in India.

8. See Adam Raz, "'We Look at Them Like Donkeys': What Israel's First Ruling Party Thought About Palestinian Citizens," *Haaretz*, June 13, 2018, www .haaretz.com/israel-news/.premium.MAGAZINE-what-israel-s-first-ruling -party-thought-about-palestinian-citizens-1.5730395.

9. See "Richard Spencer Tells Israelis They 'Should Respect' Him: 'I'm a White Zionist,'" *Haaretz*, August 16, 2017, www.haaretz.com/israel-news/richard -spencer-to-israelis-i-m-a-white-zionist-respect-me-1.5443480.

10. See Ilan Pappe, "Israel's Incremental Genocide in the Gaza Ghetto," Electronic Intifada, July 13, 2014, electronicintifada.net/content/israels-incremental -genocide-gaza-ghetto/13562.

11. See "Yair Netanyahu Says Leftists More Dangerous than Neo-Nazis," *Times of Israel*, August 16, 2017, www.timesofisrael.com/netanyahu-junior-says-leftists -more-dangerous-than-neo-nazis.

12. See Philip Weis, "Charlottesville Is Moment of Truth for Empowered U.S. Zionists (Who Name Their Children after Israeli Generals)," Mondoweiss, mondoweiss.net/2017/08/charlottesville-empowered-children.

13. Toni Morrison, "Making America White Again," *The New Yorker*, November 21, 2016, www.newyorker.com/magazine/2016/11/21/making-america-white-again.

14. See Alastair Smart, "Is It Wrong to Admire Paul Gauguin's Art?" *The Telegraph*, September 19, 2016, published on the occasion of "Gauguin: Maker of Myth" exhibition at the Tate on September 30, 2015–January 16, 2016, www.telegraph .co.uk/culture/art/8011066/Is-it-wrong-to-admire-Paul-Gauguins-art.html.

15. Meredith Mendelsohn, "Why Is the Art World Divided Over Gauguin's Legacy?" Artsy, August 3, 2017, www.artsy.net/article/artsy-editorial-art-divided -gauguins-legacy.

16. For more on this, see Malek Alloula, *The Colonial Harem*, trans. Wlad Godzich (Minneapolis, MN: University of Minnesota Press, 1986).

17. Ibid. For the most recent scholarship on Gauguin's colonial paintings, see *Gauguin's Challenge: New Perspectives After Postmodernism*, ed. Norma Broude (New York: Bloomsbury Academic, 2018).

Four. Europe and its Shadows

1. Enrique Dussel, *Philosophy of Liberation*, trans. Aquilina Martinez and Christine Morkovsky (New York, Orbis Books, 1980): 3.

2. See "With Xi's Power Grab, China Joins New Era of Strongmen," *New York Times*, February 26, 2018, www.nytimes.com/2018/02/26/world/asia/china-xi -jinping-authoritarianism.html.

3. See "Trump on China's Xi Consolidating Power: 'Maybe We'll Give That a Shot Some Day,'" CNN, March 3, 2018, www.cnn.com/2018/03/03/politics/trump -maralago-remarks/index.html.

4. See "Donald Trump Sure Has a Problem With Democracy," *New York Times*, March 4, 2018, www.nytimes.com/2018/03/04/opinion/trump-democracy -problem.html.

5. Krishnadev Calamur, "Nine Notorious Dictators, Nine Shout-Outs from Donald Trump," *The Atlantic*, March 4, 2018, www.theatlantic.com/international /archive/2018/03/trump-xi-jinping-dictators/554810.

6. See "The Unique Vapidity of the Bibi-ist Right," *Haaretz*, March 4, 2018, www .haaretz.com/opinion/.premium-the-unique-vapidity-of-the-bibi-ist-right-1 .5868012.

7. See Bruno Latour, "Europe Alone—Only Europe," trans. Stephen Muecke, www.bruno-latour.fr/sites/default/files/downloads/P-178-EUROPE-GB.pdf.

8. See Roger Cohen, "Islam and the West at War," *New York Times*, February 16, 2015, www.nytimes.com/2015/02/17/opinion/roger-cohen-islam-and-the-west -at-war.html.

9. See "Michael Flynn in August: Islamism a 'Vicious Cancer' in Body of all Muslims that 'Has to Be Excised,'" CNN, November 23, 2016, edition.cnn.com /2016/11/22/politics/kfile-michael-flynn-august-speech/index.html.

10. "UK Brexit Proposal Would Spell 'End of Europe,'" *Financial Times*, September 26, 2018, www.ft.com/content/6c89ebe2-c0e0-11e8-95b1-d36dfef 1b89a.

11. See Ivan Krastev, "3 Ideas of Europe Are Failing, but a New One Can Rise," Dialogues of Civilizations, ResetDoc, September 21, 2018, www.resetdoc.org /story/3-ideas-europe-failing-new-one-can-rise.

Five. The Postcolonial Paradox

1. Tayeb Salih, *Season of Migration to the North*, trans. Denys Johnson-Davies (London: Heinemann, 1970): 49–50.

2. Edward Said, *Culture and Imperialism* (New York: Vintage, 1993): 211–212.

3. Antonio Gramsci, *Selections from the Prison Notebooks*, ed. and trans. Quentin Hoare and Geoffrey Nowell Smith (London: Lawrence & Wishart, 1971): 702–703.

4. Ibid., 703.

5. I have examined and documented this interpolated pluralism on many occasions and most recently in my *Iran without Borders: Towards a Critique of the Postcolonial Nation* (New York and London: Zed, 2016).

6. I have studied these prerevolutionary critical thinkers in detail in my *Theology of Discontent: The Ideological Foundations of the Islamic Revolution in Iran* (New Brunswick, NJ: Transactions, 1993).

7. For a sample of Abdulkarim Soroush's ideas in English, see *Reason, Freedom, and Democracy in Islam: Essential Writings of Abdolkarim Soroush*, eds. and trans. Mahmoud Sadri and Ahmad Sadri (Oxford: Oxford University Press, 2022).

8. See Hamid Dabashi, *Iran, The Green Movement and the USA: The Fox and the Paradox* (London: Zed, 2010).

9. For the link I make between the Green Movement in Iran and the Arab Spring in the Arab world, see Hamid Dabashi, *The Arab Spring: The End of Postcolonialism* (London: Zed, 2012).

10. See Hamid Dabashi, *Post-Orientalism: Knowledge and Power in Time of Terror* (New Brunswick, NJ: Transactions, 2008).

11. See David Scott, *Conscripts of Modernity: The Tragedy of Colonial Enlightenment* (Durham, NC: Duke University Press, 2004): 2.

12. I discuss this episode in more details in my *Iran: A People Interrupted* (New York: The New Press, 2007).

13. See Amy Allen, *The End of Progress: Decolonizing the Normative Foundations of Critical Theory* (New York: Columbia University Press, 2017).

14. Ibid., 1.

15. Ibid., 5–6.

16. See Gianni Vattimo, *After Christianity*, trans. Luca D'Isanto (New York: Columbia University Press, 2002).

17. Ibid., 1–2.

Six. Europe: The Indefinite Jest

1. See Rodolphe Gasché, *Europe, or the Infinite Task: A Study of a Philosophical Concept* (Stanford, CA: Stanford University Press, 2009): 344.

2. Ibid., 1.

3. Ibid., 44.

4. Ibid., 64.

5. Ibid., 95.

6. Ibid., 96.

7. Ibid., 97.

8. Ibid., 99.

9. Ibid., 101.

10. Ibid., 103.

11. Ibid., 114–116.

12. Ibid., 124.

13. Ibid., 126.

14. Ibid., 129.

15. Ibid., 131.

16. Ibid., 134.

17. Ibid., 144.

18. Ibid., 175.

19. Ibid., 200.

20. Ibid., 211.

21. Ibid., 212.

22. Ibid., 213.

23. Ibid., 213.

24. Ibid., 222.

25. Ibid., 224.

26. Ibid., 238.

27. Ibid., 249.

28. Ibid., 250.

29. Ibid., 265.

30. Ibid., 266.

31. Ibid., 268.

32. Ibid., 281.

33. Ibid., 284.

34. Ibid., 285.

35. Ibid., 287.

36. Ibid., 289.

37. Ibid., 290–291.

38. Ibid., 291.

39. Ibid., 292.

40. Ibid., 292.

41. Ibid.

42. Ibid., 293.

43. Ibid., 293–294.

44. Ibid., 294.

45. Ibid., 294–295.

46. Ibid., 295.

47. Ibid., 297–298.

48. Ibid., 299.

49. Ibid., 300.

50. Ibid., 301–302.

51. Ibid., 339.

52. Ibid., 340.

53. Ibid., 341.

54. Ibid., 341.

55. Ibid., 341.

56. Ibid., 343.

57. Ibid., 346–347.

58. Antonio Gramsci, *Selections from the Prison Notebooks*, ed. and trans. Quentin Hoare and Geoffrey Nowell Smith (London: Lawrence & Wishart, 1971): 765.

59. An earlier version of this chapter section appeared as "Rosa Luxemburg: The Unsung Hero of Postcolonial Theory" on *Al Jazeera*, May 12, 2018, hawkingsbay-dispatch.com/2018/05/12/rosa-luxemburg-the-unsung-hero-of-postcolonial-theory.

60. Rosa Luxemburg, *The Accumulation of Capital*, trans. Agnes Schwarzschild, with Introduction by John Robinson (London: Routledge and Kegan Paul, 1951 [original German, 1913]): 297.

Seven. Mapping beyond the Postcolonial Artworld

1. Arthur Danto, "The Artworld," *The Journal of Philosophy* 61, no. 19 (1964): 571–584, American Philosophical Association Eastern Division 61st Annual Meeting, October 15, 1964.

2. Día al-Azzawi, quoted in *Día Al-Azzawi: A Retrospective, from 1963 until Tomorrow* (Doha, Qatar: Mathaf: Arab Museum of Modern Art, 2016): Front page.

3. For more details on this event, see docs.google.com/document/d/1xN170RJZaq 70ABQZyozsk93EpbooouYHgEqLiUeoIFg/edit.

4. I have explored this point in the following essay, "The Crowd, the Truth, and the Artist," *Koorosh Shishehgaran: The Art of Altruism,* ed. Hamid Keshmirshekan (London: Saqi Books, 2017): 5–11.

5. Arthur Danto, "The Artworld": 580.

6. See Hamid Dabashi, "A Portrait of the Artist as a Dead Boy," *Al Jazeera,* February 4, 2016, www.aljazeera.com/indepth/opinion/2016/02/portrait-artist -dead-boy-ai-weiwei-aylan-kurdi-refugees-160204095701479.html. See also Hamid Dabashi, "Between Ai Weiwei and Bashar al-Assad, We Wonder," *Al Jazeera,* April 26, 2018, www.aljazeera.com/indepth/opinion/ai-weiwei-bashar -al-assad-180426071333625.html.

7. See, for example, the "Introduction" to my edited volume, *Dreams of a Nation: On Palestinian Cinema* (London and New York: Verso, 2006).

8. See Zainab Bahrani, "Día al-Azzawi's Modern Antiquity," in *Día Al-Azzawi: A Retrospective, from 1963 until Tomorrow,* 12–17.

9. See Rebecca Joubin, *Two Grandmothers from Baghdad: And Other Memoirs of Monkith Saaid* (Netherlands: Weideblik Press, 2008).

10. Hans Georg Gadamer, *The Relevance of the Beautiful and Other Essays,* trans. N. Walker, ed. R. Bernasconi (Cambridge: Cambridge University Press, 186): 63.

11. Mathew Abbott's *Abbas Kiarostami and Film-Philosophy* (Edinburgh: Edinburgh University Press, 2016) is an insightful book on Kiarostami's cinema in and of itself but has nothing to do with what I am proposing here. Abbott works his way to Kiarostami through European philosophers from Ludwig Wittgenstein to Giorgio Agamben and Martin Heidegger, which is a perfectly fine thing to do—but entirely alien to my invocation of the philosophical memory of an Iranian Muslim philosopher of a very long time ago.

Eight. Is Peace Possible?

1. Walter Benjamin, *On the Concept of History,* folk.uib.no/hlils/TBLR-B/ Benjamin-History.pdf, I.

2. Walter Benjamin, *On the Concept of History,* IX.

3. Emmanuel Levinas, "Time and the Other," in *The Levinas Reader,* ed. Séan Hand (Oxford: Basil Blackwell, 1989): 45.

Conclusion

1. V. Y. Mudimbe, *The Invention of Africa: Gnosis, Philosophy and the Order of Knowledge* (Bloomington and Indianapolis: Indiana University Press, 1988): 1.
2. Jason Hickel, "How Britain Stole $45 Trillion from India," *Al Jazeera,* December 19, 2018.
3. Giorgio Agamben, *Means Without End: Notes on Politics,* trans. Vincenzo Binetti and Cesare Casarino (Minneapolis: University of Minnesota Press, 1996/200): 114–115.
4. Shakespeare, *King Lear,* act 1, scene 2.

Index